Acting Civically

Civil Society: Historical and Contemporary Perspectives

Series Editors:

VIRGINIA HODGKINSON
Public Policy Institute, Georgetown University

KENT E. PORTNEY
Department of Political Science, Tufts University

JOHN C. SCHNEIDER
Department of History, Tufts University

Susan A. Ostrander and Kent E. Portney, eds., *Acting Civically: From Urban Neighborhoods to Higher Education*

Peter Levine, *The Future of Democracy: Developing the Next Generation of American Citizens*

Jason A. Scorza, *Strong Liberalism: Habits of Mind for Democratic Citizenship*

Elayne Clift, ed., *Women, Philanthropy, and Social Change: Visions for a Just Society*

Brian O'Connell, *Fifty Years in Public Causes: Stories from a Road Less Traveled*

Pablo Eisenberg, *Philanthropy's Challenge: The Courage to Change*

Thomas A. Lyson, *Civic Agriculture: Reconnecting Farm, Food, and Community*

Virginia A. Hodgkinson and Michael W. Foley, eds., *The Civil Society Reader*

Henry Milner, *Civic Literacy: How Informed Citizens Make Democracy Work*

Ken Thomson, *From Neighborhood to Nation: The Democratic Foundations of Civil Society*

Bob Edwards, Michael W. Foley, and Mario Diani, eds., *Beyond Tocqueville: Civil Society and the Social Capital Debate in Comparative Perspective*

Phillip H. Round, *By Nature and by Custom Cursed: Transatlantic Civil Discourse and New England Cultural Production, 1620–1660*

Brian O'Connell, *Civil Society: The Underpinnings of American Democracy*

Acting Civically

From Urban Neighborhoods to Higher Education

Susan A. Ostrander and
Kent E. Portney, editors

Tufts University Press
Medford, Massachusetts
Published by University Press of New England
Hanover and London

Tufts University Press
Published by University Press of New England,
One Court Street, Lebanon, NH 03766
www.upne.com

This book was published with additional support from the Jonathan M. Tisch College of Citizen-ship and Public Service.

Library of Congress Cataloging-in-Publication Data
Acting civically : from urban neighborhoods to higher education / Susan A. Ostrander and
Kent E. Portney, editors.
    p.   cm. — (Civil society : historical and contemporary perspectives)
Includes bibliographical references and index.
ISBN-13: 978-1-58465-660-9 (cloth : alk. paper)
ISBN-10: 1-58465-660-3 (cloth : alk. paper)
ISBN-13: 978-1-58465-661-6 (pbk. : alk. paper)
ISBN-10: 1-58465-661-1 (pbk. : alk. paper)
    1. Civil society—United States. 2. Political participation—United States. I. Ostrander,
Susan A. II. Portney, Kent E.
JK1759.A34 2007
300.973—dc22   2007025158

Contents

Part Two: *Civic Engagement in Societal Institutions: Health Care and Education*

Preface and Acknowledgments

This book project represents the product of numerous contributors at Tufts and elsewhere, many of whom have participated in the Civic Engagement Research Group (CERG) at Tufts. CERG is a collection of scholars in numerous schools and departments at Tufts who share an interest in aspects of civic engagement, and is supported by the Jonathan M. Tisch College of Citizenship and Public Service. CERG is coconvened by Susan Ostrander and Kent Portney, and in its first year, by Deborah Pacini Hernandez. CERG is now in its fourth year of providing opportunities for Tufts scholars to interact with each other and with eminent scholars from other institutions. Many of the chapters in this volume were first presented as papers or works-in-progress at regular monthly meetings of CERG.

The vision of CERG is to promote high-quality research on civic engagement by scholars in many different disciplines working across the university. This vision is based on the belief that civic engagement research needs to be defined as an interdisciplinary challenge, and that promoting the interdisciplinary approach will advance our understanding far beyond what could be accomplished in any one discipline. Each discipline contributes something important, valuable, and somewhat unique to this understanding; from this happy confluence emerges a deeper and richer understanding. The essays in this volume have been written by scholars and community practitioners whose work comes out of traditions in sociology, political science, education, child development, psychology, history, public and community health, urban planning, women's studies, American studies, and community organizing; yet all are influenced by the interdisciplinary environment operating through CERG.

We would like to thank a number of people who have helped to make this volume a reality. First we thank Rob Hollister, dean of the Tisch College, for his support of CERG from the beginning. Second, Molly Mead, Lincoln Filene Professor of Citizenship and Public Service at Tisch College, who has helped guide the intellectual directions of CERG. We also thank John Schneider, editor of the civic society series at the University Press of New England, for seeing the potential for this book, and working with us to make it happen. A special note of thanks goes to Carmen Sirianni, who offered many constructive suggestions for improvement. We thank Ellen Wicklum, editor at UPNE, for all her guidance and support. And finally, we thank all the participants in the CERG speaker series from within and outside of Tufts for helping to build an exciting intellectual foundation for civic engagement research.

Contributors

SUSAN A. OSTRANDER is professor of sociology and adjunct professor in the Jonathan M. Tisch College of Citizenship and Public Service at Tufts University. She teaches courses on wealth, poverty, and inequality; nonprofits, states, and markets; community organizing; and gender. She has published widely about social justice philanthropy, women and philanthropy, class elites, and higher education civic engagement. She is the author of *Women of the Upper Class* (1984) and *Money for Change: Social Movement Philanthropy at Haymarket People's Fund* (1995), both published by Temple University Press; and the senior editor of *Shifting the Debate: Public/Private Relations in the Modern Welfare State* (1987, Transaction Press). She has served on the board of the Women's funding Network, cochaired that board; and has been involved in the work of the Boston Women's Fund for more than fifteen years.

KENT E. PORTNEY is professor of political science and adjunct professor in the Jonathan M. Tisch College of Citizenship and Public Service at Tufts University. He is the author of *Taking Sustainable Cities Seriously: Economic Development, the Environment, and Quality of Life in American Cities,* published by MIT Press in 2003, and coauthor of *The Rebirth of Urban Democracy* (Brookings Institution Press, 1993), which won the American Political Science Association's 1994 Gladys Kammerer Award for the Best book in American Politics, and the American Political Science Association Organized Section on Urban Politics' 1994 Best Book in Urban Politics Award. His journal articles include "Civic Engagement and Sustainable Cities in the United States" (*Public Administration Review,* 2005) and his coauthored article, "Mobilizing Minority Communities: Social Capital and Participation in Urban Neighborhoods (*American Behavioral Scientist,* 1997).

JULIAN AGYEMAN is associate professor of urban and environmental policy and planning at Tufts University, Boston-Medford. His research interests include the nexus between environmental justice and sustainability. He is cofounder and coeditor of the international journal *Local Environment: The International Journal of Justice and Sustainability.* With more than 120 publications, his books include *Local Environmental Policies and Strategies* (Longman, 1994), *Just Sustainabilities: Development in an Unequal World* (MIT Press, 2003), *Sustainable Communities and the Challenge of Environmental Justice* (New York University Press, 2005) and *The New Countryside? Ethnicity, Nation and Exclusion in Contemporary Rural Britain* (Policy Press, 2006).

He is a fellow of the UK Royal Society of the Arts (FRSA) and is a contributing editor to *Environment: Science and Policy for Sustainable Development,* an associate editor of *Environmental Communication: A Journal of Nature and Culture,* and a member of the editorial boards of the *Journal of Environmental Education, Sustainability: Science, Practice and Policy,* and the *Australian Journal of Environmental Education.*

LINDA V. BEARDSLEY's career in education has been guided by her belief that education can transform lives and communities. Her work has included extensive teaching experience at all levels, from early childhood classrooms through middle school, high school, and university programs. In 1992 she joined the Massachusetts Department of Education, playing a key role in implementing the Education Reform Act of 1993. In September 1997 she was appointed director of teacher education and school partnerships at Tufts University. In collaboration with university and K–12 educators, she developed the Urban Teacher Training Collaborative, a professional development school model of teacher preparation. Ms. Beardsley received her B.A. degree in English and secondary education at Simmons College and graduated cum laude in 1969. She received her master's degree in child development and early education at Tufts University in 1981. She is an adjunct faculty member at the Tisch College of Citizenship and Public Service. She is also a founding member of EdVestors, a philanthropic group funding education reform initiatives in urban schools.

JEFFREY M. BERRY is John Richard Skuse Professor of Political Science at Tufts University. Professor Berry specializes in the areas of interest groups, citizen participation, nonprofits, and public policymaking. He is the author or coauthor of *The Challenge of Democracy* (Houghton Mifflin, 9th ed., 2007), and *The Rebirth of Urban Democracy* (Brookings Institution Press, 1993), winner of the American Political Science Association's 1994 Gladys Kammerer Award for the Best Book in American Politics, and the American Political Science Association Organized Section on Urban Politics' 1994 Best Book in Urban Politics Award. His book, *The New Liberalism: The Rising Power of Citizen Groups* (Brookings Institution Press, 1999), received the Aaron Wildavsky Award, given annually by the Policy Studies Organization for the best book in the field of public policy. Recent books include *Surveying Nonprofits: A Methods Handbook* (Aspen Institute, 2003) and *A Voice for Nonprofits* (Brookings Institution Press, 2003), recipient of the Leon D. Epstein Outstanding Book Award of the Political Organizations and Parties section of the American Political Science Association. Berry is the coauthor of *Democracy at Risk* (2005), a study of civic engagement in America, published by the Brookings Institution.

DOUG BRUGGE is associate professor in the Department of Public Health and Family Medicine at Tufts University School of Medicine, director of the Tufts Community Research Center, and environmental and occupational health editor for the *Journal of Immigrant and Minority Health.* His interest is in the environmental health of low-income and minority communities in the United States. He is coeditor (with H. Patricia Hynes) of *Community Research for Environmental Health: Lessons in Science, Advocacy and Ethics* (Ashgate, 2005) and coeditor (with Timothy Benally and Esther Yazzie-Lewis) of *The Navajo People and Uranium Mining* (University of New Mexico Press, 2007).

CHARLENE A. GALARNEAU is visiting assistant professor in the Women's Studies Department, Wellesley College. Until fall 2005, she was senior lecturer at Tufts University, Community Health Program, and clinical instructor at the Tufts University School of Medicine, Department of Public Health and Family Medicine. Her teaching and research interests include ethics (religious, social, and philosophical) and U. S. health policy, gender and bioethics, and religion, health, and healing. Her current primary research argues for the inclusion of communities (local, religious, cultural) as necessary moral participants in the creation of just health care in the United States. Other research projects address the ethical dimensions of Christian medical sharing plans, citizen participation in Canadian health care, and FDA blood donation policy.

LYDIA LOWE is executive director of the Chinese Progressive Association, a nonprofit grassroots community organization that works for full equality and empowerment of the Chinese community in the Greater Boston area and beyond. She has more than thirty years of community organizing experience focused on racial equality, immigrant workers' rights, affordable housing, community planning, and political empowerment. She is a second-generation Chinese American and the mother of two girls.

HEATHER ROSS is legislative outreach coordinator at Alternatives for Community and the Environment (ACE) working to pass an environmental justice bill for the state of Massachusetts. She is a graduate of Duke University's Nicholas School of the Environment and Tufts University's Urban and Environmental Policy and Planning master's program. She has done extensive course work in environmental justice and has worked with environmental organizations in New York City and Boston. She is involved in her local community and is part of a political organization that works to elect progressive legislators that are committed to economic justice, protection of the environment, and equal rights. She has also worked with MassVOTE, a nonpartisan, political organization in Massachusetts, to empower disenfranchised communities.

SARAH SOBIERAJ is assistant professor of sociology at Tufts University. Her research examines the relationship between political and associational life in the United States. She is currently completing a book that explores public political life during presidential campaigns, investigating the mobilization of civil society during presidential elections by studying the responses of voluntary associations to the key campaign events of 2000 and 2004. Her most recent journal articles can be found in *Sociological Theory, Sociological Inquiry,* the *Sociological Quarterly,* and *Social Science Quarterly.*

DEBORAH WHITE is associate professor of sociology at Minnesota State University, Moorhead and director of Tri-College University's National Education for Women's (NEW) Leadership Development Institute. Her research interests include gender, leadership, and civic and political participation. Her published work in these areas includes "Taxing Political Life: Revaluating the Relationship Between Voluntary Association Membership, Political Engagement, and the State," with Sarah Sobieraj (2004); "Gender Inequality and National Elite Networks in Twenty-Four Industrialized Societies," with Gwen Moore (2001); and "Interpersonal Contacts" with Gwen Moore in *Gendering Elites: Economic and Political Leadership in 27 Industrialised Societies,* edited by Mino Vianello and Gwen Moore (St. Martin's Press, 2000).

JEAN YU-WEN WU is senior lecturer in the American Studies Program at Tufts University and also the program and education director of the Tufts University Office of Diversity Education Development. Her teaching and research interests include comparative race and ethnic studies, Asian American studies, civic engagement in communities of color, the impact of civic engagement education on learners, and the creation of inclusive learning environments. . Her current research focuses on how race is experienced and lived in the United States, and the impact of race and racism on teaching and learning in university classrooms. She is coeditor of *Asian American Studies: A Reader,* published by Rutgers University Press in 2000.

Acting Civically

Susan A. Ostrander and Kent E. Portney

Introduction

Key Issues in Civic Engagement Research Today

Over the past twenty years, scholars in a wide range of disciplines have begun
to recognize the importance of civic engagement in American social and political life, and have increasingly turned their attention to the wide array of issues
surrounding it. Civic engagement, as a concept and a subject of research, does
not owe allegiance to any particular academic discipline. Scholars in virtually
every social science and many humanities disciplines have sought to shed light
on some aspect of civic engagement.

Civic engagement can be broadly defined as individual and collective action
to identify and address public issues and to participate in public life. Often,
emphasis is placed on how people become involved in their communities to
consider and deal with matters of public concern. Realms of engagement include electoral politics and active participation in both local neighborhoods
and in the institutions of daily life such as schools, community organizations,
voluntary associations, and religious congregations. Virtually anyone interested in the health of civil society and politics has reason to want a deeper
understanding of civic engagement—both its theory and practice. With the virtual explosion in research about civic engagement over the last ten years, it is
not surprising that scholars from many fields have jumped into the fray.

The debates that characterize the literature on civic engagement are
pivotal to the most fundamental issues of politics, governance, civil society,
and community. They pertain to the overall health of society and the polity,
to matters of justice and equality, to who gets what from government, and to
how people develop the networks of social relationships and trust so founda-
tional to participating in public life. The recent resurgence of scholarship
about civic engagement in the United States has been stimulated by research
that purported to show a long-term secular decline in the propensity of
Americans to be, or to become, engaged in society. Whether the participation

is in politics and elections, or in civic and voluntary organizations, Americans seem at first glance to be more disengaged today than ever before. This concern about a critical decline in civic engagement has been the impetus for new research in this field, including the current volume.

The Roots of Concern about Declining Civic Engagement

In the 1980s and early 1990s, scholarly writings began to emerge that raised significant concerns about the character of civic engagement in the United States. In search of an explanation for why Americans may have become less engaged in their civic and political worlds, noted political philosopher Michael Sandel wrote that the United States had shifted its orientation "away from a public philosophy of common purposes . . . and [from] a politics of good" (Sandel 1982, 183). In 1984, political theorist Benjamin Barber theorized that an overreliance on tenets of classical liberal political thought—emphasizing individual rights over public concerns and social responsibilities—contributed to the decline in civic engagement. Barber argued that this individualized and privatized orientation sanctions what he called a thin democracy that "can conceive of no form of citizenship other than the self-interested bargain" (Barber 1984, xiii). In 1985, Robert Bellah and others argued that American society had gotten to the point where "individualism may have grown cancerous" (Bellah et al. 1985, vii) and that changes in the practices and values underlying civic engagement had produced clear and serious consequences for the country. What these scholars have in common is a concern for the character of civic engagement in the United States—and concern that that character has somehow changed for the worse.

In 1995 and 2000 Robert Putnam put forth substantial empirical evidence that civic engagement in the United States has been in serious decline. Putnam argued strenuously that there was a national crisis of declining participation in electoral politics, voluntary association membership, and face-to-face associative behavior. This erosion threatened, in his view, the essential bonds of social trust and connection—social capital—so fundamental to a vital democracy. Stated succinctly, Putnam argued: "For the first two-thirds of the twentieth century a powerful tide bore Americans into ever deeper engagement in the life of their communities, but a few decades ago—silently, without warning—that tide reversed and we were overtaken by a treacherous rip current. Without at first noticing, we have been pulled apart from one another and from our communities over the last third of the century" (1995, 27). This contention spawned a virtual cottage industry of research into the character of engagement in civil society and politics, and into the character of changes in this engagement over time. Research since Putnam has provided rich insights into the many ways in which the broad-brush picture he painted was either overstated or simply wrong. The research has become more refined and nuanced, documenting the ebbs and flows of engagement of different types and groups of people in the United States and around the world. (Putnam 2002)

Mapping Civic Engagement Scholarship: Contemporary Research Questions

The majority of the research on civic engagement focuses on a series of questions that derive from these broad concerns. These research questions represent a contemporary scholarly view of the important conceptual and empirical issues that affect American society. We have developed a brief "mapping" of these research questions to demonstrate the breadth and importance of contemporary civic engagement research and to provide a glimpse into some of the extant debates that characterize this research. Suffice it to say we provide only a glimpse; the literature dealing with each of these questions has its own extensive underlying body of research, far too voluminous to review here.

Are people in the United States actually less civically engaged than in past decades? How and why have the ways people engage changed?

Putnam initially claimed a national crisis of declining rates of participation in electoral politics (especially declining voting rates), membership in established voluntary organizations (for example, Chamber of Commerce, Parent-Teacher Associations), and face-to-face associative behavior (for example, having people to your house for dinner). Putnam's findings have been the subject of a great deal of debate and criticism, and scholars rose quickly to counter and circumscribe his claims. While agreeing that declines in voting rates are a serious concern, some argued that civic engagement at the local community level and in multiple other settings continue to be vital (for example, Sirianni and Friedland 2005; Boyte 2004). Even when people were unwilling to call what they did political many were found to be involved in neighborhood associations, schools, religious congregations, the workplace and a range of other contexts where they actively addressed public issues and concerns (Warren 2001, 10).

Overall, current thinking seems increasingly to be that civic engagement has not so much declined as changed and adapted to large-scale societal changes (Skocpol 2003). A recent study in Chicago, for example, concluded that "collective civic engagement appears to have changed rather than declined, with sources that are organizational rather than interpersonal," leading the authors to argue "that American democracy has undergone a civic *re*organization rather than simple decline" (Sampson et al 2005, 675 and 710). This reorganizing and other kinds of change are especially evident at the local community level and perhaps in places of work as well. Robert Wuthnow's (1998) research suggests, for example, that, while traditional middle-class, largely white voluntary organizations have lost members, people act in other ways. Families where both adults are employed fulltime, may engage in short-term projects related to schools, neighborhoods, and religious congregations more than to long-term membership in voluntary associations.

Raising the key question of *who* engages civically, others argue that there is little evidence that middle-class whites in the United States are any less civically engaged than in the past; rather, large numbers of low-income people and people of color, and sometimes women (Caiazza 2005), have less access and opportunity for a variety of reasons to actively participate in public life. This inequality of access, these scholars emphasize, is the real crisis in need of attention (Skocpol and Fiorina 1999; Verba, Schlozman, and Brady 1995). Others urge attention to specifying *what* kinds of civic engagement are occurring, observing that informal helping networks and church involvement are often quite strong in low-income communities and communities of color. Still others take the view that where people actually are less civically engaged (say, in electoral politics), the source of disengagement is not people's withdrawal from active engagement but rather their encountering different political arrangements that devalue and make participation more difficult—such as the playing out of political campaigns through expensive media ads more than substantive discussions of the public issues which people cared about. (Crenson and Ginsburg 2002)

One sweeping critique of Putman comes from sociologist Michael Schudsen. His argument takes off from a historical demythologizing of the idealized American past where everyday citizens supposedly regularly came together to discuss and act on public affairs. Schudsen reminds us that the mythic New England town meeting was open only to property owners and adult males. "Women, like slaves and servants, were defined by their dependence; citizenship belonged only to those who were masters of their own lives"—a category that often excluded as well Jews and Catholics (Schudsen 1998, 29). Schudsen goes on to suggest that Putnam's finding of little civic engagement may be more a factor of where and how he looked than of actual decline. Because "civic participation now takes place everywhere," Schudsen concluded that it is "premature at best" to claim a decline in civic well-being (1998, 308).

Where is civic engagement declining? What are the main reasons? What can be done about it?

One debate here is between those who emphasize more individually or culturally based explanations (and solutions), and those who emphasize more institutional or structural ones. On the individual-cultural side are arguments that people in the United States have become more concerned, for a variety or reasons, about individual achievements (say, in regard to "careers"), personal growth (say, focus on developing "the self"), and private comforts (say, mass entertainment) and less concerned about larger "civic" concerns. Explanations include a growing culture of individualism (Bellah et al. 1985; Barber 1984), and a decline in civic values and education (Ehrlich 2000). Solutions here are to encourage people to become more civic-minded and socially responsible, and to educate people (especially young people) about civic virtues and the skills needed to be effective engaged citizens.

In contrast to this emphasis on culture, the structural school of thought emphasizes major historical shifts, economic transformations, and political changes that pose increased structural obstacles to engagement. These obstacles are beyond the control of the individual (they can, however, be addressed by collective movements for social and political change). Matthew Crenson and Benjamin Ginsberg (2002) argue that governments now operate so that people's active involvement is neither needed nor valued. Instead, political elites view citizens as the "audience" targeted for public relations "impression management" about pre-set agendas, not as potential participants in the democratic action and debate aimed at creating those agendas. The 2002 work of the American Political Science Association's Standing Committee on Civic Education and Engagement argues similarly that "the political arrangements under which we live—the policies and institutions we make together as a political society—shape the incentives, interests, identities, and capacities of citizens to participate less in civic life" (Macedo et al. 2005). Other scholars highlight other barriers, such as highly concentrated global networks of economic and political power that seem beyond the reach of citizen action; and the lack of access that most people—especially low-income people and other underresourced populations—have to the resources needed for effective engagement. In this view, the targets of change for increasing civic engagement must be the structures of states and markets, and systems of structural inequalities (see Skocpol and Fiorina 1999).

How, and in what ways, is "social capital" related to civic engagement? Does increasing social capital also increase civic engagement?

Building on a concept originally developed by Pierre Bourdieu and James Coleman, Putnam (2000, 18–28; 1995, 65–69) argued that an important facilitator of civic engagement is social capital, defined as social networks and relationships of trust. (Coleman had earlier defined the term to mean social ties and shared social norms.) This work has led to an ongoing body of theory and research attempting to further define social capital, and to assess its impact on civic engagement. An important research finding here is that while bridging capital (building trusting relationships across social differences) does seem to build civic engagement and enhance democracy, bonding capital (limited to one's own race, class, and so forth) may actually serve to decrease civic engagement in ways contrary to democratic principles of inclusion. Research is increasingly focused on how to create bridging capital.

Not everyone agrees about the usefulness of social capital either as a theory, as a valid description of what goes on in society, or as a research tool. A recent study of trends in social capital in the United States found that of six studies, only Putnam's argued conclusively for decline (Costa and Kahn 2003). Foley, Edwards, and Diani (2001) have cautioned that studies of social capital may overgeneralize results and undertheorize meanings. Jennings (2006) suggests that social capital has been defined in ways that ignore the real assets of low-income communities, and used as a poor substitute for redistributing wealth, income, and power. Based on a review of literature, I. T. Thomson (2005:424) concludes that "there is no reason to assume that social capital has declined" and that the argument that it has is "hard to substantiate." Yet whether and to what extent civic engagement in one form or another helps to build social capital, remains an important conceptual and empirical issue.

How is civic engagement related to democracy? Does civic engagement result in a more just and equitable society? And if so, how?

Concern about low levels of voting behavior in the United States has contributed to a rethinking of what we mean by democracy. Barber's concept of strong democracy where citizens are actively engaged in highly participatory forms of public decision-making is posed as an alternative to earlier notions of representative and/or "republican" democracy. The concept of public work developed by Boyte and Kari (1996) represents another important expression of active citizenship. They define it as people working together on issues of common concern to create shared ways of addressing those issues. Doing public work requires the creation of public spaces where people can pursue this work collectively.

The question of whether raising the quantity and quality of participation necessarily makes for a better society seems unresolved, and largely unaddressed. Some argue that participation is a good thing in and of itself; others ask what are the outcomes of participation, for example, for creating a society that is responsive to human concerns and where there is an equitable distribution of resources. Berry, Portney, and Thomson (1993) address this question in an analysis of citywide systems of neighborhood associations in Saint Paul, Dayton, Portland, Birmingham, and San Antonio.

Simply understanding the many ways that different forms of civic engagement might privilege or disadvantage particular groups of people—especially the chronically disadvantaged and disenfranchised—is a significant challenge. Indeed, substantial energies have been expended in the empirical analysis of different kinds of "biases" in participation, including electoral participation (Verba, Schlozman, and Brady 1995: Harris 1999). The broader issue, of course, is whether there are forms of civic engagement—both political and nonpolitical—that can help overcome chronic disengagement caused by disadvantage. Several of the chapters in this volume address this question; for example, Sarah Sobieraj and Deborah White's study of the consequences for political participation of involvement in voluntary associations of different types.

What is civil society? Why has it reemerged as a central concept? How is civil society related to civic engagement? Is the concept of civil society a useful one?

Developed in the eighteenth-century Enlightenment period in Europe and long a central concept in the field of sociology, the concept of civil society has reemerged in response to "the crisis of the welfare state," and to global problems that loom so large that states and markets alone seem incapable of addressing them (Cohen 1999). This concept has recently generated an enormous body of scholarly literature that we can barely touch upon here. Walzer defines civil society as "the space of uncoerced human association, and also the set of relational networks, formed for the sake of family, faith, interest, and ideology" (Walzer 1995, 7)—a definition that feminist political philosopher Iris Marion Young criticizes because "it seems to include almost everything we know as social." She favors instead, as many do, a separation between the "activities of voluntary associational life" (that is, civil society) away from "those of both state and economy" (Young 2000, 157). At the same time, she issues a strong caution about the hope that a nonpolitical civil society alone can "promote democracy, social justice, and well-being"; she argues instead for the continued importance of the state and the role of civil society institutions in pressuring the state.

Overall, there has been much confusion about the meaning and importance of civil society and whether it does or does not include the realm of state and electoral politics. Nonetheless, agreement is widespread that civil society, whether broadly or narrowly defined, is or should be the most promising site and venue for a revitalized civic engagement (Fullinwider 1999).

One wing of civil society thinking comes from those who use it to justify a diminishing welfare state, substituting nongovernmental and commercial sectors to address public issues. This was exemplified in the United States by the policies of the Reagan administration and in Britain by those of Margaret Thatcher. The more moderate Bill Clinton and Tony Blair tempered this explicit anti-state agenda with what they called "a third way": this policy was aimed not so much at abolishing the welfare state but at forging public-private partnerships between and among local communities, voluntary associations, nonprofit organizations, civic groups, religious congregations, and so on.

It is in these ways that the concept of civil society appeals across the ideological spectrum. Liberals and progressives are attracted to this concept because it has the potential to increase democratic participation, and it acknowledges the value of nonprofit advocacy (Berry 1999, 2005) and grassroots community organizing (Warren 2001) as ways to build a democracy and social justice. For those who aim to "privatize" welfare state activities by turning them over to the market, a turn toward civil society also includes more reliance on the private for-profit sector as well as the nonprofit or voluntary sector. Some even include the state and increased civic involvement in electoral politics in their notions of civil society (O'Connell 1999). The broad concept of civil society also encompasses efforts to promote civic engagement through the educational process; institutions of secondary and higher education across the United States have begun to incorporate community service learning, active citizenship, and civic engagement into their curricula (Ostrander 2004).

What kinds of civic engagement contribute to democracy and civil society? Does the level and quality of civic engagement actually affect the character of the public policies enacted?

One debate here has been about what "politics" means and what is included in being "politically" engaged. Political theory has tended to privilege participation in electoral politics or actions related to the state, while feminist scholars have sought to expand politics to include engagement in local neighborhoods, schools, community groups, and other realms not strictly limited to governmental or electoral politics (Gittel et al. 2000; Naples 1997; Kaplan 1998; Mansbridge 1983). It is here in these more "social" realms where women—especially working-class white women and women of color—have historically been leaders. In recent years, community-based civic engagement has become a growing and important area for research and theorizing.

One significant challenge raised by civic engagement research is the search for ways that participation at the local level can connect and contribute to addressing issues beyond the local, from state to regional to national and even global. Several authors have suggested that it is well within the range of possibility that networks of neighborhood associations, primarily operating in relatively small geographic areas, could become part of a larger system capable of contributing to governance at all levels (Thomson 2001; Smock 2004).

Audience, Themes, and Lessons

Acting Civically: From Urban Neighborhoods to Higher Education is a collection of previously unpublished civic engagement scholarship from a variety of disciplinary and interdisciplinary perspectives. It is a project of the Tufts University Civic Engagement Research Group (CERG) founded in March 2003 and still codirected by the editors of this volume. A catalyst for forming and sustaining CERG has been the Tisch College of Citizenship and Public Service (formerly the Tufts University College of Citizenship and Public Service), established in 2000. Tisch College has attracted considerable national and international interest in higher education for its "infusion" model, which aims to educate students for active citizenship in every aspect of their lives: in their home communities, at work, and through political and democratic forms of participation locally and worldwide. The chapters in this volume reflect that broad perspective; the widespread interest in how Tufts University is carrying out its civic engagement initiative should thus attract readers to this volume.

Acting Civically will be of special interest to the growing number of civic engagement researchers and teachers in and out of the academy. The book will be of value to others inside and outside higher education interested in improving civic participation and developing and supporting campus and community civic engagement initiatives that include both teaching and scholarship. Activists and practitioners, community leaders, public policymakers, charitable foundation boards and staff, and civic-minded people in general will benefit from reading this book.

Teachers and their students in the wide range of courses where civic engagement is key will find this volume a useful supplement to course readings. Given the multidisciplinary nature of the work presented here, the book will be of value in the fields of political science, sociology, urban and community studies, education, American studies, ethnic studies, and nonprofit studies. Courses for which this book seems especially well suited include those that address civil society, political participation, leadership and active citizenship, social and cultural change, urban communities, community and grassroots organizing, neighborhoods and neighborhood associations, civic education and values, American political culture, community and nonprofit organizations, and collective action and social movements. Courses about race and class inequalities and how ordinary citizens can act to address them would also find this volume useful.

Acting Civically describes, analyzes, and draws lessons from a variety of organizational and local contexts where people are or have been involved in efforts to change for the better their own neighborhoods, communities, and two of the institutions that have significant impact on their lives: health and education.

The chapters suggest a number of "lessons" about promising contexts for engagement, and for those engagement methods and approaches most likely to have positive impact. Several of the chapters also address the forms of civically engaged teaching and civic engagement research most likely to explain and support these positive forms of active engagement.

All of the authors here address, implicitly or explicitly, what continues to be the principal question in the larger debates about civic engagement in America today: has civic engagement declined to a point where democracy is threatened, and, if so, what can be (and is being) done about it? All the chapters address the question of what kinds of civic engagement—including civically engaged teaching—seem most suited to achieving positive goals. In several of the chapters, those forms of civic participation that are inclusive across race and class are of primary concern. Overall, the research presented here shows that, in a wide variety of ways and in a range of settings, people *do* engage when and where they are able to find and to create places and opportunities to affect issues they care about most.

The first part of *Acting Civically* focuses on civic engagement in three different local contexts: neighborhood associations in urban areas, a community-based organization in an urban ethnic enclave, and a local campaign for social and environmental justice. A fourth chapter addresses engagement in voluntary associations more generally and the consequences of political versus non-political associational activity for different groups. In the second part we move from local contexts and associational behavior to civic engagement by and in two of society's largest institutions: health care and education. The chapters address *why* people engage, *how* they engage, *who* engages and through what vehicles, and with what *effect*. Each also offers its own conceptual and theoretical contributions to the study of civic engagement. We offer a few previews here.

Political scientists Portney and Berry, in chapter 2, see local residents motivated to act civically by their social and political identification with their neighbors. "Neighbors," they say, "represent roots and family, our most enduring and deeply felt identities." The "how" is neighbors' working to influence city politics by, for example, representing their association on citywide committees and calling city officials to account. Effects of their involvement include positive zoning decisions that control the rate of economic development in their neighborhoods and what kinds occur. In conceptual terms, Portney and Berry's research shows that engagement in neighborhood associations creates a stronger sense of community, more trust in local government, and deeper feelings of efficacy about political participation than do service or social groups, crime watch groups, or issue groups. This, they, argue, provides a strong basis to claim that neighborhood associations, compared to other kinds of civic organizations, create a solid foundation for civic engagement and democracy. This claim may be especially true for low-income people, as neighborhood associations, in contrast to other forms of engagement, address the needs and interests of all socioeconomic classes. In short, this type of civic engagement contributes positively to democratic values.

In chapter three, community activist Lydia Lowe and action researcher Doug Brugge show residents of Boston's Chinatown acting to preserve their neighborhood from aggressive land development occurring in an absence of residents' voices. The residents form a coalition to provide them with a vehicle to speak. They engage in strategies such as pickets, protests, legal strategies, and a community referendum. They succeed in blocking a large parking garage and, more important, in building a strong grassroots base of working-class leadership in their community. In broader terms, Lowe and Brugge examine the role of different approaches of grassroots community organizing to civic engagement. Their case study of Boston's Chinatown compares and contrasts community consensus-based organizing with the more "transformative" model used by the Chinese Progressive Association. Their study suggests that building a political movement toward broad-based systemic change in line with a transformative approach is more successful than focusing on "winning" particular issues because it has more potential for long-term stable and democratic forms of engagement. Based on their work in Chinatown, they take the view that methods of leadership development focused more on collective goal-setting and less on individual skill-building create forms of engagement more likely to engage low-income people of color.

Environmental social scientist Julian Agyeman and policy advocate Heather Ross, in chapter 4, describe residents of one of Boston's poorest neighborhoods displaying fear for their safety in the face of what is to them a "bio-terror" laboratory. Their fears are compounded by a lack of trust in the government's willingness and ability to protect them. The how of their engagement includes a public education campaign, a citywide coalition-building among community groups, and a grassroots organizing campaign around the dangers of the proposed lab. While the conflict remains unresolved at this writing, this coalition has won at least temporary stopgaps and become a powerful force in the community. Agyeman and Ross's narrative of a local campaign to oppose the building of a bio-safety lab in a Boston neighborhood is built around a larger argument that framing this local issue in relation to larger questions of social and economic justice builds a democratic form of civic engagement inclusive of race and class, thus bringing together a wider range of organizational support than if the focus had been exclusively environmental.

In chapter 5, sociologists Sobieraj and White caution that *how* people engage in voluntary associations matters for social equality and inequality. Who it is that is most likely to engage *politically*—through associations taking stands on political issues, for example—as opposed to nonpolitically, may replicate more than challenge existing inequalities of race-ethnicity, socioeconomic class, and gender. Sobieraj and White's research leads them to conclusions about what specific kinds of civic engagement contribute most to democracy and political participation, especially by low-income people, women, African Americans, and Latinos. Based on a study of voluntary associations, the authors support their claim that while involvement in nonpolitical associations may have other benefits, they do not result in greater political activity by participants. They conclude further that low-income people, Latinos, and women are most likely to be involved in the less political civic organizations and are thus less likely to gain the political advantages that come with them.

The chapters in the second part focus on two major societal institutions, health care and education. As did those of the first part, these chapters address the why, how, who, and with what effect people engage, as well as more theoretical and general concerns. In chapter 6, health ethicist Charlene Galarneau unearths a wide variety of early consumer participants in United States health care reform. Motivated by the need to improve community health and better distribute health services, groups such as trade unions, businesses, mutual aid societies, and local community organizations created innovative consumer-based plans and services such as medical cooperatives. Examining historical trends in civic engagement related to health care organization in the United States, Galarneau shows how civic engagement changes over time and supports a claim that civic engagement aimed at shaping U.S. health care began much earlier than most other scholars have claimed. Explaining how diverse groups of health care consumers developed early twentieth-century health plans, she draws lessons for today's civic engagement efforts and for civic engagement research. Her findings caution against a narrow focus: such may mask rich civic engagement precedents and lead to a mistaken claim that the public has only recently acted civically to shape health care and similar institutions.

In chapter 7, teacher educator and researcher Linda Beardsley explains how one university's graduate teacher training program is a vehicle for the university becoming a civically engaged actor in local cities and towns—an actor that in turn moves public school teachers, students, and their families to become agents of civic education and become more involved in their own community. Motivated by goals of strengthening teaching and bridging the achievement gap among students, public school teachers and university faculty form learning communities that uncover knowledge about local communities and issues of concern to them; they then use this knowledge to develop a curriculum from which both students and teachers learn. In documenting the collaboration between a university-based teacher education program and one region's public schools aimed at improving the quality of life of a whole community, Beardsley conceptualizes this collaboration as itself civic engagement. As the teachers learn to be teachers, they, and the university they attend, become active agents in community where they confront this volume's recurring issues of race and class.

In chapter 8, education specialist and award-winning teacher, Jean Wu, is motivated by the view that universities have the capacity to bring about cultural and social change if professors know and students are taught how to analyze systemic sources of the inequalities they encounter as they learn and serve in local communities. She and her students become active agents for change as she teaches them to use critical race thinking to question their initial reactions to some of what they see and hear in Boston's Chinatown. Using excerpts from student journals to make her argument, Wu documents the loss of commitment to civic engagement on the part of college-age students that can result if differences of race and class between the students and community residents are ignored. Her chapter is extremely revealing about students' racial misconceptions and attitudes and how good teaching can have a positive impact, potentially shaping for life the kind of civically engaged citizens that students become. For college teachers to learn to sustain civically engaged teaching, scholars writing in this field must provide more guidance in how to design, implement, and assess this kind of educational experience. In the broadest terms, Wu argues for a reconceptualization of education for civic engagement with greater attention to race and the history of race in host communities—or, more pointedly, for scholarly analysis and a set of good practices that link pedagogies of race to pedagogies of civic engagement.

Finally, in chapter 9, sociologist Susan Ostrander, turns to another aspect of higher education civic engagement: an analysis of funding by three major foundations over the past decade, Carnegie, Pew, and Kellogg. The why of civic engagement in this case develops from how foundations have historically been involved in shaping the direction of higher education, and from foundations' concern about reports of critical declines in civic engagement—especially by college-age youth. The who consists of foundations themselves (who in turn use colleges and universities as agents of broader social change), and institutions of higher education (who, for their own reasons, develop civic engagement initiatives). In regard to how they engage, the foundations that set out to urge and support these initiatives use a variety of approaches ranging from civic values education to community change. The difficulty of showing (or achieving) a clear short-term positive effect of these initiatives on actual college youth engagement is a factor, though perhaps not the main one, in these foundations' decisions to fundamentally alter or end altogether their support. Based on overtime scrutiny of changing text on foundation Web sites about existing programs and, most important perhaps, on insider interviews, Ostrander documents and seeks to explain the recent decline of support by these "big 3" to college and university civic engagement initiatives. She concludes that, more than deriving from external effects, the ending of support emerged from common internal foundation tendencies and practices. Analyzing funding shifts toward new civic engagement projects that do not favor support to higher education institutions but rather focus on K–12 civic education, community-based social change initiatives, and youth voting, Ostrander ends with implications for future efforts by higher education to find support for civic engagement initiatives.

Looking at the volume as a whole, we see a number of overarching lessons for methods and approaches for engagement emerge. The range of *who* the agents of civic action and engagement are (and can be) is wide and includes residents in neighborhood associations, founders and members of grassroots organizing groups and urban coalitions, health care consumers, trade unions, mutual aid societies, college and public school teachers and students, higher education institutions, and the funders that support them. Possibilities for *how* agents act civically also contains great variety: representing their neighborhoods on citywide bodies, planning and participating in demonstrations and protests, applying legal strategies, offering community referendums, conducting public education campaigns, providing a space for conversation and debate about political issues, building healthcare organizations responsive to consumer needs, developing civically engaged pedagogies that integrate critical race analyses, and formulating, implementing, and supporting civic education initiatives in higher education. *Why* people engage may include acting out deep identity-based connections to home and community, protecting neighborhoods from outside developers that fail to take account of residents' needs and interests, shielding self and family from threats to health and safety, working to address achievement gaps in urban education, and committing to a kind of civic education that forms a critical race consciousness in college youth. The *effects* of engagement can range from deeper beliefs and trust in a strong democracy, city plans that reflect resident concerns, strong grassroots leadership that can be a voice for the future as well as the present, and solid coalitions across organizations and neighborhoods—as well as barriers of class and race—that can be stable participants in public decision-making. Other effects include mutually beneficial collaborations between institutions of higher education and host communities. Such collaborations are vital to the shared well-being of professors, students, staff, and local residents; they are equally essential to the civically engaged scholarship and teaching that is grounded in and relevant to the day's most pressing issues and concerns.

Clearly, forms of civic engagement exist that seem capable of improving the quality of democracy and civil society. In moving toward increased and higher quality engagement of people in governmental and electoral politics, local involvement in neighborhood associations and grassroots community organizing campaigns may prove the most promising starting points—especially when local campaigns can be connected to goals of systemic change and larger issues of social justice. Local engagement also appears effective in bringing in people of color and low-income people, especially when (1) leadership development is more about setting shared goals than building individual skills; (2) issues are broadly rather than narrowly defined; and (3) that engagement is more political than not. The kinds of civic engagement most likely to lead to political participation take place in voluntary associations where political issues are discussed and stands are taken. Attending to a full range of multiple kinds of engagement can bring to light previously neglected kinds of civic participation that may provide possibilities for future forms of participation. Civically engaged teaching at the university level, whether for college students or teachers being trained to teach in public schools, should bring students and teachers directly into acting for change in host communities and directly addressing issues of race and class. Otherwise we all risk further diminishing and weakening of a strong and active democracy.

Most important, what this volume clearly shows is that civic engagement in many forms and across many places and settings is highly evident in United States society and politics. Participating in local neighborhoods and community organizations, working in social justice campaigns, being involved in voluntary associations with some level of political activity, affecting large-scale institutions (like the health care systems), conducting civically engaged teaching and learning in colleges and universities, and providing supportive resources through leading philanthropic foundations, Americans are actively shaping issues and concerns and developing ways to best address them. Higher education institutions through initiatives like Tufts' Tisch College of Citizenship and Public Service, with which all the authors of this volume are or have been in some way affiliated, can contribute in ways that benefit the larger society at the same time as they "[enhance] the credibility, usefulness, and role of universities as important institutions in civic life" (Gibson 2006, 20).

References

Barber, B. 1984. *Strong Democracy: Participatory Politics for a New Age.* Berkeley and Los Angeles: University of California Press.

Bellah, R., R. Madden, W. M. Sullivan, A. Swidler, and S. M. Tipton. 1985. *Habits of the Heart: Individualism and Commitment in American Life.* Berkeley and Los Angeles: University of California Press.

Berry, J., 1999. *The New Liberalism: The Rising Power of Citizen Groups.* Washington, D.C.: Brookings Institution Press.

———. 2005. *A Voice for Nonprofits.* Washington, D.C.: Brookings Institution Press.

———, K. Portney, and K. Thomson. 1993. *The Rebirth of Democracy.* Washington, D.C.: Brookings Institution Press.

Boyte, H. 2004. *Everyday Politics: Reconnecting Citizens and Public Life.* Philadelphia: University of Pennsylvania Press.

Boyte, H., and N. Kari. 1996. *Building America: The Democratic Promise of Public Work.* Philadelphia: Temple University Press.

Caiazza, Amy. 2005. "Don't Bowl at Night: Gender, Safety, and Civic Participation." *Signs* 30, no. 2 (winter): 1607–31.

Cohen, J. 1999. "American Civil Society Talk." In *Civil Society, Democracy, and Civic Renewal,* edited by R. Fullinwider. New York: Rowman and Littlefield.

Costa. D. L., and M. E. Kahn. 2003. "Understanding the American Decline in Social Capital, 1952–1998." *Kyklos* 56: 17–46.

Crenson, M., and B. Ginsburg. 2002. *Downsizing Democracy: How America Sidelined Its Citizens and Privatized Its Public.* Baltimore, Md.: Johns Hopkins University Press.

Edwards, M. 2004. *Civil Society.* Cambridge, Mass.: Polity Press.

Ehrlich, T. 2000. *Civic Responsibility and Higher Education.* Phoenix, Ariz.: Oryx Press.

Evans, S., and H. Boyte. 1992. *Free Spaces: The Sources of Democratic Change in America.* Chicago: University of Chicago Press.

Foley, M., B. Edwards, and M. Diani. 2001. "Social Capital Reconsidered." In *Beyond Toqueville: Civil Society and the Social Capital Debate in Comparative Perspective,* edited by M. Foley, B. Edwards, and M. Diani. Hanover, N.H.: University Press of New England.

Fullinwider, R., ed. 1999. *Civil Society, Democracy, and Civic Renewal.* New York: Rowman and Littlefield.

Gibson, C. 2006. *New Times Demand New Scholarship: Research Universities and Civic Engagement, A Leadership Agenda.* Medford, Mass.: Tufts University and Campus Compact. 24 pps.

Gittel, M., I. Otega-Bustamante, and T. Steffy. 2000. "Social Capital and Social Change: Women's Community Activism," *Urban Affairs Review* 36, no. 2 (November): 123–47.

Harris, F. 1999. "Will the Circle Be Unbroken? The Erosion and Transformation of African American Civic Life." In *Civil Society, Democracy, and Civic Renewal,* edited by R. Fullinwider. New York: Rowman and Littlefield.

Jennings, J. 2006. "Social Capital, Race, and the Future of Inner City Neighborhoods." *Working Papers.* Medford, Mass.: Tufts University Department of Urban and Environmental Policy and Planning.

Kaplan, T. 1998. *Crazy for Democracy: Women in Grassroots Movements.* New York: Routledge.

Macedo, S., et al. 2005. *Democracy at Risk: How Political Choices Undermine Citizen Participation And What We Can Do About It.* Washington, D.C.: Brookings Institution Press.

Mansbridge, J. J. 1983. *Beyond Adversary Democracy.* Chicago: University of Chicago Press.

Naples, N., ed. 1997. *Community Activism and Feminist Politics: Organizing Across Race, Class, and Gender.* New York: Routledge.

O'Connell, B. 1999. *Civil Society: The Underpinnings of American Democracy.* Hanover, N.H.: University Press of New England.

Ostrander, S. A. 2004. "Democracy, Civic Participation, and the University: A Comparative Study of Civic Engagement on Five Campuses." *Nonprofit and Voluntary Sector Quarterly* 33, no. 1 (March): 74–92.

Putnam, R. 1995. "Bowling Alone: America's Declining Social Capital," *Journal of Democracy* 6:65–78.

———. 2000. *Bowling Alone: The Collapse and Revival of American Community*. New York: Simon and Schuster.

———, ed. 2002. *Democracies in Flux: The Evolution of Social Capital in Contemporary Society*. New York: Oxford University Press.

Sampson, R. J., D. McAdam, H. MacIndoe, and S. Weffer-Elizondo. 2005. "Civil Society Reconsidered: The Durable Nature and Community Structure of Collective Civic Action," *American Journal of Sociology* 111, no. 3 (November): 673–714.

Sandel, M. J. 1982. *Liberalism and the Limits to Justice*. Cambridge: Cambridge University Press.

Schudsen, M. 1998. *The Good Citizen: A History of American Civic Life*. New York: Martin Kessler Books.

Sirianni, C., and L. Friedland. 2001. *Civic Innovation in American: Community Empowerment, Public Policy, and the Movement for Civic Renewal*. Berkeley and Los Angeles: University of California Press.

———. 2005. *The Civic Renewal Movement: Community Building and Democracy in the United States*. Dayton, Ohio: Kettering Foundation Press.

Skocpol, T. 2003. *Diminished Democracy: From Membershp to Management in American Life*. Norman, Okla.: University of Oklahoma Press.

———, and M. P. Fiorina, eds. 1999. *Civic Engagement in American Democracy*. New York: Russell Sage.

Smock, K. 2004. *Democracy in Action: Community Organizing and Urban Change*. New York: Columbia University Press.

Thomson, I. T. 2005. "The Theory That Won't Die: From Mass Society to the Decline of Social Capital." *Sociological Forum* 2, no. 3 (September): 421–48.

Thomson, K. 2001. *From Neighborhood to Nation: The Democratic Foundations of Civil Society*. Hanover, N.H.: University Press of New England.

Verba, S., K. Lehman Schlozman, and H. Brady. 1995. *Voice and Equality: Civic Voluntarism in American Politics*. Cambridge, Mass.: Harvard University Press.

Walzer, M. 1995. *Toward a Global Civil Society*. Providence, R.I.: Berhanan Books.

Warren, M. R. 2001. *Dry Bones Rattling: Community Building to Revitalize American Democracy*. Princeton, N.J.: Princeton University Press.

Wuthnow, R. 1998. *Loose Connections: Joining Together in America's Fragmented Communities*. Cambridge, Mass.: Harvard University Press.

Young, I. M. 2000. *Inclusion and Democracy*. New York: Oxford University Press.

Part One

Civic Engagement in Local Contexts and in Political versus Nonpolitical Voluntary Associations

Neighborhoods, Neighborhood Associations, and Social Capital

"Community" has become the holy grail of American civic life. It's elusive, yet precious. We seem to search for it everywhere, even though every part of our social lives already seems to fall within some community. The city we live in, no matter how large, is a community. Those who share our lifestyle or interests or political passions are part of communities we identify with. We feel connected to the environmental community, the Christian conservative community, the women's movement, or whatever political sector we identify with. Our churches, clubs, and professional associations are communities with very real bonds among members. Online chat rooms and other places in cyberspace, where we never actually meet our correspondents, are a new form of community. Even our places of employment strive to create comfortable work communities. Community has come to include so much that one might wonder if it still means anything at all. Indeed, numerous commentators have drawn this same conclusion, and have frequently suggested that the term ought to be avoided altogether (Bell and Newby 1974).

Putting an end to the chicken-franchising of the term is far beyond our powers. What we hope to accomplish in this essay is to focus attention on a most basic and enduring form of community: the neighborhoods where we live. Although we may feel connected to different people in many different ways in many different "communities," neighborhoods represent something unique. Our neighbors—quite literally, the people we physically live near—are part of our own political and social identity whether we like it or not. Neighborhoods represent roots and family, our most enduring and deeply felt identities. The financial investment in our homes or apartments makes the viability and future of this physical and emotional terrain of supreme importance to our well-being. For those with children (most adults), neighborhoods embody our greatest hopes: that neighborhood schools will help our children flourish.

Few would disagree that neighborhoods represent a singularly important community among all the communities with which we identify. Surprisingly, however, the recent outpouring of literature on civil society places no special emphasis on neighborhoods. At best, neighborhoods are conceived of as one element in a nested structure of social relationships that include individuals, families, neighborhoods, communities, cities, and society (Wallis, Crocker, and Schechter 1998). At the core of the argument about civil society is the belief that the polity benefits when there are a variety of well-functioning mediating structures situated among citizens and between citizens and their government. We are a highly diverse society and it only stands to reason that a rich, dense, and diverse set of mediating structures will work to broaden representation in the political process. Yet when it comes to choosing how they would like to work with others to solve social and political problems, Americans have a decided preference. After extensive discussions with ordinary Americans, Robert Bellah and his colleagues concluded: "Lacking the ability to deal meaningfully with the large-scale organizational and institutional structures that characterize our society, many of those we talked to turned to the small town not only as an ideal but as a solution to our present political difficulties" (1985, 204). We can't all return to small towns but the neighborhoods of our cities come closest to offering the possibilities associated with this romanticized vision of bygone America.

Civil society advocates look at modern life and warn against a decaying infrastructure of mediating organizations. Robert Putnam (1995a, 1995b, 2000) has argued that there are very real consequences to a decline in civic engagement. If people are less involved in civic organizations, less social capital is being generated. Social capital, says Putnam, is made up of the "features of social life—networks, norms, and trust—that enable participants to act together more effectively to pursue shared objectives" (1995b, 664–65; 2000, 19). Putnam's primary evidence that social capital is endangered is that popular support for voluntary organizations is on the wane. He documents a long list of organization with declining memberships, a few of which are neighborhood-based (like PTAs), but most of which have no basis in neighborhood life (like unions). Others have looked at membership trends in voluntary organizations and have found stability rather than decline (Ladd 1996 and 1999). A small army of scholars has joined the debate over civic engagement, often searching for the most valid measures of civil society and social capital (see Edwards and Foley 1997; Edwards, Foley, and Diani 2001; Skocpol and Fiorina 1999; and Wallis 1998).

Communitarians and Civil Society

We shall not try to sort out the dispute over Putnam's data; whatever the ultimate truth about membership figures, we believe that Putnam's broader argument resonates with most Americans. As Bellah and his colleagues found, Americans yearn for more community—for a greater sense of connectedness with those around them. Putnam makes a distinction between those associations that have the potential for generating social capital and those that don't. He derides sending a check to a political action committee, for example, because it "does not embody or create social capital" (1995b, 665). After making this basic distinction, however, Putnam treats all associational life that offers some potential for individuals to "connect with other people" (1995b, 665) in a unidimensional way. Clearly, he has identified a significant threshold: social capital is generated in greatest quantities through personal interaction. At the same time he ignores the communitarian literature that emphasizes the intensity of interaction as the key. Communitarians draw a different threshold. Social capital will be generated not merely by social interaction, but by commitment and involvement in community life. Being a member of the PTA isn't enough; even going to a PTA meeting and observing what is going on is not enough. Communitarians ask people to become involved and take responsibility for the well-being of their communities.

This perspective is perhaps epitomized in Amitai Etzioni's *The Golden Rule* (1996). Etzioni lays out what he sees as the fundamental character of communitarian societies, a character that he sees as necessary for such societies to generate social capital. His argument focuses on a central definition of community, which "is defined by two characteristics: first, a web of affect-laden relationships among a group of individuals, relationships that often crisscross and reinforce one another (rather than merely one-on-one or chainlike individual relationships), and second, a measure of commitment to a set of shared values, norms, and meanings, and a shared history and identity—in short, to a particular culture." Clearly, in Etzioni's formulation, social capital flows from the actions that are undertaken as an integral outgrowth of these interpersonal relations and shared values.

The emphasis on the role of actions is exemplified by Barber's *Strong Democracy* (1984). Barber attacks liberalism for sanctioning "thin democracy": a form of government that assumes that self-interest is the driving force underlying all political behavior. Liberal democracies take a cynical view of human nature and do not demand that people become active citizens. Rather, individuals are encouraged to believe that voting is sufficient participation and that cooperative forms of political participation are of little importance. "Strong democracies," on the other hand, are participatory democracies. At the heart of his idealistic plan to revive American democracy, Barber advocates neighbor-hood assemblies where individuals can meet and deliberate with those who live with them in the same community. "Without talk, there can be no democracy" (1984, 267). The neighborhood is one place where talk about politics can and should begin.

Similarly, in Mansbridge's *Beyond Adversary Democracy* (1980), modern American democracy is derided for its cynicism and for its failure to involve people in the political process. Most people rely on their legislators and inter-est groups to represent them in the adversarial bargaining between interests. What Mansbridge advocates is face-to-face interaction among citizens so that they can strive toward unitary democracy, where the aim is building consensus rather than making decisions by majority rule. Put people together in the same room and let them find their common humanity and their common purpose. The very basis for a unitary democracy, says Mansbridge, is friendship. Friend-ship provides the bond that facilitates a process of turning divergent views of citizens into unified action.

The eloquence of Barber, Mansbridge, Etzioni, and other communitarians who argue for participatory democracy, is of little value in the real world of politics unless those ideas can be cast into processes and institutions. If more social capital is to be generated, ways must be found to encourage more face-to-face interaction in the political life of Americans. We argue here, as we have elsewhere, that neighborhoods should be the focus of efforts to create more civic engagement (Macedo et al., 2005, 67–115). Following the logic of the communitarians, neighborhoods are places where we should feel comfortable talking about politics, even with those we may disagree with. Our neighbor-hoods are filled with our friends, and neighborhood-based institutions offer ample opportunities to make new friends. Neighborhoods offer the opportunity for the development of complex webs of affect-laden interactions (to use Etzioni's terms), and commitment to shared values and identity not easily con-structed elsewhere.

For the purposes of promoting civil society, not all neighborhood civic or-ganizations and political institutions are equal. Few cities have any form of neighborhood government. Neighborhood-based political organizations are al-most always voluntary organizations, such as PTAs or crime watch patrols. Neighborhood political groups are difficult to organize and their capacity and vitality can vary greatly within the same community. Grassroots organizations find that it is exceedingly difficult to overcome the collective action problem for any significant length of time.

There are a handful of American cities that have built neighborhood-based participation systems. These city programs were designed by activists and bu-reaucrats, not communitarian thinkers. Yet communitarian goals are clearly in-stitutionalized in these citywide systems. They promote talk, deliberation, and cooperative action by neighbors working together to solve problems. The assumption behind them is that neighborhood government will build a commitment to shared values that will make citizens more involved, more tolerant of those they disagree with, more trusting of the governmental process, and more educated about public policy. When these practical goals are translated into the discourse of modern social science, such systems are designed to promote "civil society," "civic engagement," and the creation of "social capital."

Cities with Neighborhood Associations

The specific systems we studied at length are in Birmingham, Dayton, Portland (Ore.), and Saint Paul.[1] As we explain at length in *The Rebirth of Urban Democracy* (Berry, Portney, and Thomson 1993), these four systems were chosen after a concerted effort to find the best citizen participation programs in the country. Using a two-stage panel survey of citizens in the four cities, a parallel set of surveys of a control group of cities without such participation systems, and elite interviews with city officials and activists, we tried to measure how successful these programs actually are. Since we first reported our results in 1993, we have continued to monitor these four cities' public involvement programs. Before turning to an evaluation of them, let us briefly describe how they are organized.

What these cities have in common—and what makes them rare among all American cities—is that they have developed programs that exist in every single neighborhood. These are citywide programs that serve the affluent, the poor, and the middle class in the exact same way. The neighborhood associations that are the foundation of these systems have real powers. They are not advisory bodies; they have substantive powers that make them significant players in city politics. For example, each of the neighborhood bodies has some responsibility for zoning decisions in their geographic area. In local politics, authority over zoning is critical to controlling the pace and type of economic development (Peterson 1981). To turn such a power over to the neighborhood associations is to make a fundamental devolution of power from city hall to community organizations. Moreover, to do so in the context of citywide systems of neighborhood associations provides the opportunity for residents to engage in some level of true power-sharing (Lopez and Stack 2001).

The neighborhood associations are often an official or quasi-official part of city government, but they are relatively autonomous from city hall. Although city hall may pay for a small central office and for a small staff of community organizers or liaison personnel, the neighborhood associations themselves are run by volunteer labor, and open meetings are the standard decision-making structure. Each system, however, is organized somewhat differently: an overview of each follows.

Birmingham has ninety-five neighborhood associations that are grouped into larger communities constituting a second tier of the system. Each of these larger communities selects representatives to sit on a Citizens Advisory Board that plays a central role in city-level decisions. Each neighborhood association distributes a monthly newsletter to all its households, and the neighborhoods collectively have significant responsibilities for deciding how to allocate certain governmental funds. The neighborhood system was instrumental in bringing African Americans and whites together in Birmingham; without a doubt it helped them to work together toward common goals, frequently proposing to upgrade predominantly African American neighborhoods rather than middle-class white ones.

Dayton has eighty-two neighborhoods that are divided administratively into seven Priority Boards. The Priority Boards have responsibility for neighborhood planning and they prepare neighborhood needs statements. Officials from city agencies are responsive to Priority Board requests and appear frequently at regular monthly meetings. Representatives of the Priority Boards sit on citywide committees that allocate budgetary resources. The city brings proposals before the Priority Boards both to solicit ideas and to sell their plans to constituents.

Portland, Oregon, has more than ninety independent neighborhood associations; like those of Birmingham and Dayton, they are organized into a second tier of the citizen participation system: District Coalition Boards. The neighborhoods all participate in an annual neighborhood needs process, culminating in a formal statement of priorities for each community. Through the district boards, neighborhoods receive technical assistance and financial support to cover the printing and distribution of communications to each resident. The neighborhood groups also place local residents on city planning and advisory bodies.

Saint Paul's system is built around seventeen neighborhood-based District Councils. Each of these neighborhood councils is a powerful political institution, and collectively they are widely respected by city officials, private developers, and political activists. Representatives from the District Councils are the sole members of the Capital Improvement Budget Committee, a citywide body with substantial influence over capital expenditures. District newspapers and an early notification system that mandates agency outreach to the District Councils are other impressive features of Saint Paul's neighborhood involvement structure.

Citizen participation structures like these four are almost nonexistent in American politics. We know of only a handful of other cities that come close to matching these systems in terms of the scope of the programs and the commitment to make them work. They are fairly elaborate programs and, even though the costs are not great, the strapped budgets of most cities may make them seem like unaffordable luxuries. Yet it is neither the complexity of the programs nor their cost that is the real impediment to adoption. Rather, these programs are difficult to institute because they are a threat to city hall; that is, to the elected officials of the city. Political power within a city may not be an exact zero-sum game, but it is certainly fair to assume that if the neighborhoods are given substantive responsibility, then the mayor, city councilors, agency heads, and bureaucrats may perceive their jobs to be somewhat diminished. And even if there were no concern at city hall about a dilution of power, strong neighborhood associations are still seen as a political force capable of sustained combat with an agency or city official.

Instructive is the experience of Los Angeles. From about 1996 to 1999, a proposal for a strong citizen participation system along the lines of the four described above had been part of the ongoing debate around government charter reform. When a long-awaited charter reform plan was put forward, the citizen participation component was initially constituted as a set of neighborhood advisory bodies rather than associations with clearly delineated authority (Rohrlich 1998).[2] This insufficiency has been the larger pattern of public involvement programs. When pressured to institute some form of neighborhood involvement system, city officials typically respond with a program designed to fail. Neighborhood advisory bodies can advise all they want, but without formal powers they amount to little. As we shall discuss later, for organizations to produce what Putnam calls "bridging social capital," they must possess some decision-making authority. Thankfully, in June 1999, Los Angeles enacted charter reform that created a new Department of Neighborhood Empowerment; this department mandated the establishment of a citywide system of neighborhood councils (Portney 2002; Musso, Weare, and Cooper 2004; Musso, Weare, Jun, and Kitsuse 2004; Sonenshein, 2006).

The citywide systems in Birmingham, Dayton, Portland, and Saint Paul represent mechanisms for channeling citizen views into policymaking processes. We have documented elsewhere what seem to be very impressive governance consequences that derive from the operation of these systems (Berry, Portney, and Thomson 1993). Yet these systems of participation can also be thought of as institutions that ostensibly promote civic engagement and generate social capital. They are certainly built around dialogue and deliberation. Based in the neighborhoods, they should promote friendship and tolerance. Presumably, participants who work with their neighbors to solve community problems should become more trusting of government, one of the forms of social capital emphasized by Putnam. Because the neighborhood associations are tied to other layers of government, participation in them offers individuals the chance to develop ties to other social networks.

Although these programs seem ideally suited to meet the objectives of contemporary communitarian thought, there is, of course, no assurance that they actually achieve their lofty goals. Indeed, their highly ambitious goals invite skepticism. Can neighborhood associations, largely run by volunteers, truly revitalize American democracy and civil society by stimulating participation, move the policymaking process away from its adversarial basis, and build trust in government? Can they provide mechanisms for generating social capital in ways that other organizations or organizational structures cannot or do not? The history of citizen participation programs since the 1960s is fairly dismal (Rosenbaum 1978; Berry, Portney, and Thomson 1993, 21–45). Are these systems of neighborhood associations really any different? As we assess these questions, we come away with a sense of optimism.

Neighborhood Associations as Social Capital

Neighborhood associations, particularly citywide systems of associations, offer more than mechanisms through which collective action can be accomplished (Mesch and Schwirian 1996). To understand the role of systems of neighborhood associations in producing social capital, as practiced in the four cities we studied, it is necessary to understand how the neighborhood associations operate in their local context. Contemporary thinking about social capital suggests that to be effective, two distinctly different processes need to operate. These processes, referred to by Putnam as "localized social capital," and "generalized or bridging social capital," play different but equally important roles in the creation and maintenance of communities capable of thriving. Localized social capital refers to the results of informal interactions that families and people living in their communities engage in over the course of their daily lives, or what Thomson (2001, 5) calls people "linking to the community." When people interact with their neighbors, whether at church, PTAs, in bowling leagues, or other venues, they develop an understanding of what they share and perhaps how they differ. These interactions take place in the context of activities or organizations that people selectively "join" in order to enjoy an experience with others who have a shared interest in the substance of the activity or organization. People who participate in PTAs share an interest in schools, students, and learning; those who participate in bowling leagues share an interest in throwing a ball down a lane at some ordered wooden objects, and so on. However, by themselves, these interactions and the resulting understanding, may not be sufficient to produce a thriving civil community.

Generalized or bridging social capital constitutes another important process in civil society. Bridging social capital refers to the connections of groups of people to other groups of people. When one neighborhood association interacts with another, when members of one church interact with members of a synagogue, when parents of children from one school interact with those of children from another school, or when neighbors contact public officials, the result produces an expanded understanding of the community. Moreover, such interactions often provide access to resources for groups that would not otherwise have them. Without bridging processes, people who live in poor inner-city neighborhoods may be engaged with each other but may be unable to create the kinds of economic opportunities the neighborhoods require. Bridging social capital also provides the foundation for the dialogue that is often identified as an important part of democratic governance: "democratic talk," as Barber calls it, or "moral dialogues," as Etzioni advocates. Because "democratic talk" involves both discussing shared values and confronting serious differences, much contemporary thinking suggests that it is integral to making society more governable.

We also distinguish between *vertical* and *horizontal* bridging social capital. Horizontal social capital involves social groups or organizations interacting with each other essentially as coequals. Several PTAs joining forces for some purpose or activity would be an instance of horizontal bridging social capital. When several citizens advocacy groups elect to form a coalition for some purpose, this is horizontal bridging social capital. Vertical bridging social capital, on the other hand, involves relations between or among functionally or geographically differentiated organizations; for example, when members of a neighborhood association interact with officials from a government agency. This distinction is important because vertical social capital is believed essential to mobilizing the widest array of resources for larger social objectives (Wallis, Crocker, and Schechter 1998, 259). The distinction is also important because vertical social capital represents the process through which residents are connected to the institutions of their governments, an aspect of social capital that is often overlooked or downplayed (Maloney, Smith, and Stoker 2001). We believe that systems of neighborhood associations in the cities we studied produce both of these types of bridging social capital.

This distinction between localized and bridging social capital finds its importance in the contention that healthy civil society requires both kinds of social capital in a sort of symbiotic relationship. As Wallis, Crocker, and Schechter (1998, 258–59) state it:

The relationship between local and bridging social capital suggests the beginning of a nested structure of social relations. The strength of bridging capital seems to rest on the strength of the local social capital being bridged. In turn, the strength of local social capital rests on the quality and frequency of informal social interactions. The common element binding local and bridging capital is a norm of civic engagement (or civic ethic). Local interactions that focus only on narrowly defined interests and fail to be guided by a broader civic agenda do not effectively bridge to other groups or ultimately achieve civil society.

Thus, civil society requires the engagement of people in organizations that develop and maintain localized and bridging functions. So the central question addressed here is, to what extent do systems of neighborhood associations perform these functions? Is there reason to believe that these systems are better able to perform these functions than collections of neighborhood associations working in the absence of any centralizing framework? Our analysis of these questions starts with an examination of how these systems work in practice.

Neighborhood Associations as Localized Social Capital

People who live in cities that have systems of neighborhood associations are virtually guaranteed to have access to ready forms of localized social capital by virtue of the existence of the neighborhood associations themselves. In each of the four cities we studied, there is a commitment to the maintenance of neighborhood associations across the entire city. Regardless of where someone lives in Portland, there is at least one neighborhood association that operates there. Every resident of Saint Paul has a nearby District Council. What goes on in these organizations can look pretty mundane. Yet many of the activities of these associations are precisely part of the process of generating localized social capital. They sponsor social events, neighborhood picnics, block parties, and other activities. But they do much more. They provide forums for residents of a given small geographic area to come together to address existing or emerging problems. When a vacant house becomes rundown and begins to attract criminal activity, the neighborhood association can, and usually does, work to rectify it. When a business wants to construct a new facility that appears inconsistent with existing uses, the neighborhood association offers a mechanism for collective response. When local problems emerge, there is a standing process for addressing them.

The neighborhood associations typically produce social capital from proactive localized activities as well. Nearly all of the associations in the cities we studied hold regular elections for officers, and provide the opportunity for residents to become engaged in the governance of that association. Residents who choose to participate can take part in the selection process. In the experiences of the four cities, the opportunities of citizen engagement are plentiful.

Clearly, not everyone participates in their neighborhood associations regardless of whether there is a system of associations in place. Our studies, which compared the four cities with systems of neighborhood associations to eight cities with no such systems, found that participation rates were essentially the same. Overall, across all the cities we studied, close to 20% of the residents participated in community activities at least once over a two-year period of time. Clearly, Portland and Saint Paul, two cities with systems of neighborhood associations, represent cities with unusually high levels of citizen engagement in community activities. But the levels of community participation there were not significantly greater than we found in Norfolk (Virginia), Louisville (Kentucky), and Buffalo (New York), cities whose neighborhood associations are not part of a larger system. And Birmingham and Dayton, two cities that have participation systems, had community participation rates that did not significantly differ from Tucson, Omaha, Colorado Springs, El Paso, Savannah, or Wichita, cities that do not have neighborhood systems. This provides at least prima facie evidence that creating systems of neighborhood associations does not improve the creation of localized social capital (Berry, Portney, and Thomson 1993, 71–98).

But there is one major caveat to this finding. When we analyzed more finely the kinds of participation people engage in by differentiating "weak participation activities" (such as attending a neighborhood picnic, or involvement in social and service organizations, or simple contacting behavior) from "strong participation activities" (such as working with neighbors to solve a community problem, or attending a meeting of a neighborhood association), we found clear differences. Residents in cities with systems of neighborhood associations were considerably more likely to engage in "strong participation activities" than residents of the other cities. Thus, the presence of systems of neighborhood associations does not seem to affect whether or not people are engaged. It does, however, affect what kinds of activities they are engaged in. As we shall discuss later, this finding has important implications for the creation of bridging social capital.

Neighborhood Associations as Bridging Social Capital

One of the distinguishing features of systems of neighborhood associations, compared to freestanding neighborhood associations, is an implied horizontal bridging function. In cities with citywide systems, there is clear linkage between and among the associations that blanket the city. In most cities without some form of citywide system, whether or not there is an active neighborhood association in a given area is somewhat idiosyncratic, owing more to the vagaries of the resident population than to the inherent differences in need. We suggest that, as is the case in many cities, the existence of a strong neighborhood association in one area and the total absence in others may well produce negative consequences for civil society. At a minimum, the sense of isolation, the inefficacy, jealousy, and lack of responsiveness that frequently accompany the absence of participatory opportunities need to be considered in an overall assessment of the production of social capital. In all of the cases we studied, there is some citywide mechanism in place to facilitate this horizontal bridging function. Neighborhood associations directly relate to each other by virtue of explicit organizational arrangements. Moreover, by virtue of possessing some formal or deferred decision-making authority, neighborhood associations necessarily produce bridging social capital. When neighborhood associations have the authority to make decisions, whether as a result of some formal city charter or de facto through the exercise of political influence, residents, citizens groups, and city officials alike take the process activities of these associations seriously.

The organizational arrangements that knit neighborhood associations together consist of some form of "second tier," or second and third tier, where representatives from neighborhood associations meet to discuss, decide about, and resolve city issues. This mildly hierarchical structure provides a formal vertical bridge to city officials, particularly the unelected officials who manage the affairs of the city. In Birmingham, the system of neighborhood associations has three tiers, where the first tier consists of the ninety-five neighborhood associations. These neighborhood associations are bridged to a second tier that consists of twenty-two formal "communities," typically composed of three to five neighborhoods. Thus, these communities provide the regular opportunity for multiple neighborhood associations to be horizontally bridged with others. These "communities" serve as the bridge to the third tier, the citywide Citizens Advisory Board. Although formally advisory in nature, this citywide board serves as a means for focusing dialogue among citizens, and between citizens and the city. Indeed, the deliberations of the Citizens Advisory Board are followed closely by administrative officials of the city, ensuring a direct vertical bridging function to city hall.

In Dayton, the arrangements are somewhat less hierarchical. The core of the system is Dayton's Priority Boards, which perform a variety of horizontal bridging functions through providing myriad constituent services directly to individual residents and to neighborhood associations in their sector of the city. There are no formal links to Dayton's neighborhood associations, but as a matter of practice, there is a clear symbiotic relationship. The culture of the Priority Boards is very clearly administrative, focusing more on the vertical than horizontal bridging functions. Most board members see their role as making city government agencies do their jobs more effectively. But there is also some duplication in the understanding of roles played by neighborhood associations and the Priority Boards. The city works through the Priority Boards and with neighborhood associations directly, providing multiple paths over the vertical bridge.

The City of Saint Paul is divided into seventeen District Council areas, where each council serves as the neighborhood association. Each council has office space and at least a half-time staffer. The councils have de facto authority over virtually all zoning and land use issues for the areas they cover. Horizontal bridging functions are performed by engaging residents in various council activities, ranging from selection of council officers and membership on committees, to attending regular council meetings, to neighborhood picnics and outings. Because the councils play such an important role in land use issues, an additional horizontal bridging results from interactions between council participants and developers who wish to propose projects. To a degree not experienced in most other cities, developers understand that before they can get approval from the citywide zoning board, approval must be obtained from the relevant District Council. Additionally, horizontal bridging occurs through the second tier of participation, the Capital Improvement Budget Committee. Officials from each of the District Councils serve on this committee to make decisions about how the city should allocate its capital expenditures. Typically, officials from each District Council come to committee meetings hoping to get funding for a specific project. Very often the result of the meetings is that consensus is reached concerning which neighborhood's projects are more meritorious and which are less.

Vertical bridging functions in Saint Paul result mainly from the role that the District Councils play in serving as a communications conduit to city agencies. Residents know that the best way to get the city to respond to constituent services is by working through the local District Council office. District Council staffers maintain close channels of communication with city departments, and routinely use these channels on behalf of residents. Moreover, when a significant issue is facing a particular neighborhood, it is commonplace for city agency officials to attend District Council meetings, communicating agency perspectives to residents, and taking residents' views back to city hall.

In Portland, the organization of neighborhood participation is far less structured and clear-cut. There are many different overlapping avenues for residents to be engaged in neighborhood and governance activities. There are more than ninety neighborhood-based associations that are loosely organized into a second tier of the citizen participation system called District Coalition Boards. But the link between neighborhood associations and the District Coalition Boards is not part of a formal hierarchy. Neighborhood associations frequently operate with a great deal of independence from the boards. Horizontal bridging occurs when the neighborhoods participate in their annual neighborhood needs process, which yields a formal statement of priorities for each community. Through the district coalitions, neighborhoods receive technical assistance and financial support to cover the printing and distribution of communications to each resident. Vertical bridging occurs through two principal mechanisms. First, neighborhood associations, working through their District Coalition Boards, maintain strong channels of communication with city agencies, particularly the Office of Neighborhood Associations. Second, the neighborhood groups frequently find that they can connect to city agencies by placing neighborhood residents on any of the large number of city planning and advisory bodies, including the citywide Budget Advisory Committees. Because there are so many opportunities for citizens to be engaged in neighborhood and government activities, there is often confusion about which are the most effective ways for residents to be heard.

Resulting Social Capital

Discussions of localized and bridging social capital would be incomplete without consideration of the people who populate the cities. There is, of course, considerable debate about whether Americans are less engaged in civic activities today than at times past. Yet even if this question could be answered definitively, there would still remain the question of whether that civic engagement makes a difference. Even if the diminished trust and sense of community experienced today were the product of reduced civic engagement, it is not clear whether stimulating engagement would reverse this trend. When the National Commission on Civic Renewal put forth its 1998 Final Report, it articulated a clear belief that civic participation constitutes the solution to the decline in social capital in the United States. The report notes: "This idea [of civic renewal]—citizens freely working together—is at the heart of the American conception of liberty, through which citizens take responsibility for improving the conditions of their lives. Civic liberty offers citizens the power to act, and it strengthens their convictions that they can make a difference" (National Commission on Civic Renewal 1998, 9).

Ultimately, the production of social capital is not measured by how many organizations there are or by how many people participate in these organizations, but rather by how people—individual citizens—relate to each other and to their cities as a result of this participation. Much of the conceptual work on civil society makes great claims about what happens to people when they are engaged in civic activities. The National Commission on Civic Renewal is not alone in making these claims. From building social trust and trust in government, to creating a deep sense of community, to solving social and community problems, to empowering citizens, civic engagement carries a great burden of expectations (Wilson 1997; Lean 1995). Yet surprisingly few studies of civil society provide any systematic analysis of the consequences for people who become engaged in civic life. Does participation, in fact, affect the way people view and relate to one another or the way they relate to their government? This is the core question we sought to address in our city studies. We wanted to know whether people who participate in the systems of neighborhood associations see the world differently than those who do not, whether they reap the kinds of benefits that advocates of civic renewal seek.

The analysis presented here is reported in much more detail in *The Rebirth of Urban Democracy*. While the fuller analysis examined a wide range of potential consequences of participation, we focus here on three variables that represent benefits predicted to accrue to citizens as a result of civic engagement. These variables—sense of community, trust in government, and political efficacy—are thought to be at the core of what civic renewal is about. If advocates of civic renewal are correct, we should find that participation in the context of systems of neighborhood associations produces increases in all three.

Sense of Community

The creation and maintenance of a relatively high sense of community among city residents is often seen as central to a connected, productive, and stable polity (Eckstein 1966; Fowler 1991). Our effort to assess the relationship between civic engagement and sense of community was conducted by asking a random sample of about one thousand residents in each city the following question, as taken from studies by Wandersman (1987):

Some people say they feel like they have a sense of community with others in their neighborhood. Others don't feel that way. How about you? Would you say that you feel a strong sense of community with others in your neighborhood, very little sense of community, or something in between?

In order to examine the relationship between participation and sense of community, we divided the residents we interviewed according to the most prevalent type of organization they participated in. We distinguished between participants in neighborhood associations, single-issue groups, neighborhood crime watch groups, social or service organizations, and nonparticipants. As shown in table 2-1, the pattern is fairly clear.

These results reveal a fairly clear tendency for participants in neighborhood associations to be more likely to feel a strong sense of community than participants in other kinds of local organizations. Although participation in all four types of organizations is associated with a strong sense of community (compared to nonparticipation), participation in neighborhood associations do better than the other three.

Of course, there is the possibility that these results do not reflect the effects of participation at all. Indeed, these organizations might attract residents who already possess a relatively strong sense of community. To address this possibility, we conducted a two-wave panel design survey in each city, where we reinterviewed each respondent approximately two years after the first interview. This reexamination allows us to identify residents who had not participated in their neighborhood associations at the time of the first interview but

TABLE 2-1.

Percentage of Respondents Indicating They Feel a "Strong Sense Of Community"

Socio-Economic Status of Respondent	Type of Organization in which Respondent was Active					Sample Size	Chi-Square
	None	Service or Social Group	Crime Watch	Issue Group	Neighborhood Association		
Low	27.1	37.8	49.3	41.3	57.3	2,490	92.41**
Middle	30.5	34.2	45.9	31.4	53.8	2,347	56.35**
High	26.1	38.8	41.9	37.4	51.3	1,282	46.88**

** Significant beyond the .01 level.

who had begun participating by the time of the second interview. In this way, we can have somewhat more confidence that the inferences we make reflect a particular direction of causation.

It becomes clearer here that participation in neighborhood associations probably plays a significant role in helping to create a strong sense of community (see table 2-2). Some respondents gained a sense of community regardless of their relation to their neighborhood associations, but the largest gains in a sense of community were reported by those who began participating in their respective neighborhood associations. Only people who continued participating in their neighborhood associations reported less loss of sense of community than new participants. Moreover, those who lost sense of community were those who never participated, or who stopped participating. The loss of a sense of community may well be influenced by powerful social and economic forces writ large, but there is evidence here that robust neighborhood associations can at least attenuate this loss. The differences are not huge, but they point to this conclusion.

Trust in Local Government

Central to creating a productive, strong, and stable polity is the extent to which citizens trust their government. Clearly, advocates of civic engagement see trust in government as a core value in need of restoration. The issue of trust, however, is complex, worthy of far more conceptual discussion than space permits here. Indeed, measuring the amount of trust that citizens have in their government can be a complicated task (Abramson and Finifter 1981; Feldman

TABLE 2-2.

Relationship between Participation in Neighborhood Associations and Change in
Sense of Community

Status of Participation in Neighborhood Associations over Time	Change in "Sense of Community"			Sample Size	Mean Value of Sense of Community*
	Lost	Same	Gained		
Continued nonparticipation	25.8	53.9	20.2	2,012	2.07
Stopped participating	25.7	58.4	16.0	257	2.30
Began participating	20.5	54.2	25.3	249	2.37
Continued participating	17.6	65.1	17.3	272	2.55

* The scale runs from 1 indicating "very little sense of community," to 3 "a strong sense of community;" 2 represents "something in between."

1983). Because of the powerful confounding effect of people's distrust of the government in Washington—and because we harbor no illusions about the ability of participation in neighborhood associations to be able to overcome this distrust—our effort here focuses on trust in local government vis-à-vis trust in the national government. In other words, we try to isolate the portion of respondents who have greater trust in local government than the national government. We do this by asking respondents:

Would you say the government in Washington is run by a few big interests looking out for themselves or that it is run for the benefit of all the people?

We also asked this question changing "the government in Washington" to the government in the respondent's city ("the government in Birmingham"). By using the results of these two questions together, we can distinguish those respondents whose trust in local government is greater than their trust in the national government (see table 2-3). To what extent is this view associated with participation in neighborhood associations?

Here the pattern of association is much less clear-cut. Participation in neighborhood associations is certainly associated with greater trust in local government, but participation in issue groups turns out to be almost as important. Both of these types of participation, however, appear to be more important than the other two forms of participation, especially for the most disadvantaged people. While high socioeconomic status people seem to exhibit the same levels of trust regardless of what type of organization they participate in,

TABLE 2-3.

Percentage of Respondents Saying Local Government Can Be Trusted More than the Government in Washington to Look Out for the Good of All the People

Socio-Economic Status of Respondent	None	Service or Social Group	Crime Watch	Issue Group	Neighborhood Association	Sample Size	Chi-Square
		Type of Organization in which Respondent Was Active					
Low	26.6	28.8	22.6	38.4	32.3	2,088	25.46**
Middle	29.6	35.1	32.4	35.0	39.5	1,956	11.88
High	31.0	36.9	34.4	37.8	38.0	1,030	6.85

** Significant beyond the .01 level.

lower socioeconomic status people seem to develop more trust in government when they participate in their neighborhood associations. Again, the differences are not great, but they do point to this conclusion.

Political Efficacy

Empowering people to take control of their governance is the third core variable. Empowerment can mean many things, but for most of us it means giving people the personal confidence and skills necessary for effective governing. To political scientists, this notion of being empowered closely resembles the concept of acquiring political efficacy. Researchers have distinguished two types of political efficacy: *internal efficacy,* which focuses on an individual's sense that he or she is capable of understanding politics and influencing the political process; and *external efficacy,* which represents an individual's belief that the government will be responsive to his or her attempts to influence it (Balch 1974; Craig and Maggiotto,1982; Abramson, 1983, 135–89). Although these two types of political efficacy represent two sides of the same coin, for the purposes of this analysis, we focus on internal efficacy because it relates more directly to the issue of whether individuals think they have the ability to influence government. To measure a person's internal efficacy, we use the standard National Election Study's survey research statement: "Sometimes government and politics seem so complicated that a person like me can't really understand what's going on." We asked respondents to agree or disagree with this statement using a five-point Likert scale (see table 2–4). If participation in neighborhood associations

TABLE 2-4.

Percentage of Respondents Disagreeing with the Statement "Politics and Government Are too Complicated."

Socio-Economic Status of the Respondent	Respondent's Score on the Participation Scale						Pearson's r
	0	1	2	3	4	5	
Low	24.0	25.7	30.0	44.2	41.2	38.4	0.118**
Middle	36.4	42.2	45.4	52.7	53.1	67.1	0.155**
High	47.1	58.0	62.3	67.3	63.1	78.7	0.174**

** Significant beyond the .01 level.

empowers people, we would expect that they would be more likely than participants in other kinds of organizations to disagree with this statement.

To examine this issue, we arrayed respondents on a scale of participation from 0 to 5, representing not only whether they participated in their neighborhood associations, but also how frequently. Respondents who received scale scores of 3, 4, or 5 all reported participating in their neighborhood associations, at least once a year but less than once a month, about once a month, or more than once a month, respectively. Respondents with 0 on the scale reported participating in no local organizations of any sort. And respondents with 1 or 2 on the scale reported participating in types of organizations other than the neighborhood associations themselves.

Here it seems fairly clear that internal political efficacy is associated with participation in neighborhood associations. Respondents in the top three categories of the participation scale are substantially more likely to disagree about government and politics being too complicated at each socioeconomic status level. Thus it seems clear that neighborhood association participants feel much more confident about their ability to understand politics and government. Of course, these results may reflect a direction of causation opposite of that suggested here. It could be that those who participate in neighborhood associations do so in part because they feel more efficacious; that is, efficacy causes participation rather than the other way around. Our analysis reported elsewhere has attempted to sort out such an implied reciprocal causation model, and the results strongly suggest that participation does, in fact, help to create internal political efficacy (Berry, Portney, and Thomson 1993, 269).

Limitations on space preclude us from fully analyzing another broad issue involving neighborhoods and social capital, namely, race relations within and between neighborhoods. We explore this elsewhere (Portney and Berry 1997), but it is important to note here that neighborhood associations also seem to play a positive role in mobilizing minority communities. Minorities participate at high rates in neighborhood associations, and neighborhood association participation is in turn linked to a greater sense of community than participation in other types of political organizations. From our fieldwork and interviews in the cities, we concluded that the neighborhood association systems facilitated interaction between predominantly minority, predominantly white, and mixed neighborhoods. Over the years, the neighborhood associations appear to have played a significant role in reducing conflict and antagonism along racial lines.

· · ·

We have sought to shed light on the extent to which civic engagement at the neighborhood level, in the context of systems of neighborhood associations, is capable of producing social capital. We have argued that citywide systems of neighborhood participation provide unique opportunities for producing localized and bridging social capital. They engage residents in ways that are more robust than most alternatives, providing clear horizontal and vertical bridging capital. Moreover, we asked what we think is the tougher question: is the production of social capital at the organizational level associated with individual-level benefits to civil society? We provided evidence from Birmingham, Dayton, Portland, and Saint Paul suggesting that systems of neighborhood associations do, in fact, translate into citizen-level benefits of increased sense of community, heightened trust in local government, and greater internal political efficacy. The implication is that, if building social capital is a worthy goal, then creating citywide systems of neighborhood associations, as proposed in Los Angeles, can be an important and effective way to accomplish this. What is perhaps less clear, and fodder for future research, is the individual-level consequences of different types of social capital. Are organizations and opportunities for localized and bridging social capital equally capable of contributing to the production of individual-level benefits? Or is it, as we suspect, that people experience the greatest benefits when they are engaged in activities that contain variety of types of social capital?

Notes

1. We also studied a fifth city, San Antonio, as it offered an alternative attempt to build citizen participation into city policymaking (Berry, Portney, and Thomson 1993). In San Antonio, COPS (Communities Organized for Public Service), a citizen action group is organized in the Hispanic neighborhoods of the city. COPS has no official role in the city although it exerts some influence on policymaking (Warren, 2001). In comparison to the city-sponsored programs, COPS's performance is disappointing across a range of evaluative criteria. Here we focus on the four city-backed programs that include all neighborhoods within their boundaries.

2. Subsequently, the Los Angeles charter reform proposal called for the creation of a Department of Neighborhood Empowerment, which would be given authority for structuring a system of neighborhood associations that could potentially have greater authority than the neighborhood advisory boards originally proposed.

References

Abramson, P. R. 1983. *Political Attitudes in America: Formation and Change.* New York: Freeman.

———, and A. Finifter. 1981. "On the Meaning of Political Trust: New Evidence from Items Introduced in 1978." *American Journal of Political Science* 25, no. 2:297–307.

Balch, G. I. 1974. "Multiple Indicators in Survey Research: The Concept of 'Sense of Political Efficacy.'" *Political Methodology* 1, no. 2:1–43.

Barber, B. 1984. *Strong Democracy: Participatory Politics for a New Age.* Berkeley and Los Angeles: University of California Press.

Bell, C., and Newby, H. 1974. *The Sociology of Community: A Selection of Readings.* London: Frank Cass.

Bellah, R. N., R. Madsen, W. M. Sullivan, A. Swidler, and S. M. Tipton. 1985. *Habits of the Heart: Individualism and Commitment in American Life.* Berkeley and Los Angeles: University of California Press.

Berry, J. M., K. E. Portney, and K. Thomson. 1993. *The Rebirth of Urban Democracy.* Washington, D.C.: Brookings Institution.

Craig, S., and M. Maggiotto. 1982. "Measuring Political Efficacy." *Political Methodology* 8, no. 3:85–110.

Eckstein, H. 1966. *Division and Cohesion in Democracy: A Study of Norway.* Princeton, New Jersey: Princeton University Press.

Edwards, B., and M. W. Foley, eds. 1997. Symposium on Social Capital, Civil Society, and Contemporary Democracy. *American Behavioral Scientist* 40, no. 5.

———, and M. Diani, eds. 2001. *Beyond Tocqueville: Civil Society and the Social Capital Debate in Comparative Perspective.* Hanover, N.H.: University Press of New England.

Etzioni, Amatai. 1996. *The New Golden Rule: Community and Morality in a Democratic Society.* New York: Basic Books.

Feldman, S. 1983. "The Measurement and Meaning of Trust in Government." *Political Methodology* 9, no. 3:341–54.

Fowler, R. B. 1991. *The Dance with Community: The Contemporary Debate in American Political Thought.* Lawrence, Kans.: The University Press of Kansas.

Ladd, E. C. 1996. "The Data Just Don't Show Erosion of America's 'Social Capital.'" *Public Perspective* 7, no. 4:1ff.

———. 1999, "Bowling with Tocqueville: Civic Engagement and Social Capital." *The Responsive Community* 9, no. 2:11–21.

Lean, M. 1995. *Bread, Bricks, and Belief: Communities in Charge of their Future.* West Hartford, Conn.: Kumarian.

Lopez, M., and Stack, C. 2001. "Social Capital and the Culture of Power: Lessons from the Field." In *Social Capital and Poor Communities,* edited by S. Saegert, J. Thompson, and M. Warren, 31–59. New York: Russell Sage Foundation.

Macedo, S., Y. Alex-Assensoh, J. Berry, M. Brintnall, D. Campbell, L. R. Fraga, A. Fung, W. Galston, C. Karpowitz, M. Levu, M. Levinson, K. Lipsitz, R. Niemi, R. Putnam, W. Rahn, R. Reich, R. Rodgers, T. Swanstrom, and K. Walsh. 2005. *Democracy at Risk: How Political Choices Undermine Citizen Participation, and What We Can Do About It.* Washington, D.C.: Brookings Institution Press.

Maloney, W., G. Smith, and G. Stoker. 2001. "Social Capital and the City." In *Beyond Tocqueville: Civil Society and the Social Capital Debate in Comparative Perspective,* edited by Bob Edwards, Michael W. Foley, and Mario Diani, 83–98. Hanover, N.H.: University Press of New England.

Mansbridge, J. J. 1980. *Beyond Adversary Democracy.* New York: Basic Books.

Mesch, G., and K. Schwirian. 1996. "The Effectiveness of Neighborhood Collective Action." *Social Problems* 43, no. 4:467–83.

Musso, J., C. Weare, and T. Cooper. 2004. *Neighborhood Councils in Los Angeles: A Midterm Status Report.* Los Angeles: University of Southern California, School of Policy, Planning and Development.

Musso, J., C. Weare, K-N Jun, and A. Kitsuse. 2004. *Representing Diversity in Community Governance: Neighborhood Councils in Los Angeles.* Los Angeles: University of Southern California, School of Policy, Planning and Development.

National Commission on Civic Renewal. 1998. *A Nation of Spectators: How Civic Engagement Weakens America and What We Can Do About It.* College Park, Md.: School of Public Affairs, University of Maryland.

Peterson, P. E. 1981. *City Limits.* Chicago: University of Chicago Press.

Portney, K. E. 2002. "Bowling in Neighborhoods: Civil Society and the Promise of Citywide Networks of Neighborhood Councils in Los Angeles." *Urban News* 16, no. 3 (fall):3–7.

Portney, K. P., and J. M. Berry. 1997. "Mobilizing Minority Communities." *American Behavioral Scientist* 40, no. 5:632–44.

Putnam, R. D. 1995a. "Bowling Alone: America's Declining Social Capital." *Journal of Democracy* 6:65–78.

———. 1995b, "Tuning In, Tuning Out: The Strange Disappearance of Social Capital in America." *PS: Political Science and Politics* 28, no. 4:664–83.

———. 2000. *Bowling Alone: The Collapse and Renewal of American Community.* New York: Simon and Schuster.

Rosenbaum, W. A. 1978. "Public Involvement as Reform and Ritual: The Development of Federal Participation Programs." In *Citizen Participation in America: Essays on the State of the Art,* edited by Stuart Langton. Lexington, Mass.: Lexington Books.

Skocpol, T., and M. Fiorina, eds. 1999. *Civic Engagement in American Democracy.* Washington, D.C.: Brookings Institution Press.

Sonenshein, R. J. 2006. *The City at Stake: Secession, Reform, and the Battle for Los Angeles.* Princeton, N. J.: Princeton University Press.

Thomson, K. 2001. *From Neighborhood to Nation: The Democratic Foundations of Civic Society.* Hanover, N.H.: University Press of New England.

Wallis, A. 1998. "Social Capital and Community Building: Part Two." *National Civic Review.* 87, no. 4:317–36.

———, J. P. Crocker, and B. Schechter. 1998. "Social Capital and Community Building: Part One." *National Civic Review* 87, no. 3:253–71.

Wandersman, A., et al. 1987. "Who Participates, Who Does Not Participate, and Why? An Analysis of Voluntary Neighborhood Organizations in the United States and Israel." *Sociological Forum* 2, no. 3:534–55.

Warren, M. R. 2001. "Power and Conflict in Social Capital." In *Beyond Tocqueville: Civil Society and the Social Capital Debate in Comparative Perspective,* edited by Bob Edwards, Michael W. Foley, and Mario Diani. Hanover, N.H.: University Press of New England.

Wilson, P. A. 1997. "Building Social Capital: A Learning Agenda for the Twenty-first Century." *Urban Studies* 34, no. 5–6:745–60.

Grassroots Organizing in Boston Chinatown

A Comparison with CDC-style Organizing

The Alinsky, or Industrial Areas Foundation, organizing model largely defined modern-day concepts of community organizing (Reitzes and Reitzes 1986), but a number of other distinct approaches and variations exist. Two important approaches to organizing in urban communities today are the *community-building* approach, typified by community development corporations (CDCs; see table 3-1 for acronyms), and another distinctive approach to grassroots empowerment organizing with roots in the radical movements of the 1960s and 1970s that Smock (2004) has labeled the *transformative model*.

This chapter describes two case examples of community organizing that are representative of the community-building and transformative approaches used in Boston Chinatown. We focus on the work of the Asian Community Development Corporation (ACDC 2005) to illustrate community building and the Chinese Progressive Association (CPA) to illustrate transformative organizing. In particular, we examine two case studies surrounding the preservation and development of Parcels C and 24 in Boston Chinatown, and the two organizations' approaches to community development, leadership development, and the use of professional, technical, or academic resources.[1]

The authors are longtime participants of the Chinese Progressive Association, our case example of transformative organizing. We make no claim, then, that our examination is an unbiased comparison of two organizing models. Instead, we attempt to make a case for the transformative approach as both contrasted with and complementary to the community-building approach as experienced in Boston Chinatown. In order to be as fair as possible in this analysis and critique, one of the authors interviewed the executive director of ACDC to confirm what we see as its community-building perspective.

TABLE 3-1.

Acronyms

ACDC	Asian Community Development Corporation
BCNC	Boston Chinatown Neighborhood Council
BRA	Boston Redevelopment Authority
CDC	Community Development Corporation
CPA	Chinese Progressive Association
CPC	Campaign to Protect Chinatown
EAFA	Edward A. Fish Associates
HSC	Hudson Street for Chinatown
MTA	Massachusetts Turnpike Authority
RFP	Request for Proposals
RHICO	Ricane Hadrian Initiative for Community Organizing
T–NEMC	Tufts–New England Medical Center

Community-Building and Transformative Organizing in Boston Chinatown

Smock writes, "Whereas the power-based model focuses on building residents' clout within the public sphere, the community-building model focuses on strengthening the internal social and economic fabric of the neighborhood itself. Community-building practitioners believe that the fundamental problem facing urban neighborhoods is their lack of internal capacity to address their own needs" (2004, 17). This approach is typical of many CDCs, like ACDC, that have helped to popularize the asset-based approach to community development. According to Smock, strengths of the community-building model include its internal focus on strengthening the community's social and economic fabric as well as its ability to leverage government and private sector support through partnerships in order to create housing, support small business development, or provide new service programs.

We argue for another distinct approach to community organizing, that also has its roots in the 1960s and 1970s, evolving particularly out of Marxist-influenced organizing within communities of color.[2] Smock (2004) loosely describes this approach and labels it the "transformative model." Characteristics of this model, exemplified by CPA, include a focus on popular education as well as a combined focus on immediate and systemic issues. Using this approach, organizers seek to make immediate improvements in the community as well as to alter the terms of public debate and raise popular consciousness toward building a longer-term social change movement.

Boston Chinatown is both an immigrant working-class neighborhood of about six thousand residents, of which 81% were Asian in 2000 (Institute for Asian American Studies, 2004), as well as the ethnic hub and strategic base of the Greater Boston Chinese community. This unique characteristic of the Chinatown community accounts for both its most important assets and its economic and political complexities and tensions. Chinatown is home to some seventy-five organizations, yet most of these organizations are ethnicity-based, not neighborhood-based, and most organizational leaders are not residents of Chinatown themselves (M. C. Liu, 1999: 35–37).[3] Such organizations have been a strength of the Chinese community in struggles for civil rights, immigrant rights, or workers' rights.

A Community-Building Model of Organizing at the Asian Community Development Corporation

The Asian Community Development Corporation (ACDC) is a community-based organization established in 1987: "The Corporation develops physical community assets, including affordable housing for rental and ownership; promotes economic development; fosters leadership development; builds capacity within the community and advocates on behalf of the community" (ACDC 2005). Notable accomplishments of ACDC include the development of Oak Terrace, a 88-unit mixed-income housing development that was completed in 1994, a series of community economic development activities, production of a video documentation project known as the Chinatown Banquet, and codevelopment of a $55 million mixed-income housing development called the Metropolitan (ACDC 2005).

Since 2002, ACDC has developed community-organizing work as an integral part of its programming, particularly helping to spearhead the community campaign for a piece of land—known as Parcel 24 and originally seized through urban renewal for highway construction—to be returned to Chinatown for housing development upon the completion of the I-93 highway reconstruction project known as the Big Dig.

While ACDC does not name its organizing approach as a specific type, its approach most closely aligns with Smock's community-building model. Key features of ACDC's work include consensus building and capacity building. Jeremy Liu, executive director of ACDC, frequently stresses that more can be achieved for Chinatown if diverse sectors of the community can work together. He notes that ACDC tries to be more than a provider: it does not merely develop affordable housing; it helps people prepare to acquire said housing.

ACDC seeks to build a community base that will support an affordable housing agenda (J. Liu 2005).

A Transformative Model of Organizing at the Chinese Progressive Association

The Chinese Progressive Association was established in 1977 by elderly immigrant residents, working mothers, and American-born youth out of a series of community-organizing campaigns in the 1970s. These campaigns concerned normalizing diplomatic relations with mainland China, seeking a voice for Chinese parents within the Boston school desegregation process, and struggling over a series of housing and land development issues (CPA 2002).

Key founders of CPA were profoundly influenced by the Black Power movement's identification with Third World liberation struggles of the 1960s and 1970s, as well as by concepts of class struggle popular in the New Left and in China at the time. CPA's founding principles included "to unite with all that can be united with to better the lives of Chinese people here in the US" and "to support just struggles against oppression."[4]

Today, CPA has a membership of more than one thousand individuals and families throughout the Greater Boston area. Its current mission is to work for full equality and empowerment of the Chinese community and to involve ordinary people in decision-making. CPA's programs include the Campaign to Protect Chinatown (which organizes residents to stabilize the community's working-class core while developing its future), a Political Empowerment Project, a Workers Center, the Chinese Youth Initiative, an Adult Education Program, drop-in services, and membership activities. CPA is often viewed as the advocate for low-income, working-class Chinese immigrants and has organized Chinatown residents around housing and land issues for nearly three decades.

Typical of transformative organizing, CPA organizers define some of their major organizing principles as (1) a long-term empowerment approach that expands power and democracy for those at the bottom; (2) development of conscious leadership based on political unity and a close relationship to the base; (3) a commitment to building the organized strength of the people; and (4) applying organizing principles to develop a democratic vision for the future (Lowe 2003).

Thus, while CPA shares the popular education philosophy and long-term social change focus of the transformative model, its core emphasis is grassroots empowerment of the most oppressed. Its three decades in the community bring unique strengths not associated with this model in Smock's case studies. Whereas the transformative organizations that Smock studied were often long on theory but short on grassroots involvement, CPA has a reputation as one of

Boston's leading community organizations in terms of the strength and depth of its community mass base, and has become "institutionalized into the community structure" (M. C. Liu 1999). Another distinguishing feature of CPA is its preponderance of women leaders.[5] Whether CPA's strong base and female leadership are the cause or the result of this strength, CPA is known for involving ordinary community members in making decisions, as described in its mission statement (see table 3–2 for comparison of CPA and ACDC).

Transformative Organizing for Parcel C

Parcel C was a one-block area contained by Oak, Nassau, and Ash Streets in the heart of Chinatown's residential section (see table 3–3 for Parcel C timeline). It is a street of mostly four-story brick row houses, which also contained a small outdoor tot lot and day care center. Less than a block away is the Josiah Quincy Elementary School, a subsidized elderly housing development, and a large low-income family housing development.

Parcel C had been a contentious site for many years. At least twice in the 1980s, the neighboring Tufts–New England Medical Center (T-NEMC) had proposed building a large-scale parking garage on the parcel, but both times had been rejected by the Boston Redevelopment Authority (BRA) after a series of community protest activities led by CPA and two other community groups. Following the second rejection of T-NEMC's garage proposal, the BRA negotiated a land swap with T-NEMC, resulting in the hospital's creating a continuous corridor down lower Washington Street in exchange for designation of two parcels of land along Oak Street for community development (Lai et al. 2000).

The two community development parcels were designated for development of housing and community services, with Parcel C as the site for a new community center. Following the defeat of the second garage proposal, the BRA selected seven agencies to codevelop the site, incorporated as Chinatown Community Center, Inc. Among the partners selected were an Asian American cultural organization, two youth recreational programs, two multiservice centers, the local health center, and CPA.[6]

When the development boom of the 1980s ended and financing for a large-scale community center could not be found, the BRA shifted its position and began to pressure the community partners to work with the adjacent hospital on a combination garage-and-community-center project, a concept that was rejected by the group. With neither financing nor BRA support, however, the community center project lost momentum. In 1993, the BRA came back to the group again with a proposal for an eight-story hospital parking garage, to which a small 10,000 square foot "community center" could be attached at the

TABLE 3-2.

Characteristics of the CPA and ACDC Approaches

Transformative Characteristics of CPA Approach

    Decide to take on garage fight with no expectation of winning

    Involve affected residents in deciding demands and strategy

    Fight for principle of respecting the Chinatown Community Plan

    Focus on democratic decision-making and grassroots leadership

    Combine mass mobilization tactics with popular education

        Outcomes

    Won open, transparent process and bilingual meetings

    Gave birth to new resident association and resident involvement

    Monitored developer accountability to vision and community

    Stopped garage and preserved land for community development

Community Building Characteristics of ACDC Approach

    Work to establish "moral site control" or claim to parcel

    Mend community fabric by reclaiming land and restoring housing

    Create community consensus by emphasizing breadth of stakeholders

    Build community capacity through technical assistance

    Convince decision-makers through knowledgeable and feasible vision

        Outcomes

    Community members gained development and political knowledge

    Leveraged land lease for below-market rate

    Parcel 24 designated for mixed-income housing

    Community developer and partner selected

TABLE 3-3.

Parcel C Timeline

1986	Community stops 1st garage proposal.
1988	Community stops 2nd garage proposal. Chinatown Community Center planned, involving CPA and six agencies.
1990	Chinatown Community Plan published, designating Parcel C for community center.
1993	3rd garage proposed, with City support. CPA and two agencies call community meeting, launch Coalition opposition campaign Coalition demands "Let the People Decide!" Parcel C vote is 1,692:42 against garage. Escalating protests continue for 18 months.
1994	Hospital and City halt garage proposal; Parcel C designated for community development.
1998	Coalition launches community visioning survey; City holds open community visioning meetings.
1999	CPA helps residents launch Chinatown Resident Association. Parcel C Request for Proposals includes resident demands. Developer (ACDC and partner) selected through open process. Parcel C project proposed as 12-story project, then 16, 19, 21, and finally 23-story project.
2002	ACDC and partner sign private Parcel C agreement, leave out nonprofit space.
2003	CPA alternates between private and public pressure to claim long-envisioned space on Parcel C.
2004	CPA and Coalition denied role in Parcel C Grand Opening.
2006	CPA completes $1.5 million capital campaign to purchase space; celebrates its Grand Opening on Parcel C.

ground level, or comparable financial compensation offered to the community partners to find space elsewhere (Lai et al. 2000).

The community center partners held a negotiation meeting with the hospital and the BRA, after which the community center group split two ways. Two agencies, desperate for space, decided to support the garage proposal. One agency had folded. Four agencies, including CPA, opposed it. Arguing that the agencies could not make such an important decision for the entire community, CPA and two other groups decided to call a community meeting to ask the area residents for their opinion. A hundred people came to the community meeting and pledged passionately to fight any parking garage proposal for Parcel C, regardless of the community benefits that might be attached (Lai et al. 2000).

From that historic community meeting, the Coalition to Protect Parcel C for Chinatown was formed. At its inception, CPA staff, who played a core organizing role, had little confidence that the garage could actually be stopped. Yet they believed that the struggle to fight for the principle of democratic decision-making was important, and that organizing the community against the garage would eventually have an impact on the outcome of that and other future projects.

While CPA's approach involved mass mobilization tactics typical of Alinsky-style organizing, the decision to place political principle and long-term organizing considerations above those of short-term feasibility distinguishes the transformative approach. For the transformative model of community organizing, expanding democratic involvement, developing new leadership, and raising the community's level of organization are often the central priorities, as was the case here. The coalition grew to consist of a cross-section of twenty community organizations and individual residents, and spanned the community's political spectrum. While a number of nonprofit service agencies declined to participate, including ACDC, many of the community's membership-based associations, both grassroots and traditional, were involved.[7]

Fight the Power: A Transformative Approach Combining Opposition Tactics and Grassroots Empowerment

For CPA and other coalition members, the struggle to stop the parking garage and preserve Parcel C was waged through intense and unrelenting opposition to both the hospital and city officials. This attitude and approach was evident in a T-shirt designed by youth participants, with the bold-letter slogan on the back: Fight the Power. In contrast to the community-building or consensual approach, CPA's unwavering focus on grassroots empowerment resulted in tensions among community leaders, some of whom had partnerships with the hospital or city government.

Yet CPA organizers and their constituents saw little alternative to this oppositional approach. Their absence from any decision-making table was a stark reality. In fact, the coalition regularly wrote, called, and tried to send messages to the mayor requesting to meet throughout the eighteen months of the campaign; it never received a single note or phone call in response.

Despite the overwhelming popular resistance to the garage, the mayor and the BRA supported the project and brushed off the opposition for a year and a half. The few community proponents of the proposal were the two agencies that sought direct benefits from the garage project and a City-initiated official advisory group known as the Chinatown Neighborhood Council.[8]

The council was designed to represent Chinatown's interests and advise city government on neighborhood affairs. Initiated as an appointed council by former mayor Raymond Flynn in 1985, it later became an elected body. The council is made up of twenty-one members, representing a variety of stakeholders and including four seats for Chinatown businesses, four seats for service agencies, four seats for organizations, five seats for Chinatown residents, and four seats for other Asian Americans living outside of Chinatown.[9] Every year, the council seated a slate backed by community business leaders in an annual community election held on Thanksgiving weekend.

The council's support of the garage was problematic for grassroots organizers. No matter how many petitions, letters, or protests they organized, city officials and the mayor pointed to the council as evidence that the community supported the project. In fact, CPA activists believed that the council had rubber-stamped development proposals for years. Thus, the campaign to stop the parking garage at its core was a challenge to the existing power structure in Chinatown and an implementation of CPA's grassroots empowerment principles, to involve people "at the bottom" in decision-making.

While residents overwhelmingly opposed the garage, the issue quickly polarized community leaders, between those traditional leaders who supported the garage and those who did not. This division was exacerbated by the mainstream media, which regularly covered the garage struggle as a story about infighting in Chinatown (Kempskie 1993). CPA organizers seized the opportunity to expose the Chinatown Neighborhood Council's lack of accountability and representation, both in its practice and composition. The polarized atmosphere made several agency leaders uncomfortable and unwilling to take a position on either side, particularly as the council enjoyed the clear support of city hall.

Altering the Debate by Fighting for Residents' Voice

Prior to 1993, CPA had developed neither an analysis of nor a focus on neighborhood-based resident organizing. But its historical focus on grassroots empowerment quickly led organizers to a deeper commitment to resident decision-making in Chinatown. With no resident organization guarding their interests, the primarily low-income working-class residents of Chinatown were simultaneously the least represented and the most impacted by development decisions.

Individual residents, especially homeowners across the street from the site, came out in force, some angry and frustrated that they were consulted so late in the process. To these residents, the fact that agencies had even negotiated with the local hospital indicated a willingness to compromise residents' quality of life in exchange for nonprofit community space. It was thus significant that the coalition and its founding organizations made an immediate decision to rally behind the residents' demand of "No garage on Parcel C," regardless of community benefits or mitigation that might later be offered.

With no resident or neighborhood association in Chinatown at the time, CPA played the core grassroots-organizing role within the coalition. Its actions included outreach to Chinatown residents and Chinese-language media, community meetings to keep residents informed and involve them in decision-making, mobilization strategies, and strategy development with other partners. An Asian American cultural and advocacy group worked with CPA to coordinate media outreach, fund-raising, and extracommunity organizing; a team of Asian American lawyers formed a legal team to direct research, monitoring of and preparation for the public comment process, and investigation of litigation strategies (Lai et al. 2000; Leong 1995–96). Through organizing residents and strengthening their voice, CPA and the coalition sought to alter the terms of the debate, in a manner typical of transformative organizing. At that point, city and community leaders emphasized the perceived inevitability of the hospital garage. They also framed the massive resident opposition as a split in the community.

In order to prove that the community was in fact united, not divided, over the garage, CPA and the coalition organized the Parcel C Referendum, a community-based plebiscite on the garage proposal, and asked the local chapter of the American Friends Service Committee to serve as an impartial monitor and administrator. "Let the people decide!" became the slogan of the Parcel C Referendum.[10] The referendum vote was a turning point for the campaign, and a massive exercise in the popular education method favored by transformative organizing. For many immigrant residents, in fact, the referendum was their first experience with voting of any kind. Using the same voting guidelines as those governing the Chinatown Neighborhood Council, the referendum vote was 1,692 against and 42 in favor of the garage. While the struggle against the garage continued to be waged for another year, the referendum created a clear popular mandate that brought more citywide allies to the coalition's side.

The decision to adopt the voting guidelines of the Chinatown Neighborhood Council was a strategic one. By using the council's own voting guidelines but exceeding the vote total of the average council election, the referendum was designed to disprove any mandate that the council might claim. To ensure that residents' voices were heard, the coalition decided to separately track and tally resident and nonresident votes. In the final tallies, however, residents and nonresidents alike overwhelmingly rejected the garage.[11]

The coalition also built citywide alliances with environmental groups as part of a legal strategy to demand a full environmental review and slow down decision-making, with other neighborhoods to build pressure on the mayor, and with a health care advocacy group to put pressure on the hospital. Following the referendum, the coalition sought the assistance of a prominent Chinese American architect to provide sketches for an alternative community use plan for the parcel, organized a Recreation Day on Parcel C to demonstrate alternative uses for the land, and continued to organize a series of creative and timely public protests.

Finally, in the fall of 1994, after eighteen months of escalating community protests, a successful media campaign, legal and technical advocacy to prolong the environmental review process, and the threat of filing a civil rights lawsuit against the City of Boston, the garage proposal was scrapped and an agreement was signed stating that Parcel C would be developed for community use. Afterward, activists speculated that the unpopular and drawn-out approval process had combined with the hospital's own budgetary issues to put an end to the garage. Stonewalled by City Hall, CPA and other coalition leaders actually had no formal role in the agreement. They first learned that the garage was stopped when a *Boston Herald* reporter called organizers for a reaction (Leong 1995/1996).

Raising Popular Consciousness in the Visioning Stage

ACDC was one of several agencies that scrupulously avoided taking a position either for or against the garage throughout the eighteen-month controversy. One member of ACDC's board of directors explained confidentially that ACDC leaders were with the protesters in spirit, but that they couldn't publicly oppose city government and thus jeopardize needed support for completion of their Oak Terrace housing project (M. C. Liu 1999, 117). In the years immediately following the 1994 Parcel C agreement, CPA and the coalition continued to have no access to city hall and lacked a clear strategy to move forward the development of the parcel. CPA and other coalition members called for an open community process to allow Chinatown residents and the community at-large to participate in planning.

Prior to the Parcel C struggle, the only mechanism for community input was the council, which did not publish its meeting dates or agenda, generally held meetings only in English, and did not allow residents or observers to speak. Seeking to reestablish the legitimacy of their processes, the BRA made the historic move of opening up the "community process" beyond the input of the council. In the fall of 1998, the BRA launched open community meetings in Chinatown to seek input into development of a Request for Proposals (RFP) for Parcel C. Ordinary Chinatown residents and community leaders who were not members of the council were able to give input for the first time. Another first was the hiring of Chinese interpreters to provide full interpretation as well as written Chinese materials throughout the process.

In the same time frame, the coalition had initiated a community survey in 1998 to learn about community members' ideas and desires for the parcel, and had brought ACDC in as a cosponsor of the survey. During the visioning process for Parcel C, CPA and other coalition activists organized residents to discuss the Parcel C survey results and to articulate their vision for the land, while the BRA led a process that involved a basic orientation to development concepts such as zoning guidelines, minimum or maximum build-out, floor area ratio, internal and external subsidies, and the financing of community benefits. Knowing little about development, CPA organized residents to debrief and arrive at opinions collectively between public meetings.

Through this process, resident activists developed a few basic principles, in addition to the more general community demand for low-income affordable housing, which they sought for inclusion in the RFP. These included (1) a moderately-scaled project, in keeping with the residential row houses and Oak Terrace apartments across the street; (2) a large multifunction community room that could be used for meetings, performances, or events; (3) a public garden or open space that would be available to the community at-large and not only future residents of the project; (4) nonprofit space for community agencies, particularly for those original community center partners who had continued to fight for preservation of the land; and (5) long-term community ownership or control.[12]

It was another historic moment when the BRA released its RFP for Parcel C. CPA and other coalition members were pleasantly surprised to see that nearly all of the points sought by residents were included (BRA 1999).

After the RFP was released, only one development group responded—a partnership formed by for-profit developer Edward A. Fish Associates (EAFA) and ACDC. In July 1999, they presented a proposal for a twelve-story project that included public open space, mixed-income housing, and 10,000 square feet of nonprofit community space, naming CPA and other former community center partners (EAFA 1999).

Development Trade-offs

While resident priorities were reflected in the RFP, a number of realities quickly began to complicate development plans for Parcel C. The original public parcel had a footprint of approximately 25,000 square feet. The BRA used its influence to assemble a larger parcel for the project, by convincing abutters to relinquish their properties in favor of building replacement facilities within the Parcel C project. Developers thus became responsible for accommodating the Boston Asian Youth Essential Services and the Boston Chinatown Neighborhood Council, which had been in adjacent properties. Hardball negotiations between these agencies and the developers ensued for several years.[13]

For-profit developer Edward A. Fish Associates (EAFA 1999) also held the advantage in its partnership with ACDC to develop Parcel C. The BRA had created a two-stage selection process in which the for-profit developer was picked first and the nonprofit second. This process effectively undercut ACDC's role and clout as a community development partner, as it had neither secured the bid nor the development site.

While CPA and resident activists who had fought the parking garage developed a unified vision for Parcel C, following the RFP's release, they had not sustained the same level of grassroots organizing and outreach to broadly unite the community around the development vision. Meanwhile, the developers used their own approach to balancing community trade-offs. From 1999 to 2002, between public meetings with the community, the Parcel C project went from an initial 12-story proposal to 16, 19, 21, and finally 23 stories in its final iteration, much to abutting residents' dismay.

EAFA/ACDC successfully secured unprecedented levels of public subsidy for this high-profile project. The affordable housing component included 115, or 46%, of units considered affordable by HUD standards. On closer analysis, however, only eleven of the affordable units serve "very low income" households typical of Chinatown residents, and seventy units serve moderate-income households.[14] With a median household income of $27,963 for Boston Asian Americans and $14,670 for Chinatown Asian Americans, most of the affordable housing on Parcel C is still unaffordable to most Chinese American residents in Boston (Institute for Asian American Studies 2004).

In 2002, unknown to most of the community, ACDC signed an agreement with its development partner to ensure the critical community benefits that they had chosen to prioritize, leaving out the envisioned nonprofit community center space, with the exception of the community room and ACDC's own office.[15] The project broke ground in August 2002.

From 2001 until the end of 2004, CPA repeatedly pressed ACDC to deliver on its informal but public promise of at-cost community space for CPA's permanent office. ACDC responded first that the developers were not yet ready to negotiate, then that it no longer had any decision-making role, and finally that there was never a particular commitment made to CPA (Smith 2004).

In November 2003, Edward A. Fish Associates issued a Request for Qualification to launch an open and competitive bidding process for what was now ground-floor commercial space. Because ACDC declined to participate as a community partner in the selection process, this role was given instead to a co-moderator of the Chinatown Neighborhood Council, who had been the community's most vocal advocate of the parking garage in 1993.[16] CPA submitted its application with ten letters of support from community agency, resident, and business leaders, only to find itself as one of two finalists, in competition with an agency that had submitted its application after the deadline. For the next six months, CPA pressured both ACDC and EAFA to honor their original commitment to at-cost community space, alternating between private and public pressure tactics while negotiating over the market-rate sale price and commercial-rate condo fees.

In August 2004, with this negotiation still in process, ACDC and EAFA celebrated the Metropolitan grand opening and denied a request from the Coalition to Protect Parcel C for Chinatown to have a speaker or any official role in the celebration. A protest of some fifty CPA members and supporters was called off just minutes before the Metropolitan grand opening. When ACDC, EAFA, and the BRA later failed to deliver on promises negotiated that day, CPA members held an impromptu sit-in at city hall and pressured the BRA to provide subsidies to lower its commercial condo fees to a nonprofit rate.[17] CPA was eventually able to purchase its space for a slightly below-market price.[18]

Contrasting Lessons from Parcel C

For ACDC, the physical development—the Metropolitan building—was the primary positive outcome of the Parcel C events, with a frame of reference that began with its involvement in the predevelopment phase. Executive Director Jeremy Liu (2005) explains that ACDC prefers concrete rather than abstract goals. Major accomplishments include the provision of more than 30,000 square feet of (primarily replacement) community space and 251 units of housing, with a mix of rental and home ownership opportunities; the units target a wide range of income levels.

A key lesson that ACDC members learned from the Parcel C experience was the need for the CDC to create more community leverage within the development partnership and to have more ongoing communication with the community during the development-planning phase. Jeremy Liu (2005) explains, "We learned that the way we were doing the project was not creating empowerment or capacity building. It was about getting a massive project done." Focusing on this lesson, ACDC set out more deliberately to plan its work around Parcel 24, an urban renewal parcel owned by the Massachusetts Turnpike Authority. Differences in ACDC's approach to Parcel 24 as compared to Parcel C included:

1. Playing a public role in a community-organizing and community-visioning campaign. ACDC's core organizing role in the Parcel 24 campaign reflected both an increased emphasis on community visioning and on its own establishment of "moral site control."[19]
2. Retaining a highly experienced development consultant to help the CDC negotiate with the for-profit developer.

3. Education to help community members better understand development realities and ongoing communication to build community support for the project.

In contrast, for CPA and core coalition activists, the most enduring victory of Parcel C was the foundation it laid for the continuing struggle for resident empowerment and the encouragement of community residents to believe in their right to a decision-making voice. Typical of Smock's transformative model of community organizing, CPA organizers renewed their focus on popular education to change the terms of the development debate, grassroots organizing to empower the most disenfranchised, and activities to link immediate struggles around particular development projects with more systemic issues.

Lessons that CPA members learned from the Parcel C experience were the value of a more organized resident voice, increased political clout, the capacity to combine grassroots organizing and professional expertise such as legal or development knowledge, and for community control mechanisms that could hold developers accountable. They also realized that popularization of the Chinatown Community Plan of 1990, a community-planning document focused on maintaining Chinatown as a working-class, family neighborhood, was vital to changing the terms of public debate about development in the Chinatown/downtown area.

Following the defeat of the parking garage and the development visioning stage, CPA worked with other core leaders to establish the Campaign to Protect Chinatown (CPC), which eventually became an ongoing program of the CPA. The Campaign to Protect Chinatown began to publish a bilingual resident bulletin, distributed door-to-door throughout the neighborhood, and to hold block or building-based meetings as a way to keep residents informed about neighborhood issues, to popularize the Chinatown Community Plan, and to educate people about the possibilities for change. For the next ten years, as development project after project came up for public review on a piecemeal basis, CPA/CPC led an effort to democratize the development review process and to popularize the Chinatown Community Plan of 1990. The work that ensued included the founding of Chinatown's first resident association, efforts to reframe public debate around downtown development, and the tripling of Chinatown's voter turn-out from 1997 to 2005.

Hudson Street for Chinatown: A Community-Building Approach

Beginning in 2002, ACDC took a visible leadership role in the campaign to establish moral site control and reclaim an area known as Parcel 24 for Chinatown (see table 3–4 for a timeline). This site was formerly a residential street of Chinatown,

TABLE 3-4.

Parcel 24 Timeline

2002	ACDC researches and plans campaign for moral site control.
	ACDC, CPA, and CRA launch Hudson Street for Chinatown.
	Coalition files state legislation.
	Community education and letter-writing campaign.
	Community design forum held.
	Coalition debates collaborative development entity, depth of housing affordability, development scale.
	Forges consensus and community development vision.
2004	ACDC decides it will bid for development without other community partners.
	Community vision published and released.
	Major points of community vision incorporated into RFP.
2005	ACDC and partner win tentative designation of parcel.

lost to eminent domain and urban renewal when homes were razed to make way for the Central Artery and Massachusetts Turnpike extension. That fall, CPA had approached ACDC to discuss developing a closer working relationship, linking organizing and development work, and to collaborate on issues of highway air rights development. ACDC, which had already been investigating the Parcel 24 issue, immediately suggested this as the focus of collaborative work.

ACDC had just received a multiyear grant from the Ricane Hadrian Initiative for Community Organizing (RHICO) project of the Massachusetts Association of CDCs to develop its community-organizing work with a focus on the Parcel 24 campaign. The goal of winning Parcel 24 back to Chinatown was compelling. With the support, training, and technical assistance of the RHICO project, ACDC staff launched into this work with zeal.

ACDC's broad approach to coalition building with residents, traditional associations, and agencies reflected its central focus on community consensus building. ACDC staff and board members saw their organization as uniquely positioned to unify the broad array of forces within an oft-contentious community. Enjoying credibility as a community housing developer with city hall—as well as the Massachusetts Turnpike Authority who owned the land—ACDC was able to quickly round up technical resources for a community-visioning process and to get the buy-in of decision-makers like the BRA and the MTA.

On the other hand, CPA and the Chinatown Resident Association, which launched the Hudson Street for Chinatown (HSC) coalition together with ACDC, brought their credibility and broad base among Chinatown residents to the effort. While each group contributed its strengths, ACDC immediately took the visible lead role, branding a number of materials in the name of both ACDC and HSC. When CPA and Chinatown Resident Association representatives questioned the omission of their groups' names from publicity materials, ACDC staff responded that there were many Chinatown organizations endorsing the HSC demands. Only after two of the more traditional associations joined the active core of HSC did ACDC begin to list participating organizations' names.

While initially deferring to ACDC's initiative, CPA and other core groups became gradually more critical of ACDC's maneuvers, thus highlighting conflicting priorities among coalition members. For CPA and Chinatown residents, a core goal was to strengthen and legitimize residents' role in decision-making within a broader community effort to reclaim the parcel for community needs. ACDC, however, had a goal to establish its own moral claim to the parcel, with its eyes on development rights. Furthermore, its community-building approach placed higher value on the breadth of stakeholders reaching consensus than on commitments to any one sector.

Because, in any community, some sectors enjoy more power and legitimacy that others, we argue that emphasis on consensus among all stakeholders will tend to favor the status quo of power relationships—in this case, weakening the leadership role of residents and grassroots organizing groups. The Parcel 24 campaign never reached the level of mass involvement of the Parcel C garage struggle, which had grown out of the community's outrage. But hundreds of people participated in a state legislative hearing, a petition and postcard campaign, community public meetings, a community charrette (bilingual community design forum) and several smaller events for over two years. Partly due to the young professional composition of ACDC's staff, the campaign was particularly able to attract the support of college students from the Ivy League campuses. CPA and other coalition members conducted extensive outreach to immigrant residents, and ACDC worked with social service agencies to bring the Parcel 24 discussion into English-language classes.

Core strategies of the Parcel 24 campaign were (1) filing of state legislation as a political tool to mandate return of the land to the Chinatown community; (2) creation of a feasible community development vision for Parcel 24; and (3) full community participation in every stage of the public input and decision-making process. The crowning achievement of the Parcel 24 campaign was the publication of a detailed and feasible development vision that had been agreed upon by all core members of the HSC coalition.

Tensions emerged in HSC around the issue of who should be the developer and who should control the development outcome. Very early in the campaign, coalition members had discussed the idea of forming a collaborative development entity that could involve diverse stakeholders and provide for a majority of resident decision-makers. ACDC said it would take the lead to unfold the complicated discussion of forming such a development entity outside of the coalition meetings through a series of interorganizational meetings. It held an initial meeting with each of the core groups, but after nearly a year of keeping the development entity off the coalition agenda, ACDC informed HSC members by e-mail that it intended to go forward as the sole community entity paired with a for-profit development partner.

While not surprised that ACDC would want to be the developer, all of the core HSC groups felt that ACDC had gone back on its earlier commitment and that their trust had been betrayed. Most expressed that they felt used by ACDC, having helped to build the Parcel 24 campaign, yet all the while positioning ACDC in the most visible role to become the sole developer (ACDC 2004). ACDC staff, on the other hand, claimed that they had simply engaged in such discussions without ever making a commitment. As a development group used to formal contracts and deals, ACDC staffers apparently had a different and more legalistic idea about what constituted a commitment. Similarly, ACDC's concept of community participation was for the community, broadly defined, to have "influence" in the development process (J. Liu 2005), while CPA sought a clear mechanism of decision-making power for Chinatown residents.

Contrasts between Community-Building and Transformative Organizing

As core members of HSC, both ACDC and CPA emphasized the importance of placing the struggle for Parcel 24 in a historical context and of developing a community vision for the land (eventually published in a bilingual vision document). ACDC, which later would bid to develop the parcel, placed greater focus on creating a detailed and economically feasible vision that could win credibility with city and highway officials. Like the community-building approach of groups described by Smock (2004), ACDC emphasized consensus building over confrontation, a diversity of stakeholders over resident empowerment, and involvement of policymakers as a strategy to leverage buy-in and support.

Jeremy Liu (2005) explains that proactive collaboration by diverse sectors of the community, combined with the know-how to create a realistic development vision, forms the community's main leverage. While ACDC also worked hard to mobilize popular support for the Parcel 24 campaign in the form of grassroots lobbying, this mass involvement seemed mainly to play a support role to the central visioning process. In a meeting of CPA and ACDC staff members to discuss Chinatown development issues, ACDC's Liu characterized the two approaches: "It comes down to the CPA versus ACDC approach to organizing — leverage through resisting or leverage through analyzing" (J. Liu 2005).

Randy Stoecker, in his critique of the CDC model of urban redevelopment, describes the dilemma: the CDCs are underfunded organizations in poor communities, yet forced to compete within the market system. This means that CDCs may be strong on legitimacy and professional and technical know-how, but in a poor position to challenge the status quo or change power relations. Stoecker (1997) opines that, because of the underlying difficulties of their position, and as landlords and developers who nonetheless view themselves as representative of the community, "the CDC model is in danger of creating weaker rather than stronger communities" (10).

Such contradictions surfaced as ACDC concretized its development plans for Parcels C and 24. In order to maximize such community benefits as affordable rental housing and nonprofit space, ACDC and its partner pushed the Parcel C project up to twenty-three stories, and created a mix of market-rate and affordable condos targeting the wealthy and upper-middle classes. This caused one longtime homeowner whose row house abutted the project to exclaim, "We were better off keeping it a parking garage!"[20]

ACDC organizers occasionally used their skills and influence to deliberately counter the voice and demands of independent organizing efforts by residents. In 2002, when Chinatown residents and abutters opposed the escalating height of the Parcel C project, ACDC published a flyer to mobilize Greater Boston Chinese community members from its homebuyers' class to attend the Parcel C community meeting in support of the project. ACDC staff printed in English and Chinese across the flyer, "If you want to own or rent a home on Parcel C, come to this important meeting" (ACDC 2002). Only after uproar from CPA and other critics did ACDC clarify that participation in the meeting would have no effect on people's chances of getting a home.

In the period leading up to the release of the Parcel 24 RFP, ACDC continued to play a strong role in advocating for a detailed HSC vision that would maximize affordable housing. Apparently due to the stringent requirements of the RFP, ACDC and its for-profit development partner became the only bidders for Parcel 24. Yet in community meetings held to describe their proposed Parcel 24 project after the release of the RFP, ACDC staff avoided directly answering resident questions that focused on the ACDC proposal's departures from the community vision.

In contrast, CPA emphasized resident decision-making and developers' accountability to the community, utilizing the community visions developed for both parcels as an organizing tool to unite the community and evaluate the development. During the development of the Metropolitan project on Parcel C, CPA organized residents and abutters to voice their opposition to the escalating scale of the project (while nonetheless realizing that they were informed of the changes too late in the process to make any substantial impact). The leadership and demand for a decision-making voice that grew out of the Parcel C struggle, however, laid the basis for the eventual establishment of the Chinatown Resident Association, increased accessibility to the development review process, and a shift in public discussion to increasingly center on implementation of the Chinatown Community Plan.

With Parcel 24, CPA focused on resident decision-making, moderate scale, sale of the land for $1, and more deeply affordable housing for low-income residents. As the HSC worked to publish a detailed community vision statement, CPA and the Chinatown Resident Association pushed for and achieved the incorporation of key resident demands into the community vision. These included a commitment to low-income rental housing, low-income (not only middle-income) home ownership opportunities, a priority on larger-sized units for families, an overall ceiling on scale and massing (particularly in the lower-scale residential section), and provisions for community control and accountability. Some of these demands, however, failed to make their way into the official RFP issued by the MTA. While CPA was only partially satisfied with the Parcel 24 planning outcome, ACDC's Liu characterized it as a "huge success" (J. Liu 2005).

Contrasting Definitions of Community Stabilization

Different approaches to community development also are revealed by examining CPA's and ACDC's affordable housing priorities. According to the 2000 census, Boston Asian Americans had a median household income of $27,963 and $14,670 for Chinatown Asian Americans (Institute for Asian American Studies 2005). Asian Americans in the nearby suburban town of Quincy, with a Chinese population of more than 10 percent, have a median household income of $49,808 (Institute for Asian American Studies 2004).

Yet the majority of recently developed affordable rental housing in Chinatown has targeted households in the income range of 60% of Area Median Income ($49,560 or above for a family of four in 2003), with home ownership opportunities focused on households above 80% of Area Median Income ($66,150 for a family of four). This places much of the affordable housing out of range for Chinese working families.

As a consequence of this disparity, CPA has advocated that city affordable housing guidelines be expressed in terms of Boston median household incomes rather than standard metropolitan statistical area figures (which are skewed upward) and that resources be targeted toward the lower end of the income scale in order to keep Boston residents in their homes. In the development plans for Parcel 24, CPA has argued for more deeply affordable housing to serve the sector most in need; such housing is key to preserving Chinatown's immigrant working-class core, even if it means producing a smaller quantity of affordable units. While supporting the growth of home ownership opportunities, CPA advocates for more low-income ownership opportunities as well as those for moderate income.

ACDC, in contrast, takes a more diversified approach to its target population. As a developer, ACDC argues that production of housing for households below 60% of Area Median Income is not financially feasible without government operating subsidies (while acknowledging that it is possible for a project to internally subsidize and produce a smaller number of more deeply affordable units). Although the HSC community vision for Parcel 24 called for the majority of affordable rental units to be affordable to households at 50% of Area Median Income and affordable condo units to begin at 60% of Area Median Income, when ACDC put on its developer hat in response to the official Request for Proposals, it retargeted its focus to a slightly higher income group for both rental and condo units. On a philosophical level as well, ACDC argues that middle-class home ownership is an equally important priority for Chinatown as a community development strategy for stabilizing the neighborhood and strengthening its leadership.

Contrasting Approaches to Leadership Development

Leadership development is an important part of community organizing for both the community-building and transformative approaches typified by ACDC and CPA. Yet the definitions and approaches to leadership development reflect the differences in the two organizing models. For ACDC and the community-building approach more generally, leadership development focuses on the education and training of residents and community members to acquire the skills and technical understanding required to advocate knowledgeably for a specific and detailed vision (J. Liu 2005). Because their community organizing strategy focuses on winning the respect of decision-makers by demonstrating community consensus, feasibility, and professionalism, the demonstration of leadership skills and technical knowledge becomes the core desired outcome of leadership development work.

ACDC implemented this leadership development approach in their sponsorship of the Parcel 24 community design forum and bilingual teach-ins on affordable housing finance. Because of the highly technical nature of development, this approach lent itself most to working with a relatively small core of activists, most often the English speakers with a stronger educational foundation, who could more easily understand and retain the development concepts. This bias toward the more skilled and educated sector also underlies the concept of bringing the Asian American middle class back to Chinatown in order to strengthen the community's leadership. On the other hand,

ACDC also developed an adult education curriculum about development concepts designed for broader use in English for Speakers of Other Languages (ESOL) classes. These learners were expected to play primarily a support role by understanding enough about the community development issues to come out for an important public hearing.

Because CPA's organizing strategy focused on increasing resident power, its leadership development work was less focused on skill development and more on unifying around a set of resident goals and priorities and demanding a place at the table. This approach empowered less-educated residents to play a vocal decision-making role in the campaign based on their commitment to the collective strategy. For both the Parcel C and Parcel 24 visioning processes, CPA-led workshops and discussions with residents focused on helping residents identify, define, and unify around priority demands or principles in order to strengthen their voice and influence on the planning process. Through discussion, mentoring, and one-on-one preparation, CPA organizers helped residents develop the confidence and prepare to take on new roles, while skills tended to be acquired through hands-on learning. This approach derives from the transformative model's emphasis on long-term leadership potential versus short-term capacity. This emphasis is rooted in the view that the community must fundamentally employ both analysis and mass mobilization to challenge the power structure sufficiently to create change.

From this longer-term point of view, for transformative organizers, the strongest leaders are not necessarily the most skillful or outspoken, but are instead those who rise to their leadership roles in the course of a struggle because of their commitment to a strong democratic vision and close ties with the people. On the other hand, CPA and resident activists found it necessary to constantly review and revisit the resident demands, because the technical nature of discussions about affordable housing finance and feasibility was often confusing to the elderly immigrants.

Contrasting Utilization of Professional, Academic, and Technical Assistance

During the Parcel C campaign, CPA and the coalition drew on a variety of technical expertise. These experts included lawyers who drafted extensive comments for the development review process and proposed litigation, an architect who developed and sketched an alternative vision for the site, and environmental experts who assessed and testified about the environmental impact of the planned garage.

In subsequent years, coalition members conducted or participated in several environmental justice projects and research studies of Chinatown. These included a study of traffic-related injuries (Brugge et al. 2002); an environmental health survey (Brugge et al. 2000); a pilot study of ambient noise (Brugge and Tai 2002); development of bilingual environmental education fact sheets; a study of gentrification and quality of life factors; and the translation of an asthma curriculum into Chinese. While this list is impressive, these activities were not well integrated into CPA's work.

CPA's staff has frequently been recruited from the base of working-class immigrants that they serve; the primary qualifications for hire focus on bilingual skills, community knowledge, and commitment to grassroots empowerment rather than on formal education or professional skills. As a result, CPA staff tend to have less formal education than their counterparts at ACDC; few have gone beyond a high school diploma or liberal arts bachelor's degree. This difference translates into less expertise to manage technical information and research.

For CPA, with its focus and strengths traditionally in grassroots organizing and protest politics, Parcel C was an important breakthrough in bringing together professional expertise with grassroots campaigning in one of the most sophisticated organizing strategies experienced by Chinatown community activists up to that time. In the years following the Parcel C experience, CPA began to consciously develop its capacity for multilevel organizing strategies employing legal, technical, or development expertise with grassroots organizing, political strategies, and mass mobilization. Its primary approach to increasing its sophistication has been through increased collaboration with professional or technical assistance providers, rather than through developing its own in-house expertise.

Incorporation of technical and professional expertise involves some challenges for the transformative organizing approach. From a philosophical point of view, technical expertise and professional skills are less central to the transformative organizing approach than to the community-building approach. The popular education approach identified with transformative organizing places its highest value on validating the experiential knowledge of ordinary community members and encouraging their voice. This approach often requires efforts to counter mainstream values and socialization, which have taught us that experts are more knowledgeable. CPA organizers know that lawyers, developers, and scientists can play an important role in a campaign. But by placing the highest priority on increasing ordinary residents' voices, this approach may tend to minimize the role or significance of professional knowledge.

In contrast, professional and technical knowledge is central to the community-building approach, which places its highest value on creating a feasible and knowledgeable vision for community development in order to achieve consensus with diverse stakeholders and with decision-makers. Senior staff at ACDC have historically held graduate degrees and an overall higher level of technical or professional skills than CPA staff. Not surprisingly, ACDC has a strong track record of utilizing professional expertise from its own staff, pro bono professional services, and through supervising both undergraduate and graduate students in the delivery of community projects. Its consensus-building approach helps to position the organization well to draw on technical resources from a range of partners.

The effort to gain community housing on Parcel 24 was a prime example of ACDC's ability to integrate technical resources effectively into its core organizing strategy and approach. With minimal financial resources and the recruitment of volunteer professionals and students, ACDC led the Hudson Street for Chinatown in a bilingual community design forum, or charrette, involving nearly forty community members. The outcomes of the charrette were immediately incorporated into the lobbying plans and the learning and discussion process became the coalition's first step toward building consensus around a common vision for the parcel. Jeremy Liu of ACDC (2005) explains that ACDC is quite good at accessing and using technical assistance; nonetheless, he acknowledges the challenges of integrating technical assistance into organizing work.

. . .

The transformative and community-building approaches to community organizing bring contrasting strengths and challenges. Transformative organizing focuses on the popular education and empowerment of the most disenfranchised sectors in order to shift the terms of public debate and to create longer-term social change. When applied in a well-integrated manner with daily involvement with the grassroots base, this approach can successfully create both short- and long-term gains, and can be particularly successful at bringing new grassroots voices into the public arena.

The transformative approach inherently challenges the status quo. By combining systemic analysis with grassroots organizing and education, the transformative approach can effectively organize the community to oppose local government policies or other authorities. On the other hand, a major challenge for transformative organizers is that of balancing the fundamental commitment to grassroots empowerment with the need for collaboration with diverse stakeholders. This challenge leads to a situation in which transformative organizing groups may at times become marginalized or at odds with other community leaders or local authorities. The tensions become more acute and complex as a group grows in its sophistication.

Similarly, the popular education emphasis of transformative organizing and grassroots empowerment creates challenges for these groups to fully integrate and maximize the use of technical and professional experts. While transformative groups often have sophisticated analyses that can appreciate the importance of professional expertise, developing the role and voice of the grassroots will generally take priority.

The community-building approach brings very different strengths to the organizing picture. The focus on internal consensus and the involvement of diverse stakeholders helps the community to leverage external resources and link with local authorities. When applied with an analysis of conditions at play, this approach can be extremely effective in securing short-term and concrete gains. The community-building approach is more likely to prioritize and be adept at utilizing professional knowledge and expertise.

A fundamental challenge of the community-building approach is its resistance to conflict, both internal and external. The drive for consensus will tend to support the status quo of power relationships, both within the community and in relationship to local authorities. Thus community-building organizers are not well positioned to engage in organizing that requires confrontation or opposition. This same phenomenon means that the priority on communitywide consensus will at times weaken the effort to empower a particularly disenfranchised sector or constituency—such as immigrant residents of Chinatown.

For CDCs as a particular type of community-building organization, the avoidance of conflict is compounded with a reliance on government funding and involvement. As organizers in the realm of community development, CDCs must also come to terms with their dual roles as both community organizer and developer, roles that contain an inherent conflict of interests. Without an appreciation of that conflict, a CDC may end up using its organizing arm to counter a community's calls for accountability.

The experiences of CPA and ACDC are examples of the transformative and community-building approaches to organizing in Boston Chinatown, and they point to key strengths and challenges within each model. By virtue of their differing priorities and philosophies, the two approaches will sometimes find themselves in conflict with one another's objectives or tactics, or in competition for the community's backing. Yet, with a deeper appreciation of the big picture and the potential contributions of each approach, we argue that a closer and more symbiotic relationship between the two approaches can also lead to significant community strength.

Notes

1. While we have attempted to cite sources for much of what we describe in the case studies, the limits on what has been written about Chinatown require us to draw heavily on our direct involvement in the events as well.

2. A few examples of this approach of which we are aware include the Boston-based City Life/Vida Urbana, the Philadelphia-based Asian Americans United, the San Francisco–based Chinese Progressive Association, and the New York–based Committee Against Anti-Asian Violence. Most began in the 1970s and were influenced by New Left movements of the time.

3. The seventy-five noncommercial organizations in Chinatown cited from a 1997 study by M. Liu included seventeen service providers (including ACDC), twenty ethnic traditional organizations, five action organizations (including CPA), five umbrella coalitions, and the remainder fulfilling religious, educational, social, and cultural purposes.

4. Chinatown Peoples Progressive Association Newsletter, no. 1, February 1978.

5. In a community often dominated by elderly male–led organizations, the majority of CPA's leadership and its top leadership positions at both board and staff levels have been female for most of its history.

6. Chinatown Community Center, Inc., included the Asian American Resource Workshop, Chinatown Boys' and Girls' Club, Chinese American Civic Association, Chinese Progressive Association, Quincy School Community Council, South Cove Community Health Center, and South Cove YMCA.

7. The Coalition to Protect Parcel C for Chinatown included the Asian American Corporation, Asian American Resource Workshop, Charlestown High School Asian Students Club, Chinese Consolidated Benevolent Association, Chinese Merchants Association, Chinese Progressive Association, Chinese Women's Club, Eastern U.S. Kung-Fu Federation/New England, Fung Luen Association, Hoi Kew Association, Kew Sing Music Club, Law Offices of Thomas Chan, Massachusetts Indochinese American Association, Moy Family Association, National Chinese Welfare Council, Oak Street and Johnny Court Residents, Quincy School Community Council, Shanghai Printing, South Cove Community Health Center, Tai Tung Tenants' Association, and Wong Family Association.

8. The two agency members of the Chinatown Community Center, Inc., which opted to support the garage were the Asian American Civic Association and the South Cove YMCA, both desperate for space.

9. Ironically, the chairperson of CPA was one of the first co-moderators of the Chinatown Neighborhood Council in 1985. She presided over the drafting of the council by-laws. At the time, leaders of the council focused on the broad inclusion of different stakeholders in recognition of Chinatown's role as both a geographic neighborhood and an ethnic hub. This rationale was the same used for determining the electorate, which defines the representatives as including "any Chinatown resident and any Asian American residing in Massachusetts." Only later would they realize that this structure could be easily manipulated by community business leaders and would end up weakening the voice of neighborhood residents.

10. "Vote! Let the people decide on NEMC's garage proposal on Parcel C!" Parcel C Referendum poster designed by Ellie Lee in 1993.

11. Total resident and nonresident votes in the referendum were 1,747: 42 in favor of the garage, 1,692 opposed, and 13 spoiled ballots. Residents voted 654 to 14 against the garage.

12. Source: Lydia Lowe, July 23, 1998 letter to community organization representatives, and June 24, 1998 notes of residents' meeting with Thomas O'Malley, Parcel C Project coordinator for the BRA.

13. According to the agency director of the Boston Chinatown Neighborhood Center, the agency utilized more than $100,000 worth of legal counsel on this negotiation process alone.

14. Area Median Income of $82,600 for a family of four is based on a Standard Metropolitan Statistical Area, which includes 127 cities and towns, many of them wealthy suburbs, and excludes single-person households. CPA and other Boston community groups have advocated for the City of Boston to change its standards for affordable housing to be calculated based on City of Boston median household income, which is $42,600 for a family of four.

15. Developers pointed to the 30,000 square feet of replacement space for BCNC and Boston Asian YES as evidence that the community center vision remained intact. Yet the RFP had clearly stipulated that 10,000 square feet of nonprofit community space would be *in addition to* replacement space for the two on-site agencies.

16. Although ACDC no longer had a partnership role, EAFA first asked ACDC to assist in the selection process of the Chinatown buyers for the space. Because two of ACDC's board members were interested in bidding on commercial space, ACDC chose to recuse itself from the entire selection process, despite earlier assurances that it was committed to advocating for CPA.

17. Commercial condo fees are assessed based on the percentage of interest shares in the condo association. Typically, this assessment would be based on the square footage of each commercial condo unit. In this case, commercial condo units were assessed at a rate nearly three times that of nonprofit condo units, through a method in which nonprofit units were assigned a valuation of $100 per square foot and commercial units a valuation of $285 per square foot, based on the rationale that nonprofit spaces were use-restricted. These values were then translated into percentage shares in the commercial condo association. As a result, CPA's space, now considered a commercial space and with a market-rate asking price, would have been charged about 34% of the total commercial condo fees when it occupied just under 18% of the total space. In contrast, another nonprofit with 49% of the square footage would pay less than 33% of the commercial condo fees. CPA asked that the condo formulas be recalculated so that all nonprofits would pay condo fees based on the square footage that they owned. The BRA and ACDC verbally agreed to this recalculation and then reneged, setting off the City Hall protest and sit-in.

18. CPA used its organizing pressure to cut $100,000 off the original asking price for its condo space and spent four years on a successful $1.5 million capital campaign to realize both purchase and build-out.

19. ACDC summary of its proposed Parcel 24 project to the Ricane Hadrian Initiative for Community Organizing, 2002.

20. This comment was made at an abutters' meeting organized by CPA and the Chinatown Resident Association for ACDC to present their latest project design; the speaker was a longtime Oak Street homeowner who had been an outspoken opponent of the parking garage back in 1993.

References

Asian Community Development Corporation (ACDC). 2002. Parcel C flier.
———.2004. Minutes of meeting with Hudson Street for Chinatown core members, July 8.

————. 2005. www.asiancdc.org; last accessed January 2007.

Boston Redevelopment Authority (BRA). 1999. *Parcel C RFP*, January 29.

Brugge D., Z. Lai, C. Hill, and W. Rand. 2002. "The Effect of Traffic on Injuries in Boston Chinatown: Lessons from Three Years of Data." *Journal of Urban Health* 79:87–103.

Brugge, D., A. Leong, A. Averbach, and F. M. Cheung. 2000 "An Environmental Health Survey of Residents of Boston Chinatown." *Journal of Immigrant Health* 2:97–111.

Brugge, D., and M. Tai. 2002. "Use of Small Area Data to Support a Community Agenda in Boston Chinatown." *Local Environment* 7:203–19.

Chinese Progressive Association (CPA). 2002. *Twenty-Five Years: Forward Together for Justice* (on file at CPA).

Edward A. Fish Associates (EAFA). 1999. *Parcel C Development–Oak Plaza: A Presentation to the Chinatown Community,* July 13.

Institute for Asian American Studies, University of Massachusetts. 2004. "Asian Americans in Quincy," October.

————. 2005. "Median Household Income by Race and Hispanic or Latino Origin in Massachusetts and Boston," March 29, Census 2000 Summary File 3 Sample Data.

Kempskie, K. 1993. "Neighborhood Split Over Parcel C." *Boston Tab*, July 20.

Lai, Z., A. Leong, and C. C. Wu. 2000. "The Lessons of the Parcel C Struggle: Reflections on Community Lawyering." *UCLA Asian Pacific American Law Journal* 6:1–43.

Leong, A. 1995–96. "The Struggle over Parcel C: How Boston's Chinatown Won a Victory in the Fight against Institutional Expansion and Environmental Racism." *Amerasia Journal* 21, no. 3:99–119.

Liu, J. 2005. Interview by D. Brugge, July 7. Notes on file with the author.

Liu, M. C. 1999. "Chinatown's Neighborhood Mobilization and Uban Development in Boston." PhD. diss., University of Massachusetts–Boston.

Lowe, L. 2003. "Radical Grassroots Organizing." Presentation to Radical Organizing Conference, March 22, Dorchester, Mass. (on file with the author).

Reitzes, D. C., and D. C. Reitzes. 1986. "Alinsky in the 1980s: Two Contemporary Chicago Community Organizations." *Sociological Quarterly* 28:265–83.

Smith, A. 2004. "CPA Claims Developer Going Back on Word," *Sampan Newspaper*, September 3.

Smock, K. 2004. *Democracy In Action: Community Organizing and Urban Change.* New York: Columbia University Press.

Stoecker, R. 1997. "The CDC Model of Urban Redevelopment: A Critique and an Alternative." *Journal of Urban Affairs* 19, no. 1:1–22.

Building Power in Minority Neighborhoods

Boston University Medical Center's Bio-safety Level Four Laboratory

This essay is a case study of building power in a minority neighborhood and associated coalition-building activities by Alternatives for Community and Environment (ACE), an environmental justice (or *just sustainability*) organization in Boston, Massachusetts. The case focuses on the tactics of a coalitional campaign to stop Boston University Medical Center (BUMC) constructing a Bio-safety Level Four laboratory. (BSL 4 lab)[1] On September 30, 2003, BUMC announced that it had won a $127 million grant offered by the National Institutes of Health (NIH) to fund the construction of the BSL 4 lab in the city's South End–Roxbury communities. NIH had received money from the Bush administration to build up the nation's bio-defense capabilities as part of its Homeland Security initiatives. It is one of two National Bio-containment Laboratories to be built with the funding provided under the administration's "Project Bio-Shield."

The proposed site of the lab is within a densely populated inner urban area and straddles two Boston neighborhoods, South End and Roxbury, the latter of which has a history of environmental stresses, injustices, mistrust of government officials, poor transit links, and little community participation in "official" urban development projects. The particular civic engagement or "power building" strategy of one of the organizers, ACE, is a common strategy used by environmental justice groups and activists: building power through a coalition of many different groups. This strategy was initially carried out through ACE's "Safety Net" program, which has, since early 2005, become a separate organization within the oppositional coalition, the "Campaign to Stop the Bio-terror Lab."[2]

Roxbury and ACE

The Roxbury community, southeast of downtown Boston, is 5% white, 63% black, 24% Hispanic,[3] 1% Asian or Pacific Islander, < 1% Native American, 3% other, and 4% multiracial, according to the U.S. Census (2000). The corresponding figures for the City of Boston are 50% white, 24% black, 14% Hispanic, 8% Asian or Pacific Islander, < 1% Native American, 1% other, and 3% multiracial (U.S. Census 2000). However, in 2003 the city officially became a "majority-minority"[4] city, with people of color making up 50.5% of the population. Alongside this demographic difference, Roxbury has higher percentages of people speaking community languages—particularly Spanish, French and French Creole, Portuguese and Portuguese Creole, and African languages— than does the City of Boston. In 1999, some 73.2% of its residents were classified as low to moderate income, as compared to 56.2% for the City of Boston.

These statistics reveal one of metro Boston's poorest neighborhoods, and an inner urban "Environmental Justice Population," as defined by the Massachusetts Executive Office of Environmental Affairs (EOEA) Environmental Justice Policy (Commonwealth of Massachusetts 2002, 5) and associated criteria:

Environmental Justice Populations are those segments of the population that EOEA has determined to be most at risk of being unaware of or unable to participate in environmental decision-making or to gain access to state environmental resources. They are defined as neighborhoods (U.S. Census Bureau census block groups) that meet one or more of the following criteria:

- The median annual household income is at or below 65 percent of the statewide median income for Massachusetts; or
- 25 percent of the residents are minority; or
- 25 percent of the residents are foreign born, or
- 25 percent of the residents are lacking English language proficiency."

Environmental Justice Populations make up 5% of the Commonwealth's land area, and take in about 29% of its population. Locationwise and unsurprisingly: "Many of these Environmental Justice Populations are located in densely populated urban neighborhoods, in and around the state's oldest industrial sites, while some are located in suburban and rural communities" (Commonwealth of Massachusetts 2002, 5).

This is the racial, ethnic, and socioeconomic milieu in which ACE, a multiethnic organization, works. ACE's mission, as defined by its 2002–2007 Strategic Plan, is as follows: "ACE builds the power of communities of color and lower income communities in New England to eradicate environmental racism and classism and achieve environmental justice. We believe that everyone has the right to a healthy environment and to be decision makers in issues affecting communities" (ACE, 2002, 1). To some, ACE may be seen as a "typical" environmental justice organization; reacting to a threat and protecting and mobilizing an underserved community. A more nuanced and fresh look at ACE, however, would tell a different story. Pellow and Brulle's (2005, 17) timely call for more "critical environmental justice studies," namely, "studies that can link theoretical models and research," speaks to two key points from ACE's mission (and shows how ACE is at the cutting edge in comparison to other, similar organizations): building power and the race versus class debate. First, ACE uses the concept of "building power" in low-income and minority communities, not the more genteel concept of "civic engagement" or "acting civically," which it sees as downplaying *powerlessness* in such communities. ACE staff use techniques such as "power mapping" to help the local community simultaneously locate, define, explore, and ultimately challenge current hegemonic power relations—in this case, the building of a BSL 4 lab. A development of this approach is that as ACE moves further into what we would call "power-based activism," their former "firefighting" approach to dealing with local issues one by one has changed. The result is that as ACE become more potent, as Agyeman (2005:164) has argued, their "programs are shifting from local and single focus, to more regional and systemic."

Second, ACE has always had a dual focus on race *and* class. As Pellow and Brulle (2005, 13) argue, "environmental injustice is and has always been, about both race and class." This may seem intuitive, too obvious to acknowledge but, as Pellow and Brulle (2005, 13) correctly note, "movement leaders have been slow to do so," preferring to focus more on race. Some, such as Pulido (1994, 17) would argue that "a distinct but prominent sub-movement is being formed that is limited to people of color." Based on our observations at the Second National People of Color Environmental Leadership Summit in Washington, D.C., in October 2002, we would say that within the "people of color" environmental justice movement that Pulido (1994) refers to, there are several race-based "factions" that hinder progress in many of the pressing issues the movement as a whole should address.

Another, different approach to critical environmental justice studies was taken by Agyeman (2005) in his case study of ACE. Concerned at the polarization of *environmentalisms,* he looked at "traditional" environmentalism (or *environmental stewardship*) through the New Environmental Paradigm (NEP) of Catton and Dunlap (1978). This is the dominant paradigm for most environmental and sustainability groups. It is strong on environmental protection, but poor on *intragenerational* equity or social justice. At the same time he looked at environmental justice, through the Environmental Justice Paradigm (EJP) of

Taylor (2000). The EJP is strong on social justice, race, and class. Agyeman found limitations in both paradigms and posited another paradigm he called the Just Sustainability Paradigm (JSP):

The "Just Sustainability Paradigm" (JSP) is an emerging discursive frame and paradigm. It is not, however rigid, single and universal, but links to both the EJP and NEP. In this sense, it can be seen as being both flexible and contingent, composed of overlapping discourses, which come from recognition of the validity of a variety of issues, problems and framings. It arises from the definition of sustainability of Agyeman et al. (2003:5) "the need to ensure a better quality of life for all, now and into the future, in a just and equitable manner, whilst living within the limits of supporting ecosystems," which prioritizes justice and equity, but does not downplay the environment, our life support system. In essence, it is malleable, acting as a "bridge" spanning the continuum between the EJP and the NEP. (Agyeman 2005, 6)

Agyeman's (2005) contention is that ACE has begun to look more like an organization espousing "just sustainability," than the slightly more limited notion of environmental justice. The basis of this thinking is that in order to be truly successful at alleviating environmental "bads" like the BSL 4 lab *and* bringing environmental "goods" to the community through substantial community-envisioned change, organizations such as ACE are taking a more *proactive, deliberative, visioning* approach more typical of sustainability and sustainable communities-based organizations. While support for this approach is now gaining traction, the antecedents of this thinking go back at least as far as 1993, when Goldman (1993, 27) suggested that "sustainable development may well be seen as the next phase of the environmental justice movement."

The analysis that follows is a critical environmental justice study. Focusing on the need to achieve a more just and sustainable community in the South End–Roxbury neighborhoods, it interrogates the power-building tactics of the ACE inspired coalition: the Campaign to Stop the Bio-Terror Lab.

The BSL 4 Lab

A press release issued on July 31, 2003, by BUMC titled "Boston University Medical Center (BUMC) Continues Building Support for Bio-safety Laboratory" claimed that only 13% of the lab would be designated for the high-security research for which the lab is classified. That is, 13% of the lab would be authorized to conduct research on the deadly biological agents that are thought to be potential biological weapons. These deadly agents, BUMC argued, such as anthrax, smallpox, and Ebola also occur naturally; therefore, searching for a vaccine would not only help in regards to biological warfare but potentially for peaceful purposes. The rest of the lab would be conducting research on other biomedical issues. BUMC, by May 2004 also claimed that it had held up to thirteen community meetings that discussed the proposed lab. At these meetings BUMC said the reason for building this facility was a response to the NIH subunit, the National Institute of Allergy and Infectious Diseases's (NIAID) request for proposals as part of the government's plan to build laboratories that would research microbes that could be transformed into tools used by bioterrorists (BUMC 2003).

The NIAID Strategic Plan for Bio-defense Research (National Institutes of Health 2002) discusses the need for more BSL 4 research facilities because of the lack of preparedness of the nation and the lack of vaccines in the event of a biological terrorist attack. The plan uses the incidence of anthrax in mail that occurred on several occasions in 2001 as an example of our lack of security in this field. NIH outlines the implications of this type of research. They note "the positive spin-offs for other diseases that will result from the large investment in research on bio-defense will be substantial" (National Institutes of Health, 2002, 12). They claim that many of the diseases to be researched "are significant public health threats in endemic areas, especially in the developing world" (National Institutes of Health, 2002, 12). Many other "societal benefits" are claimed by the report. But there also be should be disclaimers. Because biotechnology has become a market-driven industry, there is no guarantee new medicines will be priced competitively enough for developing nations or other poor people. Advancements in this area are usually guided toward treatments, drugs, and vaccines that will bring in a substantial monetary reward. The pharmaceutical companies are looking for treatments that are used by a large population affected by an ailment or condition. In the time of a terrorist attack or similar disaster, will the companies that invest in manufacturing the vaccine or treatment ask a high price? What will happen to those who cannot pay or who do not receive health care? With regards to the "positive spin-offs" within developing countries, the question of whether a pharmaceutical company will invest in the manufacturing of a vaccine, treatment, or cure is significant. Most of these countries are still affected by diseases such as smallpox because they do not have the financial resources or an effective health care system to care for their populations.

The Push for Bio-tech as a Source for Local Economic Recovery

BUMC has stood firmly by two claims that have dominated their defense against the coalition opposed to the construction of the lab. The first claim is that the construction of the lab will bring 660 permanent jobs at all levels, as well as 1,300 construction jobs of which 50% will go to Boston residents (BUMC 2003). It is not clear how BUMC will ensure that half the jobs will go to Boston residents. In a study conducted by the South End Neighborhood

Action Program (SNAP) of Action for Boston Community Development, Inc. (ABCD) published in 1991, an analysis of the economic impacts of Boston's biomedical developments was undertaken. According to their research conducted sixteen years ago, 18% of the biomedical research jobs require only a high school diploma; many of these jobs, however, are filled by college students hoping to get into the field or into medical school. SNAP included a quote from a Harvard Medical School human resources manager with regards to the hiring of semi- and low-skilled workers: "why should I hire school people when people with bachelor's degrees from Dartmouth and Harvard come to work as lab aids for a year or two at $18,000–$20,000 a year?" (SNAP 1991, 34). Given this reality, ABCD believes that in order for long-term job creation to develop out of the biomedical/biotech developments in Boston, these incoming businesses must generate manufacturing jobs that will be accessible to the low- and semi-skilled labor market. A quote taken from the Economic Development and Industrial Corporation (EDIC) report on real jobs for Boston residents used in the SNAP report contends, "A key element in Boston's ability to capture local benefits of this projected growth will be the recruitment and retention of businesses which are expanding, particularly those which are moving toward product development and manufacturing where job opportunities at all levels may be captured by Boston residents" (EDIC 1991, 31).

A report on the impacts of biotechnology on local economies that was published in 2002—eleven years after the SNAP report—found similar concerns still looming with regards to jobs for all Boston residents (Sable 2003). A study done by the Boston Redevelopment Authority (BRA) found only 6% of the jobs generated by the expansion of biotechnology developments would require high school diplomas only (SNAP 1991). The Sable report found that 40% of the Crosstown residents (which include most of Roxbury's minority and poor residents) do not have high school diplomas, thereby showing, "a fundamental skills mismatch between the needs of biotech employers and the dynamics of the labor market into which they are seeking to expand" (Sable 2003, 17). Other issues raised in the Sable report include the concern over human safety regarding industrial accidents, as the biomedical research being conducted must be closely monitored; and that those semiskilled and low-skilled workers with limited English proficiency will automatically be cut out of the job market.

The former governor of Massachusetts, Mitt Romney, was one of the early political supporters of the laboratory, along with Boston Mayor Thomas Menino and Massachusetts Senator Ted Kennedy. Romney believed, "I and my family and my children and my grandchildren are even safer in Boston following construction of this facility than perhaps we are today" (Smith 2003). Mayor Thomas Menino believes, "for Boston, the economic impact of this lab will be unprecedented, . . . the economic ripple effect will be tremendous" (Heldt Powell 2003).

The State of Massachusetts is no stranger to the biotechnology industry. In a 2002 study by the Brookings Institute titled *Signs of Life: The Growth of Biotechnology Centers in the U.S.,* Boston is ranked second in the nation as a center for biotechnology, coming in behind the San Francisco Bay Area. The other clusters are San Diego; Research Triangle Park, North Carolina; New York–Northern New Jersey; Philadelphia–Wilmington, Delaware; and Washington, D.C.–Baltimore. More than 60% of the National Institutes of Health spending for biotechnology research goes to these seven areas. The common factor for all of these areas is their proximity to universities. Multiple factors are needed for developing biotechnology industries and companies; the largest is the need for research facilities and social capital. Many of the biotechnology firms were founded by university professors. Biogen and Genzyme were the nation's first biotech companies: Biogen was founded by MIT and Harvard researchers in 1978; Genzyme was established in 1981 to continue research started at Tufts University (Cortright and Mayer 2002).

In this same study, a survey showed 83% of local and state economic development agencies viewed biotechnology as one of their top two objectives for development. College students are increasingly looking into biotechnology as an avenue toward success and wealth. The local Roxbury Community College (RCC) has created a certificate program designed to train students to become lab technicians.

The Campaign to Stop the Bio-terror Lab

Community Concerns

In an advertisement printed in the *Boston Globe* on April 20, 2004 (the date of the city council hearing on the decision to build the lab) BUMC used one full page to list "10 Things You Should Know About the National Emerging Infectious Diseases Laboratory" (BUMC 2004). Point 9 states, "the biotechnology industry in Massachusetts has contributed to half of all new industrial jobs over the past five years." Point 2 is the assurance that the engineers constructing the lab will have taken all precautions necessary for the safety and security of the lab. They state that "there has never been a community incident or accidental environmental release connected with a laboratory of this kind" and "the lab will make it safer to live in Boston," contending that it will be the most prepared city in the event of a biological terrorist attack (BUMC 2004).

It could be argued that the reason BUMC has persistently commented on these two issues is to counter campaign lead organization ACE's use of an "injustice frame."[5] Invoking the injustice frame can be dynamite in disinvested communities. It plugs the user (ACE and the campaign) into a vast, renewable source of energy from the civil rights movement. British cultural theorist Hall (1982) would call framing "the politics of signification" while Schlosberg (1999, 12) would add another important dimension, that of "recognition of the diversity of the participants and experiences in the environmental justice movement."

As a result of the advertisement in the *Boston Globe,* three major issues of concern were foregrounded by members of the Campaign to Stop the Bio-terror Lab. The first was the belief that the lab would generate local insecurity and lack of safety because of the manufacture of bio-warfare weapons. Because the lab is partially funded and connected to Homeland Security and funding for the research is being pulled from President Bush's plan to protect the nation from any type of future terrorist attacks, some antiwar, pro-peace groups are very concerned (L. Rosenwald, personal communication, February 1, 2004). Contrary to official statements, there have been some accidents in BSL 3 and 4 laboratories across the country. The Council for Responsible Genetics (CRG) has created a list of accidents, intentional releases, containment and security failures, missing samples, and environmental releases that have occurred within BSL 4 laboratories since 1994 to 2003. The 2002 anthrax mail incidents are examples where the anthrax used in the terrorist attacks came from a BSL 4 lab operating within the United States. BUMC claims that, "the BSL 4 laboratories in North America have more than 73 combined years of operation with a perfect safety record" (BUMC 2003). However, even the safest of facilities is never 100% safe and this is proven by the list of incidents generated by CRG (CRG 2004).

The second issue was what the coalition sees as BUMC's disregard for procedural justice via the NEPA-mandated environmental review process. In his testimony on April 20, 2004, during the city council hearing on the safety and security of the BSL 4 lab, Kyle Loring (then staff attorney at ACE) accused BUMC of violations for not following the proper procedures of an environmental review process. BUMC is in the process of doing an Environmental Impact Statement (EIS), which is legally required by federal (NEPA) and state (MEPA) law for all developments of this kind. However, the BSL 4 facility is being treated by its developers and the EPA as a regular building, such as a school or office. Because the City of Boston has not had to deal with such a facility in the past, there are no current city regulations that are suitable for this facility (K. Loring, personal communication, April 20, 2004). The third issue, which was largely dealt with under "The Push for Bio-tech as a Source for Local Economic Recovery" surrounds the debatable assertions of BUMC about local jobs.

In order to pull together a citywide coalition against the lab, ACE needed to develop an enabling framework around which to build the campaign. ACE staff members invested many hours engaging local community members of all racial and socioeconomic backgrounds. It is because of this, and the injustice framing of the three key campaign issues, that a citywide coalition of diverse interests and constituencies has been able to raise awareness and command media attention.

Building the Campaign

We attended four larger coalition meetings of the Campaign to Stop the Bio-terror Lab that were held once a month beginning in February through May 2004 during the period of our study. One was a "scoping" meeting for NEPA, presented by the EPA; two were public forums and one was a city council meeting. Interviews were carried out with members of the campaign, including Gene Benson (ACE staff attorney), Larry Rosenwald (concerned citizen), Professor Patricia Hynes (Boston University School of Public Health), and Sara Fass (concerned citizen and member of the Jamaica Plain Action Network [JPAN]). Most of our research was as participant observers at the meetings, and through content and discourse analyses of media and other texts including campaign materials created by the campaign and BUMC.

On March 31, 2004, we spoke to Larry Rosenwald, a professor of English at Wellesley College who was on a one-year sabbatical. During this time he wanted to work on nonviolent activism and was led to the Campaign to Stop the Bio-terror Lab by a friend with United for Justice with Peace Coalition, a campaign member. He became interested because it was a diverse coalition with many different voices. Mr. Rosenwald aligns himself politically with anti-war supporters and is opposed to the production of biological weapons. We wondered if the antiwar motive for his participation was at odds with the environmental justice frame of the campaign:

"Environmental justice" is a new idea for me, and I first heard it articulated by Patricia Hynes of BU, at a Brookline meeting on the biolab—but her account of the concept, and of the situation, was irresistibly compelling. Making one area the dumping ground for a disproportionate amount of waste, both hazardous and non-hazardous, exposing it to a disproportionate amount of risk—what other term than "environmental injustice" describes this inequitable distribution system? Cambridge already has an ordinance banning level 4 facilities and other, equally affluent and influential communities would have such ordinances soon if even the ghost of a rumor reached them that such a facility would be built within their territory." (L. Rosenwald, personal communication, March 31, 2004)

We spoke with another member of the coalition, Sara Fass of JPAN, about her involvement. JPAN is a group of Jamaica Plain (JP) residents who came together after September 11, 2001, and were concerned with war; the group consists only of JP residents. Its members oppose the wars in Afghanistan and Iraq and believe that the building of this BSL 4 lab is building a culture of terror that will only bolster support for war. Ms. Fass believes that the placement and construction of this lab is an environmental justice issue. She believes there is a connection between the continuation of American imperialism through war and the placement of a potentially dangerous lab in a predominantly minority and poor community. She felt that a campaign specifically against the high-security section of the lab is in accordance with economic injustice that is happening abroad with the war. Placing the lab in this neighborhood is racist and economically unjust (S. Fass, personal communication, April 15, 2004).

In regards to the coalition against the lab, Ms. Fass sees the coalition as being very positive. JPAN has its reasons for opposing the lab and has signed on with ACE and Safety Net as a way to protest effectively against this facility. She does see this as an environmental justice issue because residents were not allowed *procedural justice*, to participate in the siting process. She also believes that the lab will not be economically beneficial to the community, and that placing the lab in this neighborhood is racist. Ms. Fass said that this coalition is one of the most diverse campaigns she has worked on in her many years of activism. The coalition has crossed race, class, and age boundaries. It also comprises many different individuals with varying reasons for opposing the lab. Some members of the coalition are concerned residents; others are involved in more general peace and justice activism; and still others are the environmental justice activists. She believes that all members of the coalition see this as an environmental justice issue but have their own reasons for participating in the coalition (S. Fass, personal communication, April 15, 2004).

With regard to the media, Ms. Fass says it has been horrendous. JPAN has repeatedly called the *Jamaica Plain Gazette* and the *Jamaica Plain Bulletin* and both declined to cover this as a story because neither one saw it as a Jamaica Plain issue. The *Jamaica Plain Gazette* was present at the April 13 community forum only because it had taken place in Jamaica Plain and because members of JPAN insisted on this being a Jamaica Plain issue (S. Fass, personal communication, April 15, 2004).

Patricia Hynes is a professor with Boston University's School of Public Health. She was the guest speaker at five of the community meetings and forums including the public hearing held on April 20, 2004 and the delivery of an open letter to the mayor and Boston city councilors. Professor Hynes agreed to pass along a paper she had written on the issue regarding the campaign. Specifically, she sees the environmental injustice of the placement of this facility. Her reasons for calling this an environmental justice issue are many. She has worked for several years building and cultivating a relationship with the local community in Roxbury. Her concerns about this facility are twofold: she is concerned with the potentially irreparable damage to the relationships built over many years between the BU School of Public Health and Roxbury citizens *and* she is also concerned with the injustice of the location of the facility. Professor Hynes believes that "some neighborhoods function, in reality, as sacrifice zones for the benefit of the regional environment and economy, or simply because they are perceived as an easy target if they already bear a larger share of the city and metropolitan area's poverty, pollution and prevalence of illness" (P. Hynes, personal communication, April 5, 2004).

Professor Hynes also believes Roxbury already bears a disproportionate amount of the city's environmental burdens: "If we overlaid onto a map of Boston's neighborhoods, public health data, such as incidence of lead poisoning, rates of asthma-related emergency room visits, weapons injuries, infant mortality and food insecurity with social data from the 2000 census, including rates of unemployment, poverty, and minority status, we would find that Roxbury and North Dorchester are the neighborhoods most burdened with environmental illness, social vulnerability, and disparities of health and income" (P. Hynes, personal communication, April 5, 2004).

Despite the clear message coming from the campaign, however, not all the residents of Roxbury are against the construction of the lab. In Professor James Jenning's public policy class discussion at Tufts University held on March 30, 2004, Mr. Bickerstaff, a member of the Roxbury Neighborhood Council (RNC), spoke of his desire to see economic growth in Boston. He wants more answers regarding the promise of the economic benefits mentioned by the mayor, the governor, and BUMC. Mr Bickerstaff, like other campaign members is not content with the BUMC's lack of procedural justice, but he is not sure that the building of such a lab will cause disastrous results. He is a businessman who owns a barbershop in Dudley Station, Roxbury. He is also a longtime resident of Roxbury and has seen the community go through many developments. Mr. Bickerstaff was instrumental in the development of the Roxbury Master Plan. According to him, there was no mention of the plans for introducing the BSL 4 lab at the time the plan was being developed. In 2001, however, Mayor Menino and the BRA did argue that Roxbury would be a good area for major investment into a biotechnology corridor along the present Melnea Cass Boulevard, originally created for a major highway. Bickerstaff believes that the pros and cons of the situation should be considered. He mentioned the schools within the area: Timilty High School (one of the best in the city), the Vocational High School, and Roxbury Community College. The students may benefit from having such a facility located within walking distance. Yet the risks associated with such a facility being located in a densely populated area may outweigh the benefits that could be brought to the community and to Boston.

Many of the participants at the larger coalition meetings that we attended were not residents of Roxbury, but all were residents of Boston and greater Boston, showing that this issue was not only a local issue but one of metro-Boston relevance. The results of ACE and its offshoot, Safety Net, being among the leaders of the Campaign to Stop the Bio-terror Lab are twofold: first, the framing of the campaign has been that of an (environmental) injustice frame; second, many of the people involved seem to have come out of ACE and Safety Net's networks of activists built over a ten-year period of environmental justice or just sustainability organizing and strategizing.

Organizing and Strategies

Gene Benson, ACE staff attorney informed us that ACE found out about the lab after a Safety Net member received a "phone call that BUMC was holding a public meeting in the South End." Rumor has it that when members of Safety Net began asking the speaker, Mark Klempner, M.D. of BUMC about the lab and its function he responded by telling them they were not competent enough to engage in this discussion. Gene, who told us about this rumor, says the incident has become somewhat of a legend within the ACE circle. This situation reflects the unequal relationship and social isolation that has left many poor communities and communities of color such as Roxbury outside of the environmental decision-making process.

After this meeting, residents wanted to find out more about the lab; they were upset about being excluded from the discussions and the way it was presented as a done deal. The initial aim for the campaign was to stop NIH from funding the lab. The strategy was to get the information out there through posters and creating a petition signed by residents that was sent to NIH. The letter sent along with the petition outlined what residents, ACE, and Safety Net were doing to increase community participation and how they were not allowed to be involved. The staff attorneys at ACE wrote a letter of intent to sue BUMC, the BRA, and the state, claiming the lab was violating MEPA regulations. NIH responded by telling them to try harder. Soon after, NIH announced they would provide funding for BUMC to build the BSL 4 lab in Boston. After looking at the research and studies regarding biotechnology being introduced into a neighborhood, members of Safety Net decided that it would not be economical and the location was not safe for such a facility.

Residents approached local Boston City Councilor Chuck Turner who felt that the lab would not be good for the local economy; that it would bring in mostly white-collar jobs, and that blue-collar jobs would be lost even more quickly than they were already being lost. He created an ordinance that would ban BSL 4 labs in the downtown area and would prohibit research that required an NIH classification of BSL 4. Councilor Turner presented the ordinance to both the NIH and the city council. After presenting the ordinance, the strategy of the growing coalition was to get citywide support for the proposed ordinance. Two strategies evolved: the first was to get people onboard with the ordinance by joining forces with the city district committees and captains; the second was to find BUMC legally accountable for any negative consequences that might result from the construction of this lab on the community.

In order for the campaign to build an active force against BUMC, the developments of this proposed lab had to get into the public eye. BUMC claims that they communicated with the surrounding communities about their intentions. The *Boston Globe* ran an article about the lab on January 16, 2003, quoting Klempner, "we've been talking to a lot of people around the area to see what they think . . . we're confident that these things can be built to the highest standards of safety. After all, my office will be right in it." In another article released two days later in the *Boston Globe*, Ellen Berlin, the director of communications for BUMC, said the medical center had created a telephone survey to gauge the residents' feelings towards the lab but refused to release the details. She said the results of the survey were encouraging, implying that residents were in favor of the lab (Smith 2003).

It is believed by coalition members that the communication that was conducted was mostly within the neighborhoods of the South End, which is where the lab will be located. But little outreach was done into the immediately adjacent community of Roxbury. As mentioned earlier, members of Safety Net, by chance, found out about a meeting conducted by Klempner in the South End and, after they were dismissed, decided to find out more about the lab. As more information was gathered over the next couple of months, members of Safety Net decided this was not something they wanted in their neighborhood. Safety Net had already been working on the proposed Melnea Cass Boulevard biotechnology corridor, so information about these facilities had already been generated. What needed to happen was a way to talk to more than just members of the communities of Roxbury and the South End (coalition meeting, personal communication, May 7, 2004).

Building a citywide coalition was the first, and a crucial, strategy for ACE and Safety Net. BUMC is a prominent and heavily funded medical center in a city renowned for its medical centers and its nationwide dominance in NIH funding. A large part of their being chosen to house a new BSL 4 lab facility was because of their prestige and connections to other successful medical centers such as the Harvard Medical School and affiliated hospitals such as Massachusetts General Hospital, Brigham and Women's Hospital, Beth Israel Deaconess Medical Center, Children's Hospital and Tufts–New England Medical Center. What ACE and Safety Net wanted was to have a more democratic process in the developments of this facility. BUMC was conducting many of its meetings in private, as reported in the January 16 article of the *Boston Globe:* "researchers and administrators from Boston Medical Center and BU have conducted quiet discussions with scientific and community leaders, cultivating support for the lab" (Smith 2003).

To build the citywide coalition, Safety Net enlisted city district captains. The city of Boston has nine districts. Each district captain was in charge of finding a way to get information about the lab that was not generated by its supporters (BUMC) to the communities within the areas. They also did outreach to the communities in these districts asking for support in any way. In order to do this, information about the lab and its potential had to be made clear; essentially, ACE and Safety Net needed to create a framework for the campaign.

It was important to frame the issue in a way that would provide lasting momentum for the campaign. The coalition began calling the lab a *bio-terror* lab instead of a *bio-safety* lab, to link it to the belief that the lab was for creating biological warfare weapons. Community forums and meetings drew attention by questioning citizens' concern for their own safety. Framing the issue in rhetoric of unimaginable risks was usually the headline of a campaign flier or brochure. Many of the headlines read, "Health and Safety Risks are Real and Potentially Catastrophic" or "Keep Anthrax and Ebola out of Boston You Could Die and not Know Why!" With help from CRG and distinguished academic faculty from local universities, facts were collected regarding the "safety" and "security" of these labs. Most of the team at ACE and Safety Net did not have to go too far to get information about the potential dangers associated with locating this type of facility in a densely populated area.

The City of Cambridge pondered the same issue in 1976; many of the professors and citizens against the introduction of a BSL 4 lab in Cambridge were still around and eager to help. These professors included Jonathan King, Sheldon Krimsky, Ruth Hubbard, and other distinguished professors from MIT, Harvard, and Boston University. Sheldon Krimsky of Tufts University and Jonathan King of MIT were present at a forum on the bio-terror lab in the village of Brookline. Without the help of these professors, many of the surrounding communities of Boston outside of Roxbury would not have taken the message of the Campaign to Stop the Bio-terror Lab seriously. In effect, the professors legitimized the campaign's assertions to people in communities such as Brookline, which are racially and socioeconomically very different from Roxbury.

Professors Jonathan King, Daniel Goodenough, Ruth Hubbard, and David Ozonoff, along with more than 140 other professors have voiced their support by writing an open letter to Mayor Menino and the city councilors to ban "high-risk" facilities in the City of Boston. The delivery of the letter provided much-needed media attention to an issue that was being treated as if it were a done deal. The letter was titled "No Place to Hide" and was covered by most papers in the Metro area on April 13, 2004. Media opinions of the placement of the lab varied widely, ranging from the scientific, to believing that its "purpose is not to respond to genuine public health needs," to safety and security, and to seeing the location of the lab as "recklessness." Typical of professorial opinion is Daniel Goodenough, professor at Harvard Medical School, who believes that by building this lab the government is continuing to build a "culture of fear and paranoia."

According to Gene Benson, the issues that have had the most traction with residents and activists have been the safety, health, and security issue. Some residents who opposed the lab on environmental justice grounds felt that Roxbury–South End is not the place to locate such a facility because of the cumulative effects of other hazardous facilities in this area.

The question was frequently asked, "can residents and activists separate the issue of the BSL 4 lab and its location from wider biotechnology issues and the powerful money-generating industry behind them?" Gene Benson believes such separation is hard because of three factors: first, there was lack of community input from the onset; second, the level of health and safety risk is too great; and third, residents are not convinced that the types of jobs that will ostensibly be available will be beneficial. Because of the differences between "expert" and lay perceptions of risk (Fischer 2002), it is hard to ask residents to do their own risk/benefit analysis. The risks associated with this lab, at this point, outweigh the benefits, according to Benson's interpretation of the community's sentiments.

Mayor Thomas Menino and former Massachusetts Governor Mitt Romney have actively supported the construction of this facility in the hopes that it will bring much-needed jobs and revenue to the state and city. For example: "Boston Mayor Thomas Menino yesterday enthusiastically endorsed a proposal by Boston University Medical Center to build a high-security biodefense laboratory in the heart of the city." Later in the article, Mayor Menino is quoted as saying, "I'm very interested in the proposal and the benefits it could have for our city" (Smith 2003).

In many of the articles that appeared in the *Boston Globe*, the economic and job-related benefits were emphasized. Environmental justice advocates (including ACE) have dealt with the issue of "jobs blackmail" before and feel that using jobs as a way to "persuade" communities of the lab's benefits has been effectively countered by the coalition. In a report that can be obtained from ACE's Web site called "Debunking Boston University's Claims About its Proposed Bioterrorism Lab" (http://www.ace-environmentaljustice.org/Biolab-Web/Debunking.html), it is argued that the amount of construction jobs required to build the lab will be a small fraction of what BUMC is claiming. Also, ACE claims that the jobs generated by biotechnology labs and firms are mismatched with the needs and qualifications of the local community. Even if the lab were able to employ mostly local residents, ACE argues, these jobs are dangerous. Without any regulations specifically for the permitting of this type of facility, the coalition must rely on environmental protection laws that mandate public comments on proposals of federally funding facilities during environmental impact statements.

If coalition building was the first power-building strategy, the second or legal strategy began when Benson and others began realizing that the information that BUMC was providing about the lab and its function and final products was misleading. Benson began filing comments and getting information out about the lab. Most of the information that was generated by the Campaign to Stop the Bio-terror Lab was to debunk the information that was misleading or simply untrue. Along this line, the intent was to show that BUMC was not to be trusted because it was consciously and consistently providing misleading and untrue information.

At the scoping meeting required under NEPA (held February 17, 2004), BUMC gave a presentation that showed the lab as being a very positive thing for the community where researchers will be looking for the cure for HIV/AIDS and certain types of cancers as well as creating vaccines for dangerous diseases that have been used in biological warfare. Residents in support of and against the lab were given the chance to voice their opinions. Comments on the Environmental Impact Statement were to be sent to a correspondent who would take their concerns into consideration and produce a report some months afterward.

At the time of this writing, the current status is that Safety Net and ACE staff attorney Gene Benson are continuing to demand sight of the application submitted to NIH by BUMC as well as the other reports and documents that BUMC has claimed to have created before they received funding from NIH. BU has still not provided a copy of the application, a security risk analysis document, or documents for economic development assessment.

However in 2005, activity centered on the need for state legislation. ACE notes that

Massachusetts has no regulatory program for BSL4 or other high containment biological laboratories. The federal government has only self-enforcing guidelines that have been proven unsuccessful. Massachusetts has standards for other inherently dangerous facilities, such as a landfills and power plants, on where they might be located, how the location decision would be made, operations and maintenance requirements, and other appropriate standards to protect the public health and environment. But it has no such standards for high containment biological labs. (http://www.aceenvironmentaljustice .org/BiolabWeb/StateLegislation.html#Revised%20legislation%20-%20September %202005)

After a meeting of the State's Joint Committee on Environment, Natural Resources, and Agriculture on June 9, 2005, ACE began working with State Representative Gloria Fox's office and others, including groups such as the Massachusetts Public Health Association, to include many of the comments and suggestions that were made on the older proposed legislation, House Docket

4249, An Act to Protect the Public Health and Environment from Toxic Biological Agents. In September 2005, ACE completed the revision and Representative Fox gave the revised version to the committee co-chairs. The revised legislation, An Act Protecting the Public Health and Environment from Pathogenic Biological Agents and Toxins, according to ACE:

- streamlines some sections, removing unnecessary provisions;
- makes direct reference to federal guidelines so that they will be requirements of state law and regulation;
- includes whistleblower protections;
- requires municipalities in which BSL4 labs are located to have an emergency response plan related to the lab;
- requires a report on whether BSL2 labs should be regulated by the state (rather than requiring that BSL2 labs be regulated because there are so many BSL2 labs in the state and regulation of them may differ from BSL3 and 4 labs);
- includes more details on the Community Oversight Board.
    — (http://www.ace-environmentaljustice.org/BiolabWeb/StateLegislation
       .html#Legislation%20status)

.   .   .

BUMC has, from its first "meeting" with concerned community members, continued to become alarmed at the vigor of the Campaign to Stop the Bio-terror Lab. It has persistently commented on and boosted two issues: (1) job creation in an area underserved by large employers; and (2) the twin and related issues of the *safety* of the BSL 4 lab, and the greater *security* it will afford to all the residents of Boston because the city will be better prepared than other U.S. cities to deal with a biological terror attack. The coalition Campaign to Stop the Bio-terror Lab's use of the "injustice frame" (namely, the voicing of community concerns around their being singled out for yet *another* locally unwanted land use, or LULU), together with the attendant safety and security issues, and the purported economic "vitality" of the lab generated much media attention and took the campaign outside the immediate South End–Roxbury community. The campaign's other major trump card, namely BUMC's disregard for procedural justice and its associated lack of transparency over its application to NIH, has been far more difficult for BUMC to refute. Procedural justice is a key demand from environmental justice activists.

The community response, building power through an influential and far-reaching oppositional coalition, has both spread the word outside the immediately affected communities of South End–Roxbury to metro Boston, and has developed the campaign into a more diverse one, racially, socioeconomically, and in terms of background and organizational focus, as was noted by several of our interviewees. It is our contention that the injustice frame crafted by ACE and adopted by the campaign, while not a regular tactic of all the groups in the coalition, was a frame that *could* be aligned with the frames of most, if not all of the participating organizations. ACE Executive Director Penn Loh sees such coalitions as an acceptance of ACE's principles, a commitment to both a longer-term project and to a wider environmental justice movement and power building: "The way we do coalition work is pretty deep. We tend not to do stuff that's, like, coalition means signing onto something and then it's over in a year. So I'd say the way we approach coalition building doesn't lend itself to those short term marriages [of convenience], although I think that we have been fairly successful in attracting the alliance of folks who do get it and I think that's part of spreading the environmental justice and equity message" (Agyeman 2005, 166).

Notes

1. Bio-safety levels refer to the guidelines created by NIH that researchers working within the designated labs must adhere to regarding handling, and use of microbial agents. There are four levels; as the levels go up in number so does the risk. "BSL 4 is the level of security required for research on the most dangerous and exotic category of disease causing organisms. According to federal guidelines, BSL 4 pathogens pose a 'high risk of exposure and infection to personnel, the community, and the environment'" (ACE, 2004). The differences between the levels of each lab (which range from 1 to 4) are associated with the level of risk and security. The higher the number, the more safety and security measures have been placed within the lab. Eleven bio-containment laboratories conducting research on biological agents, some more dangerous than others, are being built across the country. The National Institute of Allergy and Infectious Diseases (NIAID)—which is part of the National Institutes of Health (NIH)—is funding the construction of all eleven. Two of the labs will be of the highest security level while the other nine will conduct research under less stringent security. One will be located at the University of Texas Medical Branch at Galveston and the other at Boston University Medical Center (ACE 2004).

2. Some of the organizations in the Campaign to Stop the Bio-terror Lab:
   - AFSCME local 1489 (Boston Medical Center Employees)
   - Alternatives for Community and Environment (ACE)
   - A.N.S.W.E.R. (Act Now to Stop War and End Racism)
   - Boston Animal Defense League
   - Boston Mobilization
   - Boston NAACP
   - BUGBLOC (BU Germ-Bioterror Lab Opposition Coalition)
   - Chinese Progressive Association
   - Council for Responsible Genetics
   - Dorchester People for Peace
   - The Foundation

- Grassroots Actions for Peace
- Labor for Justice with Peace
- League of United Latin American Citizens (LULAC) Massachusetts
- Massachusetts Animal Rights Coalition
- Massachusetts Nurses Association
- Neighborhood of Affordable Housing
- Roxbury Neighborhood Council
- Safety Net
- SEIU Local 2020 (Boston Medical Center Employees)
- United for Justice with Peace Coalition
- Watertown Citizens for Environmental Safety
- Women's International League for Peace and Freedom

3. The word "hispanic," although used by the U.S. Census is not the preferred word by many Latinos.

4. The word "minority," while problematic in many ways, is the term used in the U.S. Census.

5. Entman (1993, 52) argues that "framing essentially involves selection and salience. To frame is to select some aspects of a perceived reality and make them more salient in a communicating text, in such a way as to promote a particular problem definition, causal interpretation, moral evaluation, and/or treatment recommendation for the item described."

References

Agyeman, J., R. Bullard, and B. Evans. 2003. *Just Sustainabilities: Development in an Unequal World.* Cambridge, Mass.: MIT Press.

Agyeman, J. 2005. *Sustainable Communities and the Challenge of Environmental Justice.* New York: New York University Press.

Alternatives for Community and Environment (ACE). 2002. *Five Year Strategic Plan for 2002–2007.* Boston, Mass.: ACE.

———. 2004. "Facts about the Boston University Proposal to Build a National Biocontainment Laboratory at Boston University Medical Center." Accessed February 4, 2004, at http://www.ace-environmentaljustice.org.

Benson, G. [ACE staff attorney]. 2004. Interview. March 15.

Boston University Medical Center (BUMC). 2003. "BUMC Continues Support for Biosafety Laboratory." Press release. July 31.

———. 2004. "10 Things You Should Know About the National Emerging Infectious Diseases Laboratories." *Boston Globe*, April 20, A11.

Catton, W., and R. Dunlap. 1978. "Environmental Sociology: A New Paradigm." *American Sociologist* 13:41–49.

Commonwealth of Massachusetts. 2002. *Environmental Justice Policy.* Boston, Mass.: Massachusetts State House.

Cortright, J. and H. Mayer. 2002. "Signs of Life: The Growth of Biotechnology Centers in the U.S." Accessed April 12, 2004, at http://www.brookings.edu/es/urban/publications/biotech.pdf.

Council For Responsible Genetics (CRG). 2004. "Frequently Asked Questions: Biodefense Research." Accessed February 17, 2004, at http://www.gene-watch.org.

Economic Development and Industrial Corporation (EDIC). 1991. *Who Benefits from Biomed? Real Jobs for Boston Residents.* Boston, Mass.: EDIC.

Entman, R. 1993. "Framing: Toward Clarification of a Fractured Paradigm." *Journal of Communication* 43, no. 4:51–58.

Fass, S. [concerned citizen and member of Jamaica Plain Action Network JPAN]. 2004. Interview. April 15.

Fischer, F. 2002. *Citizens, Experts and the Environment.* Durham, N.C.: Duke University Press.

Goldman, B. 1993. *Not just Prosperity: Achieving Sustainability with Environmental Justice.* Washington, D.C.: National Wildlife Federation.

Hall, S. 1982. "The Rediscovery of Ideology: Return to the Repressed in Media Studies." In *Culture, Society and the Media,* edited by M. Gurevitch, T. Bennett, J. Curran, and J. Woolacott. London: Methuen.

Heldt Powell, J. 2003. "Bioterror Lab Foes Threatening Lawsuit." *Boston Herald,* September 20 and 21.

Hynes, P. [professor at Boston University School of Public Health]. 2004. Interview. April 5.

Loring, K. [ACE Staff Attorney]. 2004. Interview. April 20.

National Institutes of Health (NIH). 2002. *NIAID Strategic Plan for Biodefense Research.* Washington, D.C.: U.S. Department of Health and Human Services. Accessed April 16, 2004, at http://www2.niaid.nih.gov/Biodefense/.

Pellow, D., and R. Brulle, eds. 2005. *Power, Justice and The Environment: A Critical Appraisal of the Environmental Justice Movement.* Cambridge, Mass.: MIT Press.

Pulido, L. 1994. "People of Color, Identity Politics, and The Environmental Justice Movement." Unpublished manuscript, Geography Department, University of Southern California.

Rosenwald, L. [concerned citizen and professor at Wellesley College]. 2004. Interview. March 31.

Sable, M. 2003. "The Impact of the Biotechnology Industry's Global Production System on Local Economic Development in the Boston and San Diego Metropolitan Areas." Accessed April 16, 2004, at http://www.economia.unimo.it/convegni_seminari/CG_sept03/Papers/Parallel%20Session%201.4-2.4/Sable.pdf.

Schlosberg, D. 1999. *Environmental Justice and the New Pluralism: The Challenge of Difference for Environmentalism.* Oxford: Oxford University Press.

Smith, S. 2003. "Foes Vow to Fight Bioterror Lab." *Boston Globe,* October 1, B5.

South End Neighborhood Action Program (SNAP). 1991. *Boston: A Biomedical Frontier; Hype or Hope.* Boston, Mass.: Action for Boston Community and Development, Inc.

Taylor, D. 2000. "The Rise of the Environmental Justice Paradigm." *American Behavioral Scientist* 43, no. 4:508–80.

U.S. Census. 2000. "Roxbury Data Profile." Accessed June 12, 2004, at http://www.cityofboston.gov/DND/PDFs/Profiles/Roxbury_PD_Profile.pdf.

Could Civic Engagement Reproduce Political Inequality?

Much prior research has suggested that civic engagement channeled through even *non*political voluntary associations serves to increase political activity and involvement. However, in stark contrast to prevailing beliefs, Sobieraj and White (2004) revealed that participation in strictly nonpolitical organizations is not significantly related to political participation. The extent to which association involvement predicts political participation is, instead, dependent upon the presence of political activity within these avowedly nonpolitical organizations (for example, informal discussions about political issues, having a political issue on the agenda during association meetings, and so forth). Those without such currents of political discourse are not politically mobilizing. Given this critical finding, the research at hand turns to the landmark American Citizen Participation Study to examine participation patterns. We find that voluntary association participation is not randomly distributed, but rather that the involvement of women, Latinos, and the economically disadvantaged is more concentrated in civic organizations that are completely nonpolitical than those from dominant groups. Equally noteworthy, we find that whites, men, and the affluent have higher levels of involvement in some of the groups in which political discourse circulates, and consequently exhibit an increased propensity for political mobilization. While civic engagement undoubtedly offers important benefits for individual participants and communities at large above and beyond increasing political participation, we argue that the patterned nature of the mobilizing benefit has important implications for political inequality.

In the United States, we have experienced a crescendo of commitment to civic engagement in the past decade, believing that greater involvement in public life has much to offer to those involved and to the communities that they work to support. Many argue that one of the valuable side effects of participation is that civic engagement, specifically voluntary association participation, is often politically mobilizing, even when the association participation is non-political in nature. The research at hand builds on our finding that although participation in any type of voluntary association initially appears to be positively related to political participation, this underinterrogated finding fails to specify the elements of participation that truly promote political mobilization. We now know that in order for active involvement in voluntary associations to promote political participation, opportunities for members to participate in political discourse are essential. Further, when participants do have opportunities to engage in political discourse, the relationship between voluntary association involvement and political activity varies based on the amount of political interaction and activity that transpires within the organizations with which respondents affiliate (Sobieraj and White 2004). This finding, coupled with the increasing awareness of gross inequities in political participation that favor advantaged groups and penalize the disadvantaged (Schlozman, Page, Verba, and Fiorina 2005; Bartels, Heclo, Hero, and Jacobs 2005; Hacker, Mettler, and Pinderhughes 2005), leads us to probe the relationship between civic engagement and political mobilization further.

In this chapter, we demonstrate that while civic engagement does have great potential to serve as a catalyst for political involvement, these benefits accrue to those who are already most likely to exercise their political voice. Whites, men, and the affluent have significantly higher levels of involvement in some of the organizations that have been found to have significant positive associations with political participation, whereas the voluntary association participation of women, Latinos and the poor is significantly more concentrated in organizations in which political discussions and activities are absent.

Civic Engagement and Voluntary Association Involvement—Great Expectations

It is likely that we owe our current love affair with civic engagement to Robert Putnam (1995, 2000) who simultaneously seemed to proffer both explanation and (partial) solution to social deficits that had long seemed intractable. A decade later, politicians, religious leaders, and college administrators are consumed with promoting civic engagement and citizen education. Advocates argue that civic engagement is essential for several core reasons: (1) it promotes individual growth by providing practical experiences (improving self-confidence and feelings of efficacy in addition to proficiency in a variety of transferable skills); (2) it helps generate positive feelings about self and community; (3) it fosters stronger and more democratic communities via the development of trust, norms of reciprocity and cooperation, and a better understanding of the positionality of others in the community; and (4) it ensures that the needs of multiple voices are communicated to public officials (Verba, Schlozman, and Brady 1995). In other words, civic engagement is understood as important because it provides opportunities for individuals to develop civic skills, fosters social solidarity, and enhances the legitimacy of representative democracy.

In the United States, much civic engagement is channeled through voluntary associations, which historically have been central to American public life, as famously celebrated by Tocqueville ([1835] 1984), and remain prominent today. As a result, deep insight into voluntary associations, and participation in these associations, is essential to understanding the texture and outcomes of civic engagement in the United States. Voluntary associations make up much of the institutional infrastructure of civil society—that space apart from, yet profoundly entwined with, home and family, the economy, and the state. Wuthnow (1991, 7) describes voluntary sector participation as including "activities that are indeed voluntary in the dual sense of being free of coercion and being free of the economic constraints of profitability and the distribution of profits." Whether individuals participate by "joining" and developing a long-term relationship with an association and/or its members, whether they turn periodically to an association for short-term (or "episodic") volunteering opportunities, or whether they participate in less tactile ways via "checkbook" support of organizations whose objectives align with their own interests and concerns, voluntary associations serve as critical conduits of civic life. In addition to offering individuals a figurative (and sometimes literal) space to freely convene around shared interests, voluntary associations have long been thought to offer frameworks that facilitate the development of social cohesion, promote the expression of collective political concerns, and safeguard against the potential abuse of state power.

The U.S. Voluntary Sector

The voluntary sector in the United States is vast. There are more than 1.5 million tax-exempt organizations registered with the Internal Revenue Service (Internal Revenue Service Data Book 2005), and even this number underestimates the true number of voluntary associations: it fails to include churches, organizations with less than $25,000 in gross receipts, and those organizations that are incorporated by the government, because these organizations are not required to petition for nonprofit status or to file tax returns. In addition, the number excludes the myriad of less formal entities that may have little or no concern with establishing formal tax-exempt status. This expansive terrain contains tremendously diverse associations, many of which seem to have little in common. Trade unions, professional associations, special interest groups, Parent-Teacher Associations, fraternal organizations, religious groups/congregations, political parties, and informal social groups (for example, book clubs) are all voluntary associations united by dramatically different shared interests. Not only do these groups have radically different foci; they also vary in terms of their size, the degree to which they are formally organized, their level of activity, their exclusivity, and whether they are local, regional, national, or international, among other characteristics.

There is also significant variation in political interest and activity level across the association landscape. At one end of the spectrum, there are a variety of political organizations that focus on influencing the selection of political leaders or the decisions made by those leaders. This category includes organizations active in the election process (for example, political parties), nonpartisan organizations concerned about political life (for example, the League of Women Voters), organizations active around a particular set of political issues (for example, reproductive rights), and organizations that support a broad spectrum of political issues based on a particular political viewpoint (for example, The American Cause). Yet, the overwhelming majority of associations are not designed to monitor or influence the decision-making processes of the government. These nonpolitical associations are often subdivided into three primary categories: social welfare organizations (for example, the NAACP), member–benefit organizations (for example, farm cooperatives), and charitable organizations (including philanthropic, scientific, literary, and religious organizations as per the United States tax code). The latter category, charitable organizations, is by far the largest, comprising more than one million organizations (not including churches) (Internal Revenue Service Data Book 2005). While these organizations do not exist primarily for political activities, some do participate in the political arena. This level of engagement is regulated by stipulations enumerated in the federal tax code (see Berry 2003; Sobieraj and White 2004, for a discussion of these restrictions and their implications).

In spite of the prevalence of such distinctions, the partition between those organizations that are political in nature and those that are nonpolitical in nature is blurry at best. Political life and work often infiltrates even "nonpolitical" organizations, sometimes in overt ways (say, religious leaders promoting particular candidates for public office from the pulpit). This permeability received widespread attention in February 2006, when Internal Revenue Service investigations found illegal political activity in three-quarters of the tax-exempt organizations it studied (Strom 2006). While the organizations in question were found to have engaged in illegal levels of political activity (as per regulations related to their tax-exempt status), moderate levels of political activity (for example, lobbying) outside of electioneering are legal and occur regularly even in many organizations considered nonpolitical. Further, those associations that are not registered as tax-exempt are free to transition into and out of political activity as they choose. It must be noted as well that political bleeding into nonpolitical associations can also be far more subtle, occurring in informal conversations about politics among members (Erickson and Nosanchuk 1990). In an earlier work, we have demonstrated the variation in political activity levels that exists even within the "nonpolitical" universe (Sobieraj and White 2004). As a result, we argue that this distinction should be reconceptualized as a continuum, rather than as binary. In recognition of this, for this research we duplicate our approach in our previous work. We reject preconceived notions of which types of associations are "political" and which are "nonpolitical"; instead, we assess associations' levels of political involvement with the inside reports of those who affiliate with them. This approach will be discussed further in the data and methods section.

Nonpolitical Associations and Political Mobilization: Toward a More Nuanced Understanding

One of the most widely cited virtues of involvement in voluntary associations is that they are believed to be politically mobilizing, even when people choose to become involved in those associations that are primarily nonpolitical in nature (Olsen 1972; Verba and Nie 1972; Ehrenberg 1999; Erickson and Nosanchuk 1990; Verba, Schlozman, and Brady 1995). The belief in the mobilizing potential of nonpolitical associations is grounded in the work of Deutsch (1961) and others who have argued that certain experiences have the effect of breaking old patterns of behavior, making individuals available for new types of behavior. While Deutsch used this mobilization hypothesis to refer to modernizing societies, his perspective has also been used to argue that social participation, even in nonpolitical voluntary associations, often serves as a catalyst for political activity.

Several prominent studies have offered evidence in support of this theoretical claim. Olsen's oft-cited research on voter turnout revealed a moderately strong correlation between social participation (of any kind, not exclusively membership in formal voluntary associations) and voting. (Olsen 1972).[1] Looking at political activity more generally, Verba and Nie's landmark work on political participation in the United States presented strong evidence that nonpolitical organization membership is positively associated with political engagement. Perhaps most strikingly, they found that individuals who are active in multiple nonpolitical associations are even *more* likely to be politically active than those who are active in only one nonpolitical organization. (Verba and Nie 1972, 174–208). They attributed this result, in part, to the fact that active members of nonpolitical groups may become politically stimulated through discussions with other group members. Erickson and Nosanchuk's (1990) qualitative case study of the American Contract Bridge League arrived at similar conclusions, arguing that such nonpolitical associational activity promotes political activity by bringing participants into contact with other members who may be politically active. Most recently, Verba, Schlozman, and Brady (1995) argued that nonpolitical associations serve as spaces where political recruitment often transpires, and that these involvements provide skills and experiences that prepare members for future political activity.

Our 2004 reanalysis of the American Citizen Participation Study data revealed, however, that in stark contrast to prevailing beliefs, once relevant control variables and other measures of voluntary association involvement are taken into account, participation in strictly nonpolitical organizations is *not* significantly related to political participation. The extent to which association involvement predicts political participation is, instead, dependent upon the presence of political activity within these avowedly nonpolitical organizations (informal discussions about political issues, having a political issue on the agenda during association meetings, and so forth). In fact, the more formal and integrated an association's political activities, the greater the potential it had to be mobilizing. For example, participation in organizations that take stands on political issues was the strongest predictor of political participation, followed by participation in organizations that sometimes have political issues on meeting agendas, and then by those in which members occasionally discuss politics. Those associations without such currents of political discourse were not politically mobilizing, demonstrating that it is not the act of joining itself that supports political engagement, but rather the exposure to political dialogue (Sobieraj and White 2004). While we agree, obviously, with earlier research that has demonstrated that such political discourse can or does transpire in nonpolitical contexts (Erickson and Nosanchuk 1990; Verba and Nie 1972), we emphasize that while such interaction with politics certainly may happen in these contexts, in many cases it does not (see Eliasoph 1998). This insight forces a modified understanding of the relationship between nonpolitical association involvement and political activity.

Political Participation and Social Inequality in the United States

It is well established that social inequalities in terms of race, class, and (to a lesser extent) gender are mirrored in the world of political participation (for an extensive review on this topic, see the edited volume by Jacobs and Skocpol 2005, particularly the chapter by Schlozman, Page, Verba, and Fiorina). Indeed, the American Political Science Task Force on Inequality and American Democracy recently concluded: "We find disturbing inequalities in the political voice expressed through elections and other avenues of participation. We find that our governing institutions are much more responsive to the privileged than to other Americans. And we find that the policies fashioned by our government today may be doing less than celebrated programs of the past to promote equal opportunity and security, and to enhance citizen dignity and participation" ("American Democracy in an Age of Rising Inequality" 2004, 655).

Although we see important discrepancies in political behavior across varied axes of inequality, researchers argue that economic differences emerge as the most glaring and that the consequences of economic inequality contribute significantly to the political inequities that have been identified among members of different racial and gender categories. The participation gap between the poor and the affluent is profound, appearing not only at the voting booth (where those with family incomes over $75,000 are almost twice as likely to vote as those with incomes under $15,000), but also in campaign work, in contact with elected officials, in protest activity (where we might expect these differences to be reduced), and most dramatically in political contributions (Verba, Schlozman, and Brady 1995). Racial differences in political behavior are noteworthy, but interestingly, are almost entirely explained by differences in participatory resources (that is, education, acquisition of civic skills at work, and so forth) that are linked closely with social class (Schlozman, Page, Verba, and Fironia 2005). In terms of gender, women are slightly more likely to vote than men, but they fall behind (modestly) in other forms of political participation (Burns, Schlozman, Verba 2001). Research also has revealed that gender and race interact in the political arena; Non-Hispanic white women are the most politically active (though less active than non-Hispanic white men), followed by African American women (who are less active than African American men), with Latino women (who, again, are less active than Latino men) being the least active (Burns, Schlozman, and Verba 2001, 278).[2] While the aforementioned class-linked differences in participatory resources also explain some of the gender difference in political behavior, they do not have the same magnitude of explanatory power that we see in terms of racial differences (Schlozman, Page, Verba, and Fiorina 2005).

Given these critical political inequities, and the increasing economic disparities in the United States, questions about the relationship between civic engagement and political life are particularly important and lead us to ask additional questions about the role of civic engagement in political life, particularly for people from disadvantaged groups. Of those people who are civically engaged, who reaps the benefit of political mobilization? Who tends to be clustered in those organizations that are completely apolitical? Here we attempt to begin to answer these questions.

Hypotheses

Sobieraj and White (2004) demonstrated that the relationship between voluntary association involvement and political participation differed depending on the level of exposure to political dialogue and information. Involvement in strictly nonpolitical organizations failed to mobilize individuals to become more politically active, whereas involvement in organizations in which political activities occurred were, to differing degrees, positively related to political participation. Active participation (attending meetings, serving on boards, and so forth) in the most overtly political organizations (those that take stands on political issues), had the strongest relationship with political participation, followed by participation in organizations that sometimes have political issues on meeting agenda, and then by those in which members occasionally discuss politics. So-called checkbook participation, in which members contribute financially but do not interact with fellow members, was also significantly positively related to political participation. This essay seeks to determine who reaps the benefit of political mobilization that occurs within some voluntary organizations. We hypothesize that individuals from groups that have traditionally had the strongest voices in the political process, including men, whites, and those who are more affluent, will have significantly higher levels of participation in organizations in which political mobilization occurs than will women, people of color, and the poor. We also hypothesize that those from groups that have been traditionally underrepresented in the political process—including: women, people of color, and those who are less affluent—will have lower levels of participation overall and will concentrate their participation significantly more in nonpolitical organizations, thus missing the mobilization benefits incurred in other voluntary associations.

Data and Methods

The data used for this research was gathered by the National Opinion Research Center (NORC) for the American Citizen Participation Study. In 1990, NORC conducted 2,517 in-person interviews for the second of a two-stage survey of the voluntary activity of the American public. Machine-readable data from the in-person interviews and phone interviews conducted in the first stage are stored at the Interuniversity Consortium for Political and Social Research at the University of Michigan.[3] Respondents were asked to identify voluntary organizations with which they were affiliated and to describe the types of political activities performed by these organizations.

Measures

Voluntary Association Involvement

In the American Citizen Participation Study respondents were asked whether they were members of any of seventeen different types of voluntary associations. These included service clubs or fraternal organizations, veterans' organizations, groups affiliated with the respondent's religion, organizations representing the respondent's own particular nationality or ethnic group, organizations for the elderly or senior citizens, organizations interested mainly in issues promoting the rights or welfare of women, labor unions, other organizations associated with the respondent's work, nonpartisan or civic organizations interested in the political life of the community or nation, youth groups, literary/art/discussion or study groups, hobby clubs/sports or country clubs or other groups or clubs for leisure-time activities, associations related to where the respondent lives, organizations that provide social services in such fields as health or service to the needy, educational institutions or organizations associated with education, organizations that are active in providing cultural services to the public, and other voluntary associations. Respondents who reported membership in any of these types of associations were also asked if the organization participated in formal and informal political activities including sometimes taking stands on public issues, sometimes including political discussions on their agendas for meetings, and whether people in the meetings sometimes chatted informally about politics or government. We used this information to distinguish between four different categories of organizations (ranging from explicitly political to completely nonpolitical): (a) voluntary associations that take stands on political issues; (b) those that did not take stands on political issues but sometimes had these on meeting agendas; (c) those that did not take stands or have political issues on their agendas but whose members sometimes had informal discussions of political issues or government; and (d) those that did not take stands on, have on their agendas, or informally discuss political issues.

Levels of Participation in Voluntary Associations

To capture differences in individual activity/involvement level with these organizations, we use indicators from Sobieraj and White (2004) of the amount of participation individuals had devoted to each of the four categories of organizations described above. Respondents were asked whether they had (a) attended a meeting in the last twelve months; (b) served on a committee, given time for special projects, or helped organize meetings in the last twelve months; and (c) served on the board in the last five years. We assigned one point for each of these types of participation and then totaled the number of activities they reported participating in for each of the four types of voluntary associations.[4] Respondents who did not report being members of any voluntary association were coded as zero. Respondents who reported being members of organizations but had not attended meetings, served on committees, given time for special projects, or helped organize meetings in the last twelve months and had not served on the board in the last five years were also coded as zero for these measures, so as to distinguish simple membership from true social participation (Sobieraj and White 2004, 749).

Checkbook Participation

To measure checkbook participation we counted the number of times respondents reported being members of organizations whose meetings they had not attended but to which they had made financial contributions (other than membership dues) in the twelve months preceding the interview.

Findings

Average numbers of memberships and average levels of participation in the different types of voluntary associations varied in the ways that we predicted (see table 5-1). Almost without exception, respondents with higher incomes held more memberships and had higher levels of participation in all types of voluntary associations. Those in the highest family income bracket ($60,000 or greater) had the largest mean number of memberships and highest mean levels of participation for each type of organization. In fact, their mean number of memberships (1.58) and mean level of participation (3.19) in all organizations combined was more than *three times larger* than those of families who earned less than $15,000 (mean number of memberships = .48, mean level of participation = .87).

White had a higher mean number of memberships in all organizations combined (.98) than did African Americans (.93), Latinos (.43), and other people of color (.66). African Americans had a larger average number of memberships in organizations that take stands on political issues (mean = .49) followed by whites (mean = .44), others (.27), and Latinos (.17). Latinos had the smallest average number of memberships for all types of organizations except those that did not take stands on, have on their agendas, or informally discuss political issues. Their mean levels of participation were lower than whites and African Americans for all types of organizations. These findings indicate that Latinos are least likely to experience the mobilizing benefits that result from membership in voluntary organizations in which political exchanges occur.

TABLE 5-1.

Mean Memberships and Active Participation by Income, Race, and Gender

	Column A*		Column B*		Column C*		Column D*		Column E*		Column F*	
	Mean Number	Mean Level	Mean Number	Mean Level	Mean Number	Mean Level	Mean Number	Mean Level	Mean Number	Mean Level	Mean Number	Mean Level
Family Income												
Under $15,000	0.48 (1.45)	0.87 (2.78)	20 (0.87)	0.38 (1.79)	0.04 (0.4)	0.07 (0.71)	0.09 (0.65)	0.15 (1.21)	0.15 (0.65)	0.26 (1.26)	0.49 (0.84)	
$15,000 to 29,999	0.71 (1.67)	1.35 (3.58)	0.32 (1.14)	0.63 (2.58)	0.06 (0.38)	0.1 (0.76)	0.12 (0.56)	0.23 (1.13)	0.21 (0.79)	0.39 (1.49)	0.68 (0.95)	
$30,000 to 39,999	1.09 (2.07)	2.15 (4.59)	0.45 (1.43)	0.9 (3.23)	0.11 (0.49)	0.23 (1.16)	0.23 (0.87)	0.48 (1.91)	0.31 (0.95)	0.55 (1.73)	0.86 (1.08)	
$40,000 to 59,999	1.23 (2.05)	2.47 (4.56)	0.57 (1.37)	1.15 (3.07)	0.11 (0.57)	0.23 (1.29)	0.25 (0.91)	0.49 (1.89)	0.3 (0.95)	0.61 (2.1)	0.93 (1.16)	
$60,000 and above	1.58 (2.64)	3.19 (5.8)	0.75 (1.71)	1.53 (3.77)	0.13 (0.62)	0.26 (1.45)	0.34 (1.08)	0.7 (2.38)	0.36 (1.02)	0.7 (2.00)	1.21 (1.37)	

Race

Latino/a	0.43 (1.32)	0.78 (2.64)	0.17 (0.76)	0.34 (1.59)	0.02 (0.24)	0.04 (0.56)	0.05 (0.38)	0.1 (0.87)	0.19 (0.84)	0.3 (1.34)	0.25 (0.54)
African(American	0.93 (2.26)	1.95 (5.18)	0.49 (1.64)	1.03 (3.77)	0.09 (0.54)	0.22 (1.35)	0.17 (0.76)	0.22 (1.24)	0.24 (0.86)	0.48 (1.8)	0.47 (0.79)
White	0.98 (2.02)	1.92 (4.36)	0.44 (1.31)	0.87 (2.86)	0.09 (0.51)	0.17 (1.05)	0.2 (0.84)	0.4 (1.77)	0.25 (0.87)	0.48 (1.72)	0.86 (1.13)
Other	0.66 (1.92)	1.33 (3.85)	0.27 (1.19)	0.56 (2.48)	0.02 (0.24)	0.03 (0.44)	0.19 (0.95)	0.42 (1.99)	0.18 (0.78)	0.3 (1.35)	0.47 (0.84)

Gender

Women	0.91 (2.00)	1.79 (4.39)	0.39 (1.29)	0.79 (2.91)	0.08 (0.46)	0.15 (0.94)	0.18 (0.76)	0.35 (1.61)	0.27 (0.89)	0.51 (1.82)	0.68 (1.00)
Men	0.99 (2.05)	1.92 (4.37)	0.47 (1.35)	0.91 (2.89)	0.09 (0.54)	0.19 (1.18)	0.2 (0.84)	0.4 (1.8)	0.23 (0.84)	0.42 (1.57)	0.9 (1.16)

* *Notes to column heads*

Column A: Memberships in all organizations

Column B: Memberships in organizations that take stands on political issues

Column C: Memberships in organizations that did not take stands but have political discussions on meeting agendas

Column D: Memberships in organizations that did not take stands or have political issues on their agendas but have informal discussions of political issues

Column E: Memberships in organizations that did not take stands on, have on their agendas, or informally discuss political issues

Column F: Checkbook participation

Note: Numbers in parentheses are standard deviations. Effective sample size is 2,514 weighted cases. Verba and his colleagues oversampled blacks, Latinos, and political activists. We replicated Verba, Schlozman, and Brady's method of reweighting, described in *Voice and Equality: Civic Voluntarism in American Politics* (1995: appendix A) in order to make the sample representative of the adult population of the United States.

Women also appear to be less likely than men to be exposed to political discourse through their voluntary association involvement. Men had more memberships on average than women, and reported higher average levels of political participation than women in organizations that take stands on political issues, that sometimes have political issues on meeting agenda, and those in which members informally discussed political issues. Women surpassed men in mean number of memberships and mean level of participation in organizations in which no political activities occurred.

The analysis then focused on determining whether gender, race and ethnicity, and income were significant predictors of levels of active participation in each of the four types of voluntary organizations and in level of checkbook participation. It also allows us to determine whether racial differences in levels of membership can be explained by differences in family income. Table 5-2 presents the coefficients from weighted least squares (WLS) linear regression analyses. Family income was a significant predictor of level of active participation in each of the four types of organizations and of level of checkbook participation. For each increase in income, the magnitude of the difference with those whose family incomes were less than $15,000 in level of participation increased as well. The largest differences occurred in active participation in organizations that take stands on political issues. For instance, those whose family incomes were at least $60,000 had levels of active participation that were 1.16 times larger than those whose family incomes were less than $15,000. This is particularly noteworthy since Sobieraj and White (2004) found that increases in active participation in organizations that take stands on political issues, compared to participation in other voluntary associations, was most strongly associated with increases in political participation.

As regards income and gender, there were few significant racial and ethnic differences in level of active participation. Latinos reported significantly lower levels of active participation in organizations that did not take stands or have political issues on their meeting agenda, but have informal discussions of political issues. African Americans reported significantly higher levels of involvement than whites in groups that take stands on political issues. However, Latinos, African Americans and other people of color had significantly lower levels of checkbook participation. These differences existed beyond what could be explained by differences in income. Checkbook participation, despite seeming to lack opportunities for in-person interaction between members, is a significant predictor of whether respondents contact local or national officials, participate in informal activities aimed at addressing community issues, and vote (Sobieraj and White 2004). These findings demonstrate that its mobilizing effects are being experienced disproportionately by whites.

Women and men did not differ in their level of active participation in organizations that take stands or have political issues on their agenda, or in which members occasionally discuss political issues. As a result, women seem to be

TABLE 5-2.

Unstandardized Coefficients from Regression of Levels of Participation on Income, Race, and Gender

	Column A*	Column B*	Column C*	Column D*	Column E*
Family Income[a]					
$15,000 to 29,999	.26*	.03	.06	.14*	.12
	(.11)	(.04)	(.07)	(.07)	(.07)
$30,000 to 39,999	.53**	.16**	.30**	.31**	.29**
	(.13)	(.05)	(.07)	(.08)	(.07)
$40,000 to 59,999	.77**	.15**	.31**	.37**	.34**
	(.12)	(.04)	(.07)	(.07)	(.07)
$60,000 and above	1.16**	.19**	.52**	.47**	.62**
	(.13)	(.05)	(.08)	(.08)	(.08)
Race[b]					
Latino/a	−.32	−.09	−.22*	−.10	−.51**
	(.19)	(.07)	(.11)	(.11)	(.11)
African American	.36**	.07	−.11	.05	−.31**
	(.13)	(.05)	(.08)	(.08)	(.08)
Other	−.26	−.13	−.03	−.15	−.39**
	(.22)	(.08)	(.13)	(.13)	(.13)
Gender [c]	.01	.02	−.01	−.14**	.18**
	(.08)	(.03)	(.04)	(.05)	(.04)
Constant	.36**	.06	.19**	.31**	.53**
	(.09)	(.03)	(.06)	(.06)	(.06)
Adjusted R^2	.04	.01	.03	.02	.07

* *Notes to column heads*
   Column A: Level of active participation in voluntary associations that take stands on political issues.
   Column B: Level of active participation in voluntary associations that did not take stands but have political discussions on meeting agendas.
   Column C: Level of active participation in voluntary associations that did not take stands or have political issues on their agendas but have informal discussions of political issues.
   Column D: Level of active participation in voluntary associations that did not take stands on, have on their agendas, or informally discuss political issues.
   Column E: Level of checkbook participation.

Note: Numbers in parentheses are standard errors. Effective sample size is 2,517 weighted cases. *p<.05, **p<.01 (two-tailed tests).
   [a] Omitted category: under $15,000. [b] Omitted category: white. [c] Omitted category: women

TABLE 5-3.

Unstandardized Coefficients from Regression of Proportion of Participation in Nonpolitical Organizations on Income, Race, and Gender

	Proportion of Participation in Nonpolitical Organizations
Family Income[a]	
$15,000 to 29,999	−2.01
	(3.79)
$30,000 to 39,999	−4.52
	(3.96)
$40,000 to 59,999	−8.59*
	(3.78)
$60,000 and above	−7.73*
	(3.90)
Race[b]	
Latino/a	11.34*
	(5.59)
African American	−.03
	(3.69)
Other	.41
	(7.29)
Gender[c]	−6.73**
	(2.09)
Constant	35.37**
	(3.29)
Adjusted R2	.01

Note: Numbers in parentheses are standard errors. Effective sample size is 2,517 weighted cases. *p<.05, **p<.01 (two-tailed tests)
 [a] Omitted category: under $15,000
 [b] Omitted category: white
 [c] Omitted category: women

equally likely to experience the mobilizing benefits of these political activities. Women, however, did devote significantly greater effort than men to totally nonpolitical organizations, whereas men had significantly greater levels of checkbook participation. In these instances where they differ, women's participation is concentrated in organizations that fail to mobilize political participation while such is not true for men.

As indicated in table 5-1, women, people of color, and those who are less affluent participate in fewer organizations overall. Our final analysis demonstrates that, within the more limited pool of organizations in which they are involved, their participation tends to be more concentrated than that of men, whites, and the more affluent in strictly nonpolitical organizations (table 5-3). We find that the proportion of total participation that was spent in organizations that did not take stands, have political issues on meeting agendas, or informally discuss political issues was significantly greater for women than for men.[5] Latinos devoted a significantly higher proportion of their participation to these nonpolitical organizations than did whites. Those in the two highest income brackets of $40,000 to $59,999 and $60,000 and above spent significantly lower proportions of their participation on nonpolitical organizations than did those whose family incomes were less than $15,000. These findings provide evidence that some who are already disadvantaged by social and economic inequalities are further disadvantaged by concentrating their participation in voluntary associations that fail to promote their political mobilization.

Discussion

Interestingly, while the disadvantaged are often thought to have the voluntary sector as a space for potential empowerment (through social movement participation, via leadership in the nonprofit sector, and so forth), it is the privileged who appear to be taking advantage of civic engagement in ways that may most magnify their efficacy. We find support for some but not all of our hypotheses. There were fewer significant gender and racial differences than had been hypothesized, but we do find that Latinos, women, and the economically underprivileged concentrated their participation more so in organizations in which political exchanges were absent, and thus missed out on the mobilization benefits incurred in other voluntary associations. Most striking were the differences in levels of participation among income groups. The poor are significantly less represented in each type of voluntary organization. It is essential that we recognize that the relationship between voluntary association involvement and political activity not only varies depending on the degree and type of association participation, but that these variations are patterned in ways that disproportionately favor those who are already on top of a range of social hierarchies. These disparities not only mirror many of the patterns of inequality that we find in other forms of political participation (contacting public officials, protesting, and so forth), they may, in fact, contribute to them.

We recognize that civic engagement is far more than a means to an end with political mobilization as the ultimate goal. There are many other important benefits to individual participants and to the community when people are involved in public life. Participation affords opportunity for the free exchange of ideas and allows individuals to further their interests more effectively by joining with others with common interests and goals. The organizations themselves offer countless societal benefits by promoting social interactions and providing the public much-needed resources such as charitable and cultural services. Given the aforementioned disparities in political equality, however, we think that these trends are significant. Research has demonstrated time and time again that those who participate in the political process and those who do not have different political concerns and priorities (for a review, see Schlozman, Page, Verba, and Fiorina 2005). If civic engagement is to truly enhance the legitimacy of representative democracy (as many hope), it is essential that it make the democratic process more inclusive. Based on the findings of this research, such may not be the case. A more realistic understanding of the range of dramatically different engagement contexts and outcomes is essential to help us understand the role that civic engagement can play in social life, as well as its limitations.

Notes

1. Olsen (1972) makes the case for the presence of a causal relationship by establishing that the social participation transpired prior to the election of interest.
2. The authors do not have systematic national data on Asian Americans.
3. A detailed description of the research design can be found in Verba, Schlozman, and Brady (1995, appendix A).
4. For instance, if someone attended meetings and served on the board of two organizations that take stands on political issues, their score for level of participation in that type of voluntary association would be four (Sobieraj and White 2004, 749).
5. This variable was measured by dividing the measure of level of active participation in organizations that did not take stands, have on meeting agenda, or informally discuss political issues by the sum of their level of active participation in all four types of organizations. The proportion was then converted to arcsin values as proportions are not free to vary widely about the mean, and thus violate an assumption needed for this statistical procedure. Transforming the proportions to arcsin values gives the values of the variable more theoretical freedom to vary.

References

"American Democracy in an Age of Rising Inequality." 2004. APSA Task Force Report. *Perspectives on Politics* 2, no. 4:651–66.

Bartels, L. M., H. Heclo, R. E. Hero, and L. R. Jacobs. 2005. "Inequality and American Governance." In *Inequality and American Democracy: What We Know and What We Need to Learn,* edited by L. Jacobs and T. Skocpol, 88–155. New York: Russell Sage Foundation.

Berry, J., with D. Arons. 2003. *A Voice for Nonprofits.* Washington, D.C.: Brookings Institution.

Burns, N., K. L. Schlozman, and S. Verba. 2001. *The Private Roots of Public Action: Gender, Equality, and Political Participation.* Cambridge, Mass.: Harvard University Press.

Deutsch, K. 1961. "Social Mobilization and Political Development." *American Political Science Review* 55:493–514.

Ehrenberg, J. 1999. *Civil Society: The History of an Idea.* New York: New York University Press.

Eliasoph, N. 1998. *Avoiding Politics: How Americans Produce Apathy in Everyday Life.* Cambridge: Cambridge University Press.

Erickson, B., and T. A. Nosanchuk. 1990. "How an Apolitical Association Politicizes." *Canadian Review of Sociology and Anthropology* 27, no. 2:206–20.

Hacker, J. S., S. M. Mettler, and D. Pinderhughes. 2005. "Inequality and Public Policy." In *Inequality and American Democracy: What We Know and What We Need to Learn,* edited by L. Jacobs and T. Skocpol, 156–213. New York: Russell Sage Foundation.

Internal Revenue Service Data Book. 2005. http://www.irs.gov/pub.irs-soi/05databk .pdf (accessed May 15, 2006).

Jacobs, L. and T. Skocpol, eds. 2005. *Inequality and American Democracy: What We Know and What We Need to Learn.* New York: Russell Sage Foundation.

Olsen, M. 1972. "Social Participation and Voter Turnout: A Multivariate Analysis." *American Sociological Review* 37:317–33.

Putnam, R. D. 1995. "Bowling Alone: America's Declining Social Capital." *Journal of Democracy* 6, no. 1:65–78.

———. 2000. *Bowling Alone: The Collapse and Revival of American Community.* New York: Simon and Schuster.

Schlozman, K. L., B. I. Page, S. Verba, and M. P. Fiorina. 2005. "Inequalities of Political Voice." In *Inequality and American Democracy: What We Know and What We Need to Learn,* edited by L. Jacobs and T. Skocpol, 19–86. New York: Russell Sage Foundation.

Sobieraj, S., and D. White. 2004. "Taxing Political Life: Reevaluating the Relationship Between Voluntary Association Membership, Political Engagement, and the State." *The Sociological Quarterly* 45, no. 4:739–64.

Strom, S. 2006. "I.R.S. Finds Sharp Increase in Illegal Political Activity." *New York Times,* February 25.

Tocqueville, A. [1835] 1984. *Democracy in America.* Edited by Richard Heffner. New York: Mentor.

Verba, S., and N. H. Nie. 1972. *Participation in America: Political Democracy and Social Equality.* New York: Harper and Row.

Verba, S., K. L. Schlozman, and H. E. Brady. 1995. *Voice and Equality: Civic Voluntarism in American Politics.* Cambridge, Mass.: Harvard University Press.

Wuthnow, R., ed. 1991. *Between States and Markets: The Voluntary Sector in Comparative Perspective.* Princeton, N.J.: Princeton University Press.

Part Two

Civic Engagement in Societal Institutions:
Health Care and Education

Consumer-Sponsored Health Care Plans

Early Twentieth-Century Public Participation in U.S. Health Care

> Consumer-sponsored plans . . . were organized out of the belief that the right
> to health is a basic human right just as much as is the right to food and shelter
> and clothing. We have demonstrated that it is possible for a small portion of
> the population to assure themselves this right . . . , that preventive medicine
> and necessary medical treatment can be provided when economic and organ-
> izational barriers to medical service have been removed.
> —Harry J. Becker, president, Group Health Association, testifying at a U.S.
> Senate hearing on a proposed national health program (1946)

During the first half of the twentieth century, literally thousands of diverse consumer groups—mutual aid societies, medical cooperatives, and local community organizations as well as employee benefit associations, businesses, and trade unions—created, sponsored, and managed health care plans that provided needed care to millions of group members and their families. Known as *consumer* plans because they were established by laypersons—not medical professionals—these distinct plans brought highly innovative health care delivery and financing arrangements to both rural and urban areas of the United States. Important if undervalued in their time, these consumer plans also had a significant impact on later twentieth-century health policy (MacColl 1966).

In this chapter I examine these early consumer groups and their health care plans as powerful examples of public participation in U.S. health care. Public participation, like civic engagement (and I use these terms interchangeably) is an umbrella term representing many forms of individual and community involvement in our collective life. In the health realm, individuals and communities commonly engage in public health efforts to improve community health, in health care planning to better distribute and utilize health care resources, in community development strategies to build community, and in self-care organizations' efforts to fill the unmet health needs of particular groups (Rifkin 1981). Despite the fact that these early twentieth-century consumer health care plans are rich examples of such involvement, conventional descriptions of civic engagement in U.S. health care consistently omit them (Sirianni and Friedland 2001; Emanuel 1991; Kari, Boyte, and Jennings 1994; Morone 1990).

A typical narrative of civic engagement in health care begins in the 1960s with community health centers and their federal mandate to operate with "maximum feasible participation" by means of patient-dominated governing boards.[1] As we shall learn, some architects of these War on Poverty–Office of Equal Opportunity (OEO) programs had been key players in the earlier consumer plans. Moving forward in time, this common historical description documents citizens as priority-setters in the regional planning efforts of the 1970s health systems agencies (HSAs), attends to Oregon's inclusion of (some) citizen perspectives and values in its 1980s revamping of the state's Medicaid program, and notes the subsequent spawning of a dozen similar state-based health decisions movements where citizens debate the values inherent in various proposed and actual health care policies. Finally this narrative tells of the more recent Healthy Communities and Healthy Cities programs that form local coalitions to define community health needs and create compatible solutions. Some narratives recognize the more diffuse though no less important efforts of the consumer/patient rights movement, the women's health movement, the persons with disabilities movement, and similar efforts to increase public participation in health policy decision-making. Missing from this conventional chronicle are the earlier consumer plans.

Multiple factors likely contribute to why this earlier period has not received its historical due. Sirianni and Friedland (2001, 19), for example, assume that "patient empowerment and community involvement were virtually nonexistent in the face of professional dominance until the early 1960s." Similarly Kari et al. (1994, 3–4) understand that a long-standing reliance on medical expertise and authority thwarted civic involvement. While these assumptions of professional dominance obscure consumer involvement, further masking may take place with the assumption that local civic engagement parallels federal engagement—as is suggested by the fact that these conventional narratives tend to highlight consumer activities of the 1960s and the 1990s, in other words, periods of substantial effort in federal health care reform.[2]

In addition, a constellation of empirical realities are likely to have contributed to the plans' historical anonymity: the plans served a relative small number of persons; they operated independently and without a centralizing "trade" association; they were opposed and eventually superseded by commercial and physician-sponsored plans; and they were largely privately, not publicly, funded endeavors. Also civic engagement research has tended to focus on relatively recent civic involvement.

To dispel this common perception that significant public participation in health care began in the 1960s, I draw on varied historical sources from the early twentieth century to reveal a prior and unusually energetic period of consumer-sponsored health care innovation. Federal health-related agencies, state and local governments, economists, philanthropists, physicians, and successive historians of medicine have documented the work of these groups in reports, articles, books, and educational pamphlets.

Starting with a description of the early twentieth-century medical context, I then focus on the leading types of consumer groups and offer illuminating specific examples. Three modes of consumer participation are discerned: consumers as financial contributors, as directors or governors responsible for these plans, and as patients or recipients of care. I take up some of the internal and external constraints on these plans with special attention to the role of the medical profession. Finally, this historical recovery effort surfaces the legacy and lessons of these early consumer groups both for later health care reforms and for civic engagement research.

The Early-Twentieth-Century Medical Landscape

Lay creation of health care plans was motivated primarily by the great need for medical care. Medicine's inability to meet this need meant that medical care was ripe for organizational and financial innovation. The then-dominant solo-physician, fee-for-service model of medical practice was becoming increasingly complex and expensive due to the proliferation of medical specialties, hospitals, and new technologies. Sick persons with adequate financial resources sought individual practitioners for treatment, but preventive care was rare. Sick persons without adequate financial resources negotiated payment with their doctor, relied on the few urban dispensaries, or went without care. Some persons, regardless of financial status, received substandard care due to the lack of physicians or hospital facilities in their geographic areas.

Health insurance as we know it today did not exist in the early twentieth century. Some commercial accident or "sickness" insurance was available but these misleadingly named policies provided cash benefits to wage earners that had lost income due to injury or illness; very few policies offered coverage for physician or hospital expenses (Numbers 1978; Goldmann 1948; Wisconsin Legislature 1919, 22–24). In 1911, the first state workman's compensation laws took effect requiring employer responsibility for employee medical expenses associated with work-related injury.

The successful enactment of compulsory health insurance in several west-ern European countries also contributed to the rise of consumer plans. Inspired by these reforms, a vocal movement in the United States advocated for passage of national health insurance in this country. That Progressive Era effort (1916–1920) failed legislatively but nonetheless heightened popular awareness of the inadequacies of current health care and motivated a search for voluntary, private, health plan alternatives (Numbers 1978; Burrow 1977).

In 1927 a group of concerned physicians, hospital representatives, public health officials, social scientists, and members of the public formed the Com-mittee on the Costs of Medical Care (CCMC) to study the economic dimen-sions of the lack of adequate medical care services. Supported by eight philan-thropic foundations, CCMC committed itself to a five-year research agenda involving numerous studies and ultimately more than two dozen published re-ports. CCMC's final report, *Medical Care for the American People*, was pub-lished in 1932 during the deepening economic crisis of the Depression. It pro-vides an unusually comprehensive view of extant health care services including consumer-sponsored plans (CCMC 1932).

Between 1928 and 1931, CCMC surveyed 8,758 white families (39,183 in-dividuals) repeatedly over a twelve-month period to ascertain their incidence of illness, the medical care they received, and the cost of this medical care.[3] This survey found that 38.2% of all respondents received no medical, dental, or eye care over the course of the year. This lack of care ranged from 13.8% in the highest income group to 46.6% in the lowest income group (CCMC 1932, 9).

Moreover, the CCMC recognized these numbers as underestimates of actual levels of care in several ways. First, having excluded "Negroes" from this sur-vey, CCMC reasoned, "It is well known . . . that the 10 per cent of our popula-tion who are colored have health problems which are, on the whole, consider-ably more serious than those of whites. . . . Because Negroes generally are poorer than whites, it is safe to assume that on the average they receive rela-tively less medical service than that received by the two lowest [white] income groups." Second, CCMC notes that "many of the persons who are counted as having had medical care may have had extremely little." Third, the study did not address the quality of care received; and fourth, the study dealt only with physical health concerns; it did not ask about the need or receipt of medical care related to "mental hygiene" (CCMC 1932, 9–11).

The central outcome of CCMC's research was that "even less-than-average charges for medical service . . . are more than many of our families can bear." CCMC focused its analysis and recommendations on the uneven and unpre-dictable costs of care, concluding, "No fact is more clearly demonstrated by the Committee's studies than this one: that the costs of medical care in any one year now fall unevenly upon different families in the same income and popu-lation groups. The heart of the problem, therefore, is equalizing the financial impact of sickness." More emphatically, "On the present fee-for-service basis, it is impossible for 99 per cent of the families to set aside any reasonable sum of money with positive assurance that that sum will purchase all needed medical care" (CCMC 1932, 13–19).

CCMC's proposed solution called for the costs of medical care to be financed by *consumer groups* rather than by individuals or families. Specifically, it recommended "that *organized groups of consumers unite in paying into a common fund* agreed annual sums, in weekly or monthly installments, and *in arranging with organized groups of medical practitioners* working as private group clinics, hospital medical staffs, or community medical centers, to furnish them and their families with virtually complete medical service. By 'organized groups of consumers' the Committee means industrial, fraternal, educational, or other reasonably cohesive groups" (CCMC 1932, 121; emphases added).

This model of consumer-sponsored plan, known at the time as a prepaid group health plan was "no theorist's dream" (MacColl 1966, 2) or even an "untried experiment" (CCMC 1932, 124). Extensive CCMC research had identified many small, independently organized groups of consumers who were sponsoring health care plans involving the prepayment of defined fees and contracts with physician group practices and hospitals, in contrast to the solo-practitioner, fee-for-service norm of the day. Thus CCMC asserted: "All the proposed methods have been extensively tested, nearly all of them in the United States. Many of them the Committee has studied in actual operation" (CCMC 1932, 124). In the next section, we examine some of these diverse consumer groups and the plans they created.

"Organized Groups of Consumers Unite"

In the early twentieth century, many working- and middle-class groups formed around commonalities as diverse as occupation, workplace or employer, ethnicity, culture, religion, national origin, and/or geography. Industry-related groups (business establishments, employee benefit associations, and trade unions), as well as mutual aid societies and local nonprofit associations were among the groups that responded to the pressing need for medical care by creating health care plans for their group members. Some of these previously organized consumer groups—predominantly industry-related groups and mutual aid societies—expanded existing group benefits such as death (funeral cost) benefits and the cash benefits of accident and sickness insurance, to include new health care plans that provided actual health care services. Other consumer groups such as medical cooperatives formed expressly for the purpose of providing needed health care services.

Industry-Related Groups

The industrial workplace was the site of many of the earliest consumer plans established by employers, employee benefit associations, and by both entities working together. In the late nineteenth century, in geographically remote regions where lumber, mining, and construction companies operated, necessity motivated novel approaches to health care delivery. Absent local medical services in these isolated areas, some industrial employers hired one or more "company doctors" to provide medical services for employee work-related injuries. Most companies covered the expenses of these "contract practices" by regularly deducting a compulsory fixed fee from employee paychecks. In exchange workers received a defined set of medical services. The range of services offered varied widely from company to company and could include general medical, medical specialty, hospital, and/or nursing services. Although employers formed these plans and employee participation was involuntary, together they functioned as an organized lay group engaged in providing otherwise unavailable health care.

An unusually comprehensive employer-sponsored medical service was offered in Binghamton, New York, by the Endicott-Johnson Corporation, a shoe manufacturer and leather tanning business. In 1918, the company established a medical service for its more than 19,000 employees and their dependent family members. The medical program offered the clinical services of about forty physicians: twenty-six nurses, five dentists, five pharmacists, as well as hospital services contracted through local hospitals (Julius Rosenwald Fund 1936, 16–18; Falk, Rorem, and Ring 1933, 469–70).

Given the medical need and the success of these plans in meeting some of this need, the number of industry-based medical plans grew rapidly. Many companies also expanded benefits to include medical services for non–work-related health concerns and expanded eligibility to include members of worker families. In 1938, industrialist Henry J. Kaiser contracted with Sidney Garfield, M.D., to provide medical services to the 5,000 workers building the Grand Coulee Dam in eastern Washington. Soon thereafter the Kaiser Company added urban shipyard worksites, built hospitals for its workers, and created a prepaid group health plan under the auspices of the Permanente Foundation. Medical benefits were extended repeatedly to cover employee non–work related health problems, then family members, and then new member groups such as unions and local colleges (Hendricks 1993). Like most employer-sponsored plans, it was the Kaiser management, not the employees, who held the primary authority for creating and directing these group health plans (Hendricks 1993; Williams 1932, 28).

In contrast, employee benefit associations established and managed their organizations' provision of benefits—usually funeral, and accident and sickness benefits although some associations also offered medical services. Started as an alternative to "passing the hat" when a worker was injured or sick, these employee associations emerged prior to the passage of state workmen compensation laws in 1911 and peaked in number in the 1920s (Plumly 1947; Williams 1932, 278-90). The Stanocola Employees Medical and Hospital Association began in 1924. Affiliated with the Standard Oil Company in Baton Rouge, Louisiana, this employee association established and owned a clinic and hired seven physicians and two nurses to serve its 2,200 members. Employees paid $3 per month for clinic services, home visits, and for hospital services with a $250 cap per hospitalization. Association membership was voluntary and approximately three-quarters of eligible employees joined. Association governance was by an eleven-member board of directors elected by the membership (Goldmann 1948, 162-64; Williams 1932, 289-90).

In the early 1930s, twenty-seven railroad employee hospital associations worked with railroad companies to provide hospital services to workers constructing the rail system. A network of company-built and -owned hospitals, including affiliated community hospitals along the rails, was supported in large part by employee association dues deducted from the rail workers' payroll. Family members were not eligible for "free" care like employees but could receive care at discounted rates (Williams 1932, 193-215).

Though primarily concerned with wages and working conditions, a few local trade unions offered medical services similar to those of employee benefit associations. Among the earliest was a 1913 clinic financed by the International Ladies Garment Workers' Union for two purposes: to give health examinations to potential union members and to evaluate union members' claims to sickness benefits. In 1919 this clinic became a dental clinic named the Union Health Center, which in 1928 added medical services. Six years later the Union Health Center served more than 19,000 persons in 40,000 annual office visits (Julius Rosenwald Fund 1936, 22-24; Plumly 1947, 16-24).

Mutual Aid Societies

In the mid-nineteenth century, many immigrant groups bound by language, culture, and/or national origin, organized to form mutual aid societies for the social, educational, recreational, and medical benefit of their members. Sometimes national, but more often local associations offered funeral benefits and financial support for sick and/or disabled members and their families. A few of these clubs offered free hospital or tuberculosis sanatoria care but at this time very few, if any, offered general medical benefits (Williams 1932, 270). Later in the nineteenth century as the industrial medical plans took hold in rural areas, parallel plans emerged in urban working-class communities. Mutual aid societies began providing medical care through contracts with local physicians.

French and German immigrants in San Francisco formed some of the earliest mutual aid societies. In 1851, La Société Française de Bienfaisance Mutuelle de San Francisco (the Society) was founded with 300 members (Harris 1932). Medical services were arranged and one year later, the Society built its own hospital. By 1943, the Society had 9,500 members (Julius Rosenwald Fund 1936, 61). Similarly the German General Benevolent Society "resulted from the desire to alleviate the sufferings of German-speaking peoples, numbering 5,500 in 1853, and also to supply certain cultural and nationalistic needs." Four years later the German Hospital opened in San Francisco (Schwartz 1965, 451; Harris 1932, 114–15).

In Tampa, Florida, in 1891, Centro Asturiano was established and later became the largest of five such clubs in that city (Avnet 1944, 5; Julius Rosenwald Fund 1936, 50–52). It provided social and medical services for its 3,000 male, largely Spanish-speaking, and wage-earning members. Males of other than "Latin" descent were allowed to join and "some forty different nationalities" did so (Plumly 1947, 53). An affiliated club, Beneficencia Asturiana, enrolled 4,500 "dependents": women and children related to Centro members. For $2 per month, members received "office calls and home calls by members of the medical staff, drugs used or prescribed by the physicians, laboratory tests, all necessary hospitalization for acute or chronic conditions, x-ray diagnosis and treatment, and surgery" (Julius Rosenwald Fund 1936, 50). These centros were "democratically run by elected representatives of the membership" and "constitute[d] the earliest example in the United States of voluntary self-supporting, non-profit consumer organizations gradually undertaking, as a primary function, full medical care for members" (Avnet 1944, 5).

Also in Tampa, the 4,500 members of the Italian Club received general and specialty medical care and limited surgical and hospital benefits for 65 cents per week (Plumly 1947, 53–54). The Jewish Worker's Circle in Chicago contracted with physicians at Mount Sinai Hospital to provide office medical services to its 1,000 families (Falk, Rorem, and Ring 1933, 463). Fraternal orders and lodges functioned much like other mutual aid organizations, providing medical care benefits through "lodge practice" (Goldmann 1948, 37–38).

Industrial and mutual aid society health care plans grew in number and influence in the late nineteenth and early twentieth centuries. By the early 1930s, between 1 and 1.5 million employees and their dependents nationwide were receiving "more or less complete medical care from organizations operated under industrial auspices" (Falk, Rorem, and Ring 1933, 462). Though the provision of medical services was rarely the central function of mutual benefit associations and fraternal lodges, thousands of these organizations served an unknown but significant number of medically needy persons in both urban and rural communities (Burrow 1977, 120–22; Starr 1982, 206–9).

This nonmedical sponsorship of contract and lodge practice was controversial among physicians; some claimed it violated professional medical ethics (Burrow 1977; American Foundation 1937, 1061–1100). On the one hand, it provided care to many patients who could not otherwise afford it. It also provided income and clinical experience to physicians who might not otherwise have received such. On the other hand, physicians competed by price for these contracts, thus reducing physician income. The quality of care was compromised by overwhelming patient caseloads, and group members had little choice of physician.

Medical Cooperatives

The cooperative movement in the United States gained notable strength throughout the Depression. This democratic, service-oriented philosophy inspired the shared acquisition of needed farm goods and services and over time came to be applied to medical services. In Elk City, Oklahoma, in 1929, local farmers worked with a local physician to organize the first medical cooperative, the Community Hospital Association (CHA). Soliciting the purchase of initial shares from several hundred families, these community leaders formed the cooperative, built a hospital, and hired several physicians to work together in a group practice. Cooperative members paid regular dues to the cooperative and received defined therapeutic and preventive medical care as well as hospital care. Five years later the CHA comprised 600 family memberships (Shadid 1992).

The Bureau of Cooperative Medicine and this Elk City physician actively promoted the formation of medical cooperatives in western rural communities where medical needs were great. A 1949 survey found 101 rural cooperatives nationwide serving an estimated 40,250 users (Johnston 1950, 5–15).

Medical cooperatives were consumer-controlled and governed democratically by a members-only board of directors using the Rochdale Principles of Cooperation as their guide.[4] Doctors working in cooperatives were adamant about preserving their professional autonomy and member boards were careful to distinguish their responsibilities from medical responsibilities. "The Guide for Member Plans" issued by the Cooperative Health Federation of America was clear: "There must be no interference in the practice of medicine by the lay board. The traditional relationship of physician and patient must be preserved. Provisions to this effect shall be included in the bylaws of all member organizations" (Johnston 1950, 89–90). In short, consumer boards tended to the economics and administration of the cooperative while physicians tended to the treatment of disease and injury of its members.

In the wake of the Depression, the federal Farm Security Administration (FSA) sponsored hundreds of rural health cooperatives as part of a package of loan, housing, and medical programs created to rehabilitate financially devastated farm families. Poor health was understood to be an obstacle to economic self-sufficiency so the FSA negotiated with local farmers and physicians to create medical cooperatives for FSA loan borrowers. FSA programs were intended to be flexible in the hope of accommodating local needs and as "an expression of the FSA's commitment to participatory democracy" (Grey 1999, 55). Starting with two small mutual aid groups in the Dakotas, in 1936 and 1937 respectively, the FSA medical cooperatives blossomed to their 1942 peak with more than 650,000 rural residents being served in one-third of all rural U.S. counties (Grey 1999).

Urban consumer groups, similarly motivated by a lack of affordable health care, also began organizing medical cooperatives. The first urban cooperative, the Group Health Association, was started in 1937 by a group of federal employees in Washington, D.C. (Goldmann 1948, 169–72). A decade later, the Group Health Cooperative of Puget Sound opened in Seattle, Washington (Crowley 1996).

Community Plans: Local and University

Community residents also developed local community-based plans to address their medical needs. Local philanthropic organizations in Brattleboro, Vermont, and in New Bedford, Massachusetts, created community health associations that contracted with local providers to offer hospital and/or nursing services. In Roanoke Rapids, North Carolina, a unique collaboration among several employers resulted in a plan that covered nearly all employed persons in town (Williams 1932, 227–44).

Universities provided another opportunity for the emergence of innovative consumer health plans. Reminiscent of remote industrial workplaces, universities have large concentrations of temporarily located young persons with significant health care needs. By 1931, some 153 universities and colleges had organized to provide at least acute medical care for their students during the academic year (Falk, Rorem, and Ring 1933, 464). At the University of California, 9,800 students received medical, dental, lab, and X-ray services, hospitalization, physical therapy, and drugs for the nine-month school year (CCMC 1932, 93). Some universities extended services to faculty, staff, and their families, leading CCMC to speculate, "It is also not beyond the range of possibility that the medical services of the university group might be extended to include the general population of the community in which the educational institution is established" (Falk, Rorem, and Ring 1933, 465).

Each of these types of consumer group developed plans responsive to local need. Employers, employee associations, and mutual benefit societies created the first plans in the mid-nineteenth century and they proliferated in the early twentieth century. In 1936 the Julius Rosenwald Fund, a philanthropy that funded CCMC, reported: "A growing number of requests arise from organizations of consumers—fraternal, industrial, educational, and social groups—as to methods whereby they can secure medical care or pay for it on some cooperative basis" (Julius Rosenwald Fund 1936, 4). The 1940s, as one observer put it, was "the decade of action" for consumer plans (Plumly 1947). Rural cooperatives multiplied, employer-based plans expanded to local communities, and union health programs grew alongside those of employee benefit associations.

"In Paying into a Common Fund . . . and in Arranging with Organized Groups of Medical Practitioners"

Consumers participated in these plans in three significant ways. First, each group member paid regular fees. The pooling of these financial contributions enabled the second form of participation: member receipt of needed medical and hospital services. Third, consumers engaged with these plans not only as patients, but also as governors, directors, and/or administrators. Just who within these lay groups had the authority to direct the plans ranged widely, from employers with sole decision-making power in some employer-sponsored plans to patient-members controlling medical cooperatives utilizing well-known principles of democratic governance. Falling within this spectrum of governance were the shared employer-employee decision-making processes of employer-employee health plans, the employee management of health plans in employee benefit associations and unions, and the consumer–group member governance of mutual aid societies and FSA programs.

Each of these modes of consumer participation represented a radical change in the physician-dominated medical care of the day. The primary consumer objective was pragmatic: to gain financial access to needed medical services through the sharing of financial risk. For some, consumer involvement was also a matter of philosophical principle. James Peter Warbasse, a physician-leader in the cooperative health movement, was resolute, "It is only natural that the people who need the services, who pay the bills, who suffer the pains, and who do the dying, should control the business. The service motive in medicine means consumer control" (Warbasse 1951, 6).

Obstacles to consumer plans were generated both internally and externally. From within, most group health plans were not fully inclusive or democratic. They typically served only persons able to pay the monthly fees, although a few served both members and nonmembers. Member eligibility criteria sometimes excluded the sickest persons, who were assumed to be the most costly in terms of medical expenses. At root, these plans were local attempts to expand access to health care, not local or national efforts to provide universal access to health care.

As in the CCMC survey, racism excluded African American residents from most consumer health plans. In response, some black groups established distinct programs: in 1932, the Flint-Goodridge Hospital in New Orleans offered black schoolteachers and other employee groups a hospitalization plan for a "penny-a-day." The annual fee for the plan was $3.65 and by 1943, some 5,000 persons had joined (Hine 1989, 74). Black women's clubs, especially in the South, supported black nursing schools, medical schools, hospitals, and tuberculosis sanitoria in their efforts to improve the health status of African American communities (Hine 1989; Neverdon-Morton 1989).

Despite collaborative agreements between local families and physicians, farmer participation in the FSA medical cooperatives was weak (Mott and Roemer 1948). Farmers gave input regarding plan benefits, sometimes sat on billing review committees, and filed grievances as needed. Yet the program "ced[ed] substantial control to doctors. For example, setting fee schedules, policing physicians' behavior, monitoring their use, and billing were largely left to local physicians and county medical societies" (Grey 1999, 55). This medical dominance in FSA programs hinted at the generally contentious relationship that existed between medical professionals and consumer plans.

The greatest external obstacle to consumer plans came from the formidable and organized physician resistance to them based on strong ideological and economic interests. Physicians and hospitals often worked with commercial insurance companies to sponsor their own health care plans while simultaneously challenging the legal and political standing of consumers to do likewise. Local medical strategies to eliminate consumer plans included the blocking of professional licensing of consumer plan–associated physicians by local county medical societies, the denial of physician memberships to professional associations, and refusals to grant local hospital privileges (Starr 1982, 299–310).

Organized medicine also worked vigorously at the state level to pass legislation prohibiting or restricting lay control of health care plans. State laws governing cooperatives often did not specifically include "health" cooperatives, and organized medicine worked to pass laws barring nonprofessionals from forming any type of health plan. In an unusual contrast, after overturning earlier prohibitive legislation a 1945 Texas law specifically allowed the establishment of lay cooperative hospitals in communities of less than 2,500 residents. The effect of this supportive legislation was reflected in a 1949 survey that found 52 rural health cooperatives in Texas, more than seven times the number in any other state (Johnston 1950, 5–15).

While the 1930s and 1940s witnessed a proliferation of consumer plans, the potent medical opposition forced some plans to close down. Other consumer plans managed to work around the law with assurances to the medical community that laypersons would control only the business of medical services, not the clinical professional aspects (Shadid 1992). Physician antagonism toward consumer-controlled health plans weakened considerably in 1943 when the U.S. Supreme Court found the American Medical Association to be in violation of antitrust laws in its less-than-subtle attempt to constrain the operation of the Group Health Association (Starr 1982, 305–6). Despite this ruling, much damage to consumer-sponsored plans had already been done.

By the early 1950s most consumer plans were in decline, including the FSA health cooperative program, which ended in 1946. The 1940s "decade of action" had been an active one for commercial and physician-sponsored plans too. A hospital-based nonprofit plan created by a group of Dallas schoolteachers and Baylor University Hospital developed into the first Blue Cross plan, and from 1940 to 1945, Blue Cross's membership grew from 5 million to 23 million members (Plumly 1947, 65). In contrast in 1946 consumer-based plans served approximately 3 million persons (U.S. Senate 1946, 110).

At the same time, for-profit commercial insurance companies began offering group indemnity insurance plans, which became a popular employee benefit during the wage freeze of World War II. Employer and union contracts increasingly included these health insurance plans. In the face of efforts to pass national compulsory health insurance legislation in the 1930s and 1940s, voluntary private plans, especially those organized by physicians and hospitals, gained political support as the "moderate" alternative. In this context where all plans competed for public, professional, and reformer attention, physician, hospital, and commercial health plans grew much more rapidly than consumer plans (Hirshfield 1970, 98; Reed 1958).

Innovation by definition involves novelty and inexperience and these features made consumer plans inherently high-risk ventures. Some medical cooperatives served needy nonmembers, straining limited resources. Cooperatives required an uncommon commitment to democratic cooperative principles and to processes that were sometimes unknown and distrusted (Johnston 1950).

Needless to say this midcentury medical, legal, and economic climate was inhospitable to consumer-sponsored plans that challenged the medical status quo. Of this era, Hirshfield (1970, 72) notes, "Programs that solved real problems in medical care distribution and, in addition, were least disruptive to the traditional medical care system won public and professional support and survived. Those which failed to solve problems effectively or which seemed to disrupt the medical care system too radically were rejected and failed."

Legacy and Lessons

Of this groundbreaking period, historian Rickey Hendricks (1993, 16) has observed: "Reform came from the base of the national medical care pyramid, from patients, consumers, and unorthodox practitioners, rather than from the elite of the medical profession." Dubbed "voices in the hinterland" (Hirshfield 1970) and "insignificant straws in the economic gale then sweeping the country" (Avnet 1944, 9), consumer health care plans were not widely recognized as important organizational and financing innovations in their time. This disregard persisted despite the fact that for years, several million U.S. residents received needed medical care that they otherwise might not have received. These plans also helped to financially sustain many families that would have been devastated by medical expenses.

The legacy of these consumer plans has become more evident over time as they have directly and indirectly shaped subsequent health care policies. Some medical and administrative personnel in the FSA health cooperatives program later worked in the 1960s Office of Economic Opportunity and its nascent neighborhood health center program. In one recognizable inheritance, the leaders of both believed that "promoting local leadership and inculcating democratic values in poor communities would advance their larger goal of social change and community renewal" (Grey 1999, 180).

The organizational model of the prepaid group health plan survived and hybridized over time. The Kaiser Permanente plan served as a prototype for the original health maintenance organization introduced in the early 1970s. A few consumer plans continue operation today. One example is Group Health, formally known as the Group Health Cooperative of Puget Sound, which serves more than half a million residents in Washington and Idaho and is governed by a member board of trustees (Crowley 1996).

Lessons for civic engagement research and for health care policy also surface. This historical research confirms that contemporary, conventional, civic engagement narratives yield relatively limited understandings of civic groups and their activities. Expanded narratives that include preceding eras and seemingly unsuccessful "hinterland voices" are required for more comprehensive analyses and insights into the actual resources, challenges, and tensions of public participation.

As for lessons for healthcare, in the twenty-first century calls for public participation in health care are being reinvigorated by a growing lack of access to high-quality care and by frustration with health care's limited mechanisms for community influence.[5] This situation "opens up new possibilities to make explicit the imperative that citizens must be actively engaged in health-problem solving and in developing health policy" (Kari, Boyte, and Jennings 1994, 2). The sheer existence of these early consumer plans, albeit short-lived, makes plain that organized groups of nonmedical personnel were capable of founding and governing innovative health care institutions. The seemingly inconceivable notion today that diverse groups of consumers could lead health care plans in meeting significant health care needs becomes downright plausible when we realize that nearly a century ago, literally thousands of U.S. consumer groups did just that.

I am grateful to Susan Ostrander for her insightful feedback in pursuit of clarity and relevance in earlier drafts and to two anonymous reviewers for their helpful comments.

Notes

1. This typical narrative is a composite of conventional descriptions of public participation in health care. Not every narrative includes all or only the consumer activities mentioned in this section.
2. The relationship between federal and local civic engagement in health care warrants further investigation as public participation in health care does appear to have been enhanced by federal sponsorship of local programs. See for example the Farm Security Administration health cooperatives described later in this chapter.
3. Notably, "white" here means "all-but-negro." The CCMC study reports that "Although the term 'white families' is used, only negro families were excluded." The reason given states, "The negro population was not included because it was considered that the procedure [survey method] adopted could not procure satisfactory information from negro families" (Falk, Rorem, and Ring 1933, 5). No justification for this claim is offered.
4. The Rochdale Principles guided the governance of cooperatives by means of certain standards: for example, each member has one vote, and profits are reinvested for the good of the members (Warbasse 1923, 22).
5. The current "consumer-driven" health care movement, though rhetorically similar to early twentieth-century consumer-sponsored care, is in fact largely market- and medicine-driven (see Davis 2004). For distinctive entries to the vast literature on the role of communities in U.S. health care, see Minkler 2002; Bayne Smith et al. 2005; Schlesinger 1997; and Light 1997.

References

American Foundation. 1937. *American Medicine: Expert Testimony out of Court.* Vol. 2. New York: American Foundation.

Avnet, H. H. 1944. *Voluntary Medical Insurance in the United States: Major Trends and Current Problems.* New York: Medical Administration Service.

Bayne Smith, M., J. Y. Graham, and S. Guttmacher. 2005. *Community-based Health Organizations: Advocating for Improved Health.* San Francisco, Calif.: Jossey-Bass.

Burrow, J. G. 1977. *Organized Medicine in the Progressive Era: The Move toward Monopoly.* Baltimore, Md.: Johns Hopkins University Press.

Committee on the Costs of Medical Care. 1932. *Medical Care for the American People: The Final Report of the Committee on the Costs of Medical Care.* Chicago: University of Chicago Press.

Crowley, W. 1996. *To Serve the Greatest Number: A History of Group Health Cooperative of Puget Sound.* Seattle, Wash.: Group Health Cooperative of Puget Sound, in association with University of Washington Press.

Davis, K. 2004. "Consumer-directed Health Care: Will It Improve Health System Performance?" *Health Services Research* 39:1219–33.

Emanuel, E. J. 1991. *The Ends of Human Life: Medical Ethics in a Liberal Polity.* Cambridge, Mass.: Harvard University Press.

Falk, I. S., C. R. Rorem, and M. D. Ring. 1933. *The Costs of Medical Care: A Summary of Investigations on the Economic Aspects of the Prevention and Care Of Illness.* Chicago: University of Chicago Press.

Goldmann, F. 1948. *Voluntary Medical Care Insurance in the United States.* New York: Columbia University Press.

Grey M. R. 1999. *New Deal Medicine: The Rural Health Programs of the Farm Security Administration.* Baltimore, Md.: Johns Hopkins University Press. Group Health Cooperative, http://www.ghc.org (accessed October 8, 2004).

Harris, H. 1932. *California's Medical Story.* San Francisco, Calif.: J. W. Stacey.

Hendricks, R. 1993. *A Model for National Health Care: The History of Kaiser Permanente.* New Brunswick, N.J.: Rutgers University Press.

Hine, D .C. 1989. *Black Women in White: Racial Conflict and Cooperation in the Nursing Profession: 1890–1950.* Bloomington, Ind.: Indiana University Press.

Hirshfield, D. S. 1970. *The Lost Reform: The Campaign for Compulsory Health Insurance in the United States from 1932 to 1943.* Cambridge, Mass.: Harvard University Press.

Johnston, H. L. 1950. *Rural Health Cooperatives.* FCA Bulletin 60 and PHS Bulletin 308. Washington, D.C.: U.S. Department of Agriculture, Farm Credit Administration, Cooperative Research and Service, and Federal Security Agency, Public Health Service, Division of Medical and Hospital Resources.

Julius Rosenwald Fund. 1936. *New Plans of Medical Service: Examples of Organized Local Plans of Providing or Paying for Medical Services in the United States.* Chicago: Julius Rosenwald Fund.

Kari, N., H. C. Boyte, and B. Jennings. 1994. *Health as a Civic Question.* Civic Practices Network, http://www.cpn.org/topics/health/healthquestion.html (accessed October 8, 2004).

Light, D. W. 1997. "The Rhetorics and Realities of Community Health Care: The Limits of Countervailing Powers to Meet the Health Care Needs of the Twenty-First Century." *Journal of Health Politics, Policy and Law* 22:105–45.

MacColl, W. A. 1966. *Group Practice & Prepayment of Medical Care.* Washington, D.C.: Public Affairs Press.

Minkler, M., ed. 2002. *Community Organizing and Community Building for Health.* New Brunswick, N.J.: Rutgers University Press.

Morone, J. A. 1990. *The Democratic Wish: Popular Participation and the Limits of American Government.* New York: Basic Books.

Mott, F. D. and M. I. Roemer. 1948. *Rural Health and Medical Care.* New York: McGraw-Hill.

Neverdon-Morton, C. 1989. *Afro-American Women of the South and the Advancement of the Race, 1895–1925.* Knoxville, Tenn.: University of Tennessee Press.

Numbers, R. L. 1978. *Almost Persuaded: American Physicians and Compulsory Health Insurance, 1912–1920.* Baltimore, Md.: Johns Hopkins University Press.

Plumly, H. L. 1947. *Budgeting the Costs of Illness.* New York: National Industrial Conference Board.

Reed, L. S. 1958. "Group Payment since the Committee on the Costs of Medical Care." *American Journal of Public Health* 48:991–94.

Rifkin, S. B. 1981. "The Role of the Public in the Planning, Management, and Evaluation of Health Activities and Programmes, including Self-care." *Social Science & Medicine* 15A:337–86.

Schlesinger, M. 1997. "Paradigms Lost: The Persisting Search for Community in U.S. Health Policy." *Journal of Health Politics, Policy and Law* 22:937–92.

Schwartz, J. L. 1965. "Early History of Prepaid Medical Care Plans." *Bulletin of the History of Medicine* 39:450–75.

Shadid, M. A. 1992. *Crusading Doctor: My Fight for Cooperative Medicine.* Reprint ed. Norman, Okla.: University of Oklahoma Press.

Sirianni, C., and L. Friedland. 2001. *Civic Innovation in America: Community Empowerment, Public Policy, and the Movement for Civic Renewal.* Berkeley and Los Angeles: University of California Press.

Starr, P. 1982. *The Social Transformation of American Medicine.* New York: Basic Books.

U.S. Senate, Committee on Education and Labor. 1946. National health program: Hearings on S. 1606.

Warbasse, J. P. 1923. *Co-operative Democracy.* New York: MacMillian.

Warbasse, J. P. 1951. *Cooperative Medicine.* 5th ed. Chicago: Cooperative League of the U.S.A.

Williams, P. 1932. *The Purchase of Medical Care through Fixed Periodic Payment.* New York: National Bureau of Economic Research.

Wisconsin Legislature, Special Committee on Social Insurance. 1919. *Report of the Special Committee on Social Insurance.* Madison, Wisc.: Democrat Printing Company, State Printer.

7

Linda V. Beardsley

Teacher Education as Civic Engagement

Building Bridges and Community through Professional Development Schools

As our nation charts its course in these early years of the twenty-first century, no discussion topic elicits more debate and differing opinions than a discussion of public education. There is, however, one area of agreement that seems to unite scholars, practitioners, policymakers, and families: an effective teacher is essential to promoting student success. Although there is considerable debate in both academic and political circles regarding the best way to prepare teachers to be effective, this essay is rooted in the belief that training effective teachers requires collaboration between a university-based teacher education program and the public schools in which pre-professional teachers do their required practice teaching. Traditionally, this collaboration has been more like the parallel play of toddlers than the truly shared experience of scholars and practitioners interested in PreK–16+ education. The world of theory and scholarship (the university program) operates separately from the world of practice (the public school classroom). Conversations among higher education faculty and district educators when they happen (*if* they happen), are confined to conversations about the progress of the pre-professional teacher. Seldom do collaborations between universities and school districts engaged in this work deepen to become authentic partnerships committed to improving the education profession, the scholarship of the field, and the quality of life within a community through improvement of its schools. The reasons given for this lack of true partnership usually focus on the very different natures of the "cultures" of these two institutions (the private academy and the public schools) even though these two institutions are committed to the same context: intellectual life and education.

A poem by Emily Dickinson creates an instructive image for those who believe that it is possible and essential to bridge the gap between these institutional cultures. The poem describes a person walking carefully along a wooden structure, aware of her progress "from plank to plank" as the night sky looms expansive from above and the moving sea swirls precipitously beneath her feet. At one point, the walker confesses to moving carefully forward even though she wondered if the next plank "would be my final inch." The reader feels relieved at the close of the poem, as the final lines suggest the planks have been successfully crossed and courage has prevailed. However, the walker is left with a "precarious gait / Some call it experience."

This essay describes how Tufts University's education department, particularly its graduate teacher education program for high school certification, has made the commitment to see teacher education as civic engagement and how it has tried to deepen its relationships with schools in urban communities through the development of Professional Development School sites for preparing teachers. In developing this model, in acknowledging the role *community* plays in supporting schools and the achievement of youth, the teachers prepared in these sites become teachers for whom teaching for civic engagement becomes a strong pedagogical value. I shall suggest here that universities cannot help becoming *civically engaged* in a community when they partner with that community's schools. The public schools reflect the daily concerns and challenges, the traditions and history, and the future vision of the community that supports them. These are the kinds of challenges that universities and school districts must be willing to face together: challenges that often force the academy and the community to confront issues of class and race, political and economic realities—those "planks" that cause the partners to walk with "precarious gait" between the idealism of the "stars" of scholarship and the rushing realities of the sea of civic life.

The establishment of the Professional Development School model to prepare prospective teachers to consider themselves teachers in a community, not only in a school, is work that is deeply grounded in the history of teacher education in the academy. It is also grounded in the belief that teachers become influential members of the communities in which they teach. Here I shall weave together some of the theoretical strands that give the work of preparing teachers its shape, color, vitality. First, I shall describe *why* collaboration between public schools and universities, particularly in the work of preparing K–12 teachers, is often characterized by frustration and unfulfilled promises, and *how* the Professional Development School model of teacher preparation promises a way to bridge these two distinctly different cultures. Second, I shall describe the theoretical foundation of the nature of civic engagement and community that is engendered when a university teacher education program and the public schools are both committed to the importance of education as preparation for civic life. Finally, I shall provide a brief glimpse of the narrative that recounts the story of one liberal arts university's experience learning to see the preparation of teachers *for* civic engagement *as* civic engagement. This narrative relates how the education of future teachers brings life to the scholarship, shaping and refining the partnerships Tufts University has established. Together these strands provide both a strong tether for connecting research and practice in teacher education and a strong connecting cord to anchor the work of the university within real communities.

Collaborating Alone: The Marginalization of Teacher Education

In his eloquent and provocative study of civic life in the United States, *Bowling Alone: The Collapse and Revival of American Community*, Robert D. Putnam (2000) promotes the notion of *social capital* that exists and enriches civic life. Certainly, educators and educational institutions represent one of the strongest aspects of that social capital in our communities. Educating future teachers should be work in which both universities and public school districts take great pride. Educating future teachers seems to provide a natural context for sharing intellectual capital, for collaborating as a community of scholars who believe deeply in the transformative power of education as essential to participation in civic life. Educating future teachers should be a satisfying collaboration between academia and local schools. But just as Putnam uses the changes in patterns of bowling from league participation to less social contexts to describe changes in civic life in the United States, educators have tended to stay close to their own camps. A process that should engage both the university and the school sites in significant conversations about the purpose of education, about the best ways to structure schools and the shape of academics and intellectual life, is reduced to requests by the teacher education program to "place" a student teacher in a classroom in the school site and then asking a university supervisor to make occasional visits to observe the "progress" of that student teacher. The relationship, which should be the hallmark of the education of future teachers, is often as awkward and tentative as an adolescent's first date. To understand why relationships between the academy and public schools are so difficult to establish, one must consider the history of teacher education in the United Sates and the ways that history blights the roots of teacher education at both the university level and within the public schools.

Normalites

The prevailing history of teacher education frames preparing teachers as focused on "practice" instead of intellectually rigorous scholarship, on training for skills rather than on developing ideas and theoretical foundations. Christine A. Ogren (2000) offers a challenging and compelling study of the history of teacher preparation in her essay, "A Large Measure of Self-Control and Personal Power: Women Students at State Normal Schools During the Late Nineteenth and Early Twentieth Centuries." She begins by describing the rise of the normal school: "In the mid-nineteenth century, to train teachers for the growing number of common (elementary) schools, education reformers drew upon European models such as the German teacher seminary and French *école normale*"(211). Normal schools were established in Massachusetts, New York, and Connecticut; by 1890 there were more than one hundred state normal schools across the United States that provided preparation for young women, most often from rural or working-class backgrounds, to become classroom teachers at little or no cost. Ogren's study of "seven regionally and racially diverse state colleges and universities that began as normal schools" provides insight into an aspect of teacher education history that many contemporary teacher educators either choose to ignore or portray negatively (Ogren 2000, 213). Whereas a "normal school education" provided generations of young women the opportunity to develop their intellect, their voices, and strong professional spirit, traditional and "prestigious" colleges and universities regarded normal schools as providing a civic service rather than as preparing a new generation of intellectuals to inspire and teach young people. She also notes there is often little recognition and acknowledgment of the role normal schools and their graduates may have played in the development of feminist perspectives. What is clear is that as normal schools evolved into state colleges in the early twentieth century, they "gained status by offering bachelor's degrees and then [by] adding programs in fields other than education, they shed some of the characteristics that contributed to their protofeminist atmosphere. . . . Teacher preparation and women students occupied much less space on campus" (Ogren 2000, 225–26).

One of the reasons that the women's "literary circles and pedagogy study groups" of the normal schools gave way to "sororities and football games" of the newly minted state colleges is that teacher education became the province of women, and therefore, less important and intellectually rigorous than other professional preparation. It was widely assumed that teacher education in normal schools focused on how to teach basic knowledge and life skills to young people. The curriculum did not focus on deep understandings and debates about the shape of knowledge in academic disciplines. However oversimplistic and even erroneous these assumptions may be, this is the view of normal schools that has "stuck" and carried through to current notions of teacher education in the academy.

The "split" between the "worlds of knowledge and worlds of pedagogy" described by Frances Maher and Mary Kay Tetreault (2000) as setting the stage for the marginalization of teacher education in universities is a dichotomy well known to teacher educators in higher education institutions. Philosophically, this dichotomy can be understood as a product versus process debate. Knowledge is a "disinterested search for universal truth"; pedagogy focuses on how we acquire or construct a knowledge base that is constantly evolving: "This split between the world of knowledge and the world of pedagogy is not merely philosophical; it also defines the role of the field of education in almost all institutions of higher education. Instead of viewed as a subject relevant to the whole academy, education is seen as having to do only with the training of teachers of children and adolescents and research on schools as institutions—topics considered less prestigious than the study of any other aspects of our society" (Maher and Tetreault, 2000, 194–95).

The devaluation of education as a field of study and professional acumen, coupled with the tradition of teaching being "women's work," leads to a continual struggle of educators to have university administrators see education studies and teacher preparation as intellectually rigorous work. "Education leaders also favored women teachers because of the association of teaching, particularly of children, with mothering, widely considered in the nineteenth century to be women's *only* proper adult role. Many still see teaching, unlike other professions, as a collection of natural processes, inherent in the female role of nurturer to the young more associated with caregiving than with stimulation and intellectual growth" (Maher and Tetreaut 2000, 199). It would seem from these two research strands that the work of teacher education is undervalued based on its history as an appropriate *feminine* occupation, although this history is one that Ogren and others continue to explore. By doing so, researchers may uncover some strong models to study in order to understand how the search for truth through study became associated with universities and men and how teaching young students became associated solely with women and divorced from knowledge. Understanding these origins can help us build new connections between teacher education and a view of the teacher as strong contributor to the quality of community life.

From Collaborating Alone to a Collaborative Consciousness

How does the marginalization of teacher education programs on college campuses contribute to the difficulty universities and school districts have in working together? The reasons can usually be framed in two ways. First, partnerships between universities, particularly those associated with teacher education programs, are established with little financial support from university administration or support from a broad range of arts and sciences, research or tenured faculty. Therefore, they often lack the resources necessary for authentic research or substantial follow through. Second, universities often venture into work with K–12 schools with little understanding of the specific vision and goals that a particular community has for the work of its public schools (Ogren, 2000). Both of these barriers result from the struggle in academia to grapple with the role of education programs in liberal arts and research universities. In teacher education programs, universities and school sites collide in the effort to ensure preservice teachers have classrooms in which to practice teach.

When universities have attempted to work more broadly with a school, their tone has often been one of what Goodlad (1993) describes as "noblesse oblige." In his landmark study of fourteen settings included in the National Network for Education Renewal in which universities were engaged with K–12 schools to train teachers and improve schools, he found that when universities and school systems attempt to join their cultures and share the work of renewing schools, they demonstrate every aspect and challenge of educational change documented in the literature. As public schools across the country struggle to meet the increasing demands of student achievement and the reality of dwindling local resources, they often turn to universities—institutions seen as the "gold standard" of education—to help them resolve their issues at the K–12 level. But without a clear commitment and deep understanding of the issues and community values, these attempts to connect often prove disappointing to schools (Haycock, 1994; Pickeral, 2003). Each instance of disappointment and frustration only contributes to the growing public distrust of higher education and academia and the public's lack of confidence that the academy is able to help solve challenges faced by real communities in the "real world" (Cochran-Smith, 2003).

So how do we move teacher education from this "collaborating alone" model of teacher education to deeper, more community-based relationships that seek to support improving public schools? The key seems to be in creating an intellectual interest in working with public education on college campuses. Indeed, creating this interest should be one of the goals of all university-based teacher education programs. This interest begins on the college campus itself in acknowledging teachers as intellectuals and developing models of teacher preparation that include close collaboration of arts and sciences faculty with their education department colleagues. Although this collaboration will not resolve the knowledge-pedagogy split, it can create a context for conversations that provide a deeper understanding of the debate and open dialogue about how these issues are shaped in K–12 education. Universities can take the lead in discussing what it means to be an educated citizen, a community problem-solver, a public intellectual.

As Alexander Astin has characterized it, the idea of "excellence' in higher education today is associated with institutions that value "the *demonstration* of intellect." What if more financial resources, and higher reputations were granted to institutions committed to "the *development* of intellect?" In such a world the myriad processes of successfully engaging students, from kindergarten through graduate school, in the active pursuit of knowledge would have much more central place. We need to challenge traditional institutional hierarchies held in place by stereotypes and inequalities of gender, race, and class. Only then may we reposition teacher education in the academy, grasp how integral the teacher-training function is to our civic and personal well-being and demand of our education system that it be committed to excellence in the processes as well as in the products of knowledge. (Maher and Tetreault, 2000, 201).

In fact, the reconsideration of the role of teacher education in the academy and the rededication of the university to this endeavor, become an opportunity for a university to rethink its connections to the K–12 school districts in which its teacher education students practice teach. It becomes an opportunity for a kind of *institutional civic engagement* that sets a tone of commitment to community and intellectual leadership. This commitment moves the model of "collaborating alone" to a potentially powerful community connection.

Teacher Education as Institutional Civic Engagement

Universities who acknowledge the fundamental collaborative nature of teacher education and who commit to establishing meaningful relationships with the K–12 public schools in which teachers in training develop their teaching skills, are acknowledging their membership in the broad education community. This community shares an essential belief in the power of education, the value of learning and teaching, the necessity of nurturing intellectual life. Within the context of this community, important conversations can unfold, conversations that express the variety of ideas people have about education, its role in the lives of children and their families, the methodologies that are effective and content that is critical. In most communities across the United States, the public schools are central institutions. Not only are their budgets most often the largest line items in the larger community budgets; they often serve as spaces where central conflicts and debates over community values are played out. For example, some school district administrators attempt to design extended-day programs and find themselves inciting a debate about child care and work schedules (usually of mothers) in the community. As communities include an increasing number of families whose first language is not English, schools find that they need to find resources to translate school information and policy documents into a number of different languages and focus on how to make families from diverse cultures feel comfortable interacting with the community's schools. Discussion of how best to meet the needs of all students within a school often incite discussions about how inclusive a community is in general for learning- or physically disabled people. These complex, compelling issues are challenging for schools, but also indicative of how the public schools in a community are often lapped by the first waves of social change and values.

The notion of schools as public spaces where diverse ideas are exchanged is expressed in Maxine Greene's writings—notably, *Dialectic of Freedom,* in which she envisions the importance of schools as public spaces within the communities they serve, as places of "dialogue and possibility" in which "diverse human beings can appear before one another as, to quote Hannah Arendt, 'the best they know how to be.'" She continues: "Such a space requires the provisions of opportunities for the articulation of multiple perspectives in multiple idioms . . . out of which something common can be brought into being. It requires, as well, a consciousness of the normative as well as the possible; of what *ought* to be, from a moral and ethical point of view and what is in the making, what *might* be in the always open world" (Greene 1988, xi).

Such a passage stirs the imagination of the educator and the philosopher to see schools as places in which people are in "search of themselves," are, in fact, *invited* to search for themselves and discover the ways their interests and talents can best serve the wider community. But such an idealistic vision of school is often tempered by the realities of resources within the community and by the tension that exists in framing the role of public schools within our culture. Is it the role of the public schools to educate people to question the established practices and institutions of our communities? Or is it the role of the public schools to perpetuate the status quo? Within the framework of this debate, the university teacher education program can choose to become "civically engaged." Through building authentic partnerships with public schools through teacher education, universities can build the foundations of trust necessary for having the conversations about how public schools can become spaces for dialogue about community. Encouraging communities to see public schools as places for civic dialogue and engagement (especially in the midst of an era of increasing standardization of education) requires a special kind of teacher education, one that can only happen when the university program sees itself as engaged in the community and in the schools in a substantial way.

Public Education: "An Apprenticeship for Civic Life"

Sonia Nieto writes of the ways in which schools and civic life have been linked in our imaginations as people who live in a democracy:

Public education and democracy have been firmly linked in the popular imagination since at least 1848 when Horace Mann in his twelfth annual report to the Massachusetts State Board of Education declared, 'Education then, beyond all other devices of human origin, is a great equalizer of the conditions of men.' . . . Half a century later, and just a few short years before the Harvard Education Review published its inaugural issue, John Dewey's progressive notions about education cemented the link between education and democracy. According to Dewey, schools could serve not only to level the playing field, but also as an apprenticeship for civic life. (Nieto 2005, 43)

Nieto points out that in the current stage of education reforms across the nation, most recent reforms have been at odds with this sentiment. Both national and state legislators, policymakers in both federal and state departments of education have pushed an agenda of focusing on testing, rubrics, standardized curriculum designed to ensure that all students are able to achieve the same high standards regardless of the zip code in which they receive their education. These standards-based reforms appear to reflect the tenets of democratization, to come from a "good place" in the hearts of policymakers. But the continuing underachievement of students from diverse racial, cultural, linguistic backgrounds, the well-publicized *achievement gap,* provides evidence that these standards-based reforms are not really supporting the intellectual growth of all students. Increasing numbers of students from diverse backgrounds and the growing disparity of wealth in our communities create a changing context and set of challenges in public K-12 education that must be addressed. As institutions who plan the programs and curriculum that prepare future teachers, university teacher education programs must deal with these challenges facing our public schools. The disparities are particularly evident in urban schools, school districts in which universities have historically been involved with very little progress toward improving student achievement. Through teacher preparation and engagement in urban schools and communities, universities can take a leading role in preparing teachers to face these critical civic issues and address the complex economic, educational, and social issues that challenge us all.

Nieto describes the theoretical frameworks that have shaped the prevailing notions of teaching and learning in diverse communities. These include genetic and cultural inferiority (Jensen1969), economic and social reproduction theories (Spring 1972; Katz 1975), cultural incompatibility theory (Baratz and Baratz 1970), sociocultural explanations (Heath 1983), and students as caste-like minorities (Ogbu 1987). Each of these theoretical frameworks introduces prospective teachers to a discourse that provides barriers to preparing all students to become contributors to their communities. The continuing achievement gap demonstrates why teaching requires a deep knowledge of culture and community. One need only look at the history of three efforts to address inequalities in schools and reduce the achievement gap — desegregation, bilingual education, and multicultural education—to realize that truly democratic and progressive practices in education are often challenged, particularly at the local level, within the schools themselves. Families and community stakeholders tend to believe that what *they* did in school is the "right way" to learn. The changes needed to make education truly better (inclusive practices, smaller schools, multicultural approaches) are the very things that often challenge public beliefs about how education works. Because progressive ideas and novel theoretical notions often pose ideas that are contrary to what people think about schools, significant changes in school structure or student achievement seldom happen.

Quite often, if teachers endeavor to change their practice, they find themselves in conflict with what families and the community expect from schools. This conflict quickly erodes public support for education—a devastating consequence, as public schools depend on local tax support (Goodlad 1997). Yet reform efforts that aim to express the connection between education and democratic ideals—such as desegregation, bilingual education, and multicultural education—are efforts that serve civic life and strong democratic communities. They express the "democratic value of tolerating differences" and recognize the role that cultural differences have played in shaping the communities in which our young people are growing up and searching for themselves (Nieto 2005). Why then, should these efforts be fading in our schools? How can universities prepare teachers to be committed to the vision that Dewey proposed in the early twentieth century that still rings true as we contemplate our schools of the twenty-first century?

Professional Development Schools

Over the past several years, teacher educators have begun to develop models of teacher training similar to the "residency model" used to train medical professionals. This model, called a Professional Development School (PDS), is based on the premise that training people for lifelong professional careers—in specialty fields like medicine and education—is the joint responsibility of institutions of higher education and the organizations in which those new professionals will serve. In education, this joint responsibility is best demonstrated through close and sustained partnerships between the university's teacher education program and selected schools in which new teachers are prepared for teaching careers. Generally, these PDS models are formed around the following objectives: (1) to provide effective training for new teachers; (2) to provide new insights and research possibilities for university faculty; and (3) to provide inquiry and support for veteran teachers to continue to develop their practice. This work, made possible by a close collaboration of the K–12 and university community, should result in high levels of student learning (Levine 1992).

John Goodlad (1988) initially described the potential of PDS relationships to transform the education community using an image of the "simultaneous renewal" that is possible for both K–12 schools and university partners (cited in Teitel 2003, xxi). In his book *The Professional Development School Handbook,* Lee Teitel (2003) provides an overview of the history of the PDS movement, its links to the development of teaching hospitals (Levine 1992), and the ways in which Alexander Flexner was influenced by John Dewey's work to establish this teaching hospital model of training for medical personnel in partnership with university faculty: "As hybrid institutions formed by universities and school partners, they bridge the gap between sectors and between theory and practice" (Teitel, 2003, xiii).

This notion of the PDS as "bridge" between the very areas that have created tensions within university settings brings hope and promise to those who seek innovative ways to train teachers. But the PDS "bridge" is seldom one of strong, rising steel girders. Instead the bridges that form between schools and universities in PDS partnerships are more in keeping with Emily Dickinson's precarious "planks." Tenuously, cautiously, and slowly, the dialogue between teacher educators and practitioners must begin, ever mindful of the gulf that historically divides the missions of these two education institutions. Yet if we truly believe that education and public schools are critical to the life of our democratic system, then the bridge must be begun, the planks laid, the first steps carefully taken.

Creating a Learning Community

Returning to the notion of "collaborating alone," we acknowledge that the first step to bridge building must be an agreement to collaborate in an authentic way. We can return to Putnam's notion of creating social capital to find encouragement and rationale for this. As Putnam (2000) describes the dimensions that connect us to one another, *bridging* becomes an inclusive model for relationships—in contrast to *bonding,* which often ends up creating an exclusive society that shuns opposing ideas or new perspectives. "Bridging networks . . . (is) better for linkage to external assets and for information diffusion" (22–23). Surely, this is the kind of relationship we want K–12 schools and teacher education programs to form to ensure effective teacher preparation and improved schools.

But what vision can help us build that bridge? What are these planks, precariously placed, cautiously tried? In the establishment of a PDS model, the partners must commit to the vision of establishing a true *learning community*. This term is often used in education to express the ideal that within a project, *everyone* is learning. In a learning community, learning is an exchange, a continual dialogue; everyone has something to learn, and, in turn, everyone has something to teach. As described by Sandra Enos and Keith Morton, the decision for universities and communities to enter a partnership that is framed as a learning community is an inherently risky business: "in an authentic partnership, the complex dynamics of the relationship mean that the partners face the continuing possibility of being transformed through their relationship with one another in large and small ways" (Enos and Morton 2003, 20). In the case of the PDS, learning is happening in layers across the school and university. University students are learning to become teachers; their mentors are learning to become skilled supervisors, to articulate their practice in new ways, to try novel methods and learn new content. University faculty are learning about the daily lives of teachers and families in K–12 schools, how theoretical models play out as communities prepare their youngest community members. University administrators are learning how their institutions can work in neighboring and host communities. Public school students are learning from a diverse group of educators. The web of learning is complex, elegant, contiguous, and each participant faces the possibility of never looking at the worlds of K–12 or university education in the same way again.

This sense of membership in a learning community and the possibility for change are what can initially bring the K–12 schools and the university teacher education program together. Yet for the partnership to persevere, there must be a sense of respect for the expertise that each member of that community brings to the learning process. There must be a sense of trust that each member of the community has something to learn as well as some expertise to contribute to the learning of others. One of the best-known models of this expanded notion of community is the model developed by Yale psychiatrist James Comer (1980). In this learning community model, schools, families, and agencies work together to support the education of their community's children. The model features substantial ways to involve families and teachers working together, so that a community's trust in and commitment to the schools becomes integral to the way the community views its mission. There is pride and a sense of the valued social capital invested in the schools. A PDS committed to being a learning community, reflects Putnam's assertion that "social capital at the neighborhood or community level clearly has an impact on child learning" (Putnam 2000, 304).

Once a university teacher education program and a school site agree to be a learning community, there needs to be a vision that provides a focus for the learning. To maintain this focus in a substantial way requires continual and frank conversations between the partners. These conversations often include discussions about how the schools want education to look in their classrooms and what the teacher education program wants its new teachers to know and be able to do. As these conversations unfold, they often demonstrate the vision of schools as places for public debate. The idea of schools as central to the communities that support them becomes the impetus for becoming involved in both the schools and the community. Thus, the PDS provides an opportunity for teacher education programs to see preparing teachers as civic engagement: through modeling this kind of commitment to the public schools and community, the programs prepare teachers to inspire civic engagement in their students and their families. The PDS model that finds meaning and intellectual rigor in this type of teacher education moves away from teacher education as collaborating alone and moves forward to a meaningful civic engagement that pervades each level of the learning community.

Tufts University's PDS Model: The Urban Teacher Training Collaborative as Civic Engagement

In Massachusetts, as in most of the nation, education policy in the last decade of the twentieth century began with promoting ideas of equity and a belief that all students can learn and ended with the rhetoric of accountability and the reality of the *achievement gap* among students of color in urban schools. With an increased consciousness about this achievement gap and the need for teachers to be prepared to teach in urban schools, teacher education faculty at Tufts University began discussions of how best to address education reform tenets with prospective teachers. Prompted in part by a series of diversity workshops (required of all university departments in the 1997–98 academic year), they quickly realized that addressing such issues as closing the achievement gap requires considerably more than delving into academic conversations about race and case studies of urban practice—especially among a mostly white faculty working with mostly white students in mostly white, suburban schools. The faculty talked about the need to cultivate strong relationships with urban schools—schools with diverse populations of students, and staff—schools that were working to be successful with all students and were creating a culture of teaching as a transformative process for urban youth. To become an influence on educator preparation on the national scene, the faculty had to acknowledge that the "pulse" of how well education in the United States is faring is often taken at the wrist of urban school districts. The faculty agreed that if we fail to prepare teachers to make schools work in our centers of commerce, culture, and diversity, then we have failed to provide a vision for all our schools and for the future of our nation. In these discussions, the Urban Teacher Training Collaborative (UTTC) began.

The next step for the Tufts Teacher Education faculty was to identify urban schools that shared their vision of teachers becoming change agents within schools and significant contributors to the civic life of the communities in which they were teaching. The Fenway High School and Boston Arts Academy, two public pilot schools in the city of Boston, were identified as potential UTTC sites because they reflected in their daily work with students, teachers, and families, the vision of teaching as civic engagement that shaped the Teacher Education program at Tufts University. These schools exemplified the commitment to providing a strong education for urban students in order to ensure the well-being of urban communities. (Complete discussion of the establishment of the UTTC can be found in Teitel [2003]).

Beginning the UTTC with these two urban high schools as partners, Tufts Teacher Education program committed itself to working with schools that were unflinching in their pursuit of academic excellence for urban students. Moreover, these high schools were committed to maintaining a partnership with a university teacher education program to "round out" the learning community within their schools. From the outset, the headmasters at Fenway High School and Boston Arts Academy were able to articulate their missions and how the interns and university program could support the implementation of their missions in the schools. The structures, roles, and resources that became successful hallmarks of the UTTC were developed because the initial school sites were clearly committed to civic engagement of their students and faculty, and knew the kinds of pedagogy and support that the university and its faculty could contribute. In turn, the Tufts Teacher Education faculty respected the ideals of the school site people and felt privileged to have the opportunity to work closely with such dedicated educators who demonstrated the civic responsibilities of teachers.

After working successfully with Fenway High School and Boston Arts Academy for two years, Tufts sought to establish a PDS model with Malden High School. Malden, an urban rim community seven miles north of Boston, was once a predominantly white, working-class community. At the close of the twentieth century, it had become a gateway community to immigrant families from all parts of the world. In the face of these changing demographics of the school population, the district leadership began an extensive school restructuring process through participation in the Breaking Ranks Initiative, which mirrors the successful "small school" practices of the Fenway High School and Boston Arts Academy (NASSP 2006). The aim of this restructuring is to improve instruction and assessment, by providing more personalized attention to the students and their learning.

Malden High School administration and faculty hoped that by becoming a part of the UTTC the university and other school partners could help address the compelling issues uncovered in the restructuring process. For example, some veteran teachers at the school challenged the idea of restructuring the traditional high school and making classrooms more inclusive; annual analysis of the scores from the Massachusetts Comprehensive Assessment System reveals that students of color, particularly African American students, are failing at an alarming rate; students of color are underrepresented in physics and calculus courses. The Tufts Education faculty identified these challenges as typical challenges to be met in partnering with a traditional comprehensive school like Malden High School. These challenges were being openly discussed and addressed at the other UTTC partner schools, identified as progressive and models of innovative urban education. It would prove to be a strategic and instructive challenge to see if the structures and roles of the PDS model in the Boston sites could translate to Malden. University faculty envisioned that administrators and faculty at Fenway High School and the Boston Arts Academy could offer advice and support to Malden administrators and faculty as they continued their restructuring.

Teachers as Influential Community Leaders

Finding a common idea to connect these three different partner schools was essential to constructing that bridge between the university and the public districts. Both the Boston pilot schools and Malden High School are sites that seek to prepare racially, ethnically, and economically diverse students to contribute to their communities. As we know, public schools have historically been viewed as places in which immigrants learn about the civic structure of the community; public schools were seen as places that helped immigrants from a variety of cultures assimilate into a common culture, namely, the culture of the public school. In many instances, this process of assimilation has meant that students and their families are asked to leave their own cultural heritage, their own community at the schoolhouse door, getting the message from teachers and administrators that their culture, their language, their experience are somehow less important, less valued, even *inappropriate* to be shared with the civic culture of their adopted school and community (Nieto 2005; Banks 2001; Shor 1992). Likewise, students who are from the so-called mainstream culture of the community learn that their own culture is "right." Their culture, their heritage, their language and history are powerful, and therefore potentially diminished by adopting more open attitudes toward other cultures. This "assimilationist conception of citizenship will not be effective in the 21st century because it is based on a serious fallacy" (Banks 2001, 7). What research has revealed, is that when marginalized groups are allowed access to learning the mainstream culture, the rules of civic engagement, they "give up" their own cultures in order to become comfortable living in their new communities. The result is not a happy and productive "melting pot" but a situation that promotes division and misunderstanding in communities (Apter 1977).

These divisions and misunderstandings often play out most dramatically in public schools (Tatum 1992). Therefore, it becomes critical that students learn to understand the range of cultural, social, and economic backgrounds of all members of their communities. Students in diverse schools have an unprecedented opportunity every day to explore racial, ethnic, and linguistic differences authentically rather than in case studies and textbook readings. With the guidance of skilled and reflective teachers, they learn to reflect on the issues in their diverse communities, and also about the larger issues of the nation-states and eventually the global world in which they live. This global awareness has become increasingly important in the twenty-first century. As part of its mission to prepare prospective teachers, the UTTC requires them to explore how knowledge is constructed and how it is influenced by cultural assumptions, community values, biases, and the shape of academic disciplines. As Banks (2001) writes: "Understanding the knowledge construction process and participating in it themselves helps students to construct clarified cultural, national, and global identifications to become knowledgeable, caring, and active citizens in democratic societies" (10).

And so, the Tufts University PDS model, the Urban Teacher Training Collaborative, came to have at its heart a purposeful commitment: empowering future teachers to educate their students to understand knowledge from many perspectives and to be critical thinkers, problem solvers, and participants in their communities. In order to do this, teachers needed to learn to see themselves not only as teachers in a particular school building and classroom(s), but as teachers in the community that supported that school. In many ways this vision of the teacher as an influential community member reflects the tenets of civic education as expressed by the Center for Information and Research on Civic Learning and Engagement (CIRCLE). Established in 2001 with funding from the Pew Charitable Trusts, CIRCLE is now based in the University of Maryland School of Public Policy and funded by the Carnegie Foundation. CIRCLE conducts and funds research focused on young people aged 15–25 to learn more about the patterns of civic engagement of this age group. In 2003, CIRCLE published a summation of current findings, including a definition of the skills and knowledge of "competent and responsible citizens" and the ways schools and community involvement shape the attitudes of young people toward civic engagement. Their findings reflect the work of visionary educators. Competent and responsible community members "are informed and thoughtful" and aware of "public and community issues; and have the ability to obtain information and think critically, and enter into dialogue among others with different perspectives" (Carnegie Corporation and CIRCLE, 2003, 4). Competent and responsible community members are eager to participate in their communities to solve community issues and "accomplish public purposes."

This summation echoes Maxine Greene's (1998) vision of the schools as public spaces in which these ideals of civic engagement can be learned and fostered. Learning about the communities in which students live should be an essential part of the work educators do. These educators believe in the connection between education and creating just communities. Understanding the relationship between teaching young people to become engaged in their communities and the potential for change in our communities is, for visionaries like Maxine Greene, at the heart of teaching for social justice: "[To teach for social justice] is to teach so that the young may be awakened to the joy of working for transformation in the smallest places, so that they may become healers and changers in their worlds" (xlv).

The teacher's concern for creating a classroom in which engagement and participation, inquiry, and problem solving are essential to the learning process is critical to establishing a classroom that allows students to practice the essential ideals of community activism. When they do not acknowledge the ways in which our K–12 classrooms prepare (or do not prepare) young people to be engaged in their neighborhoods, educators miss the opportunity to use classrooms as the primary social environment in which we promote democratic ideals and civic engagement (Gross and Dynneson 1991). As Deborah Meier, noted educator and MacArthur Foundation award winner observes: "[School] is where we learn how public life is lived, where we fit (or don't) in the pecking order and how decisions are made and power exerted" (Meier 2004, 98).

In fact, in every aspect of their knowledge and practice, educators model for the young members of a community how to participate in a social, civic life by organizing schools and classrooms that reflect principles of democracy (Dewey 1916). As Shor writes: "The teacher is the person who mediates the relationship between outside authorities, formal knowledge, and individual students in the classroom. . . . Education is more than facts and skill. It is a socializing experience that helps make the people who make society" (Shor 1992, 13 and 15). And Nieto adds: "[T]eaching is *about and for . . . democracy.*" . . . teaching is a way to make concrete the ideals that are the very bedrock of our civilization. . . . Dedicated and excellent teachers find many ways to focus on equality and democracy as part of their pedagogy and curriculum" (Nieto 2003, 123; emphasis in original).

Three Essential Tenets for Teacher Education as Civic Engagement

Tufts University and its partners in the UTTC wanted its teachers, both experienced and newly prepared, to model education *as* civic engagement and *for* civic engagement. To carry out this plan, it proposed three tenets that the teacher education model would espouse. Each of these important components would set new teachers on a lifelong journey and prepare them to chart a course for their own students that would lead to lifelong learning about civic life and commitment to community *and* to social justice. First, teachers would need to learn to see their own ethnicity and background in order to truly see the ethnicity and color of their students, and how these issues may influence approaches to learning (Delpit 1995; Cochran-Smith 2000; Banks 2001; Beardsley and Teitel 2004). Second, it is critical that teachers deeply understand the academic subjects they are teaching, the origins of the theories and conventions that underlie the canon and values of that subject. This scholarship is critical so that teachers can weave other conceptions of the discipline into their teaching to reach students from various backgrounds. This notion is a powerful plank in our bridge in that it begins to address that issue of "true knowledge" versus how we construct knowledge through pedagogy. It is respectful of multiple perspectives as it promotes searching for commonalities as well as distinctive ideas. Third, teachers must learn about the communities in which they teach so that their curriculum can reflect the values and interests of the community. This adds to the narrative, the relationship that their students can develop with the discipline and content they are learning (Shakespear, Beardsley, and Newton 2003). Teacher education programs model these approaches in the ways they interact with the schools in the partnership. Involvement in the community breaks down the notion that the teacher education program or the school sites are the only sources of knowledge in PDS. Community people and community resources have a great deal to contribute to the knowledge and understanding of teachers (Teitel 2003). With these planks in place to bridge the historical differences in K–12 and university relationships, the work of the UTTC began. It continues today to shape the civic engagement of the university and the partnership.

Features of the UTTC that Support Civic Engagement

Whereas the UTTC model has many of the usual "trappings of a PDS partnership" (Teitel 2003), it developed some special features in order to support its commitment to civic engagement and involvement in the community. These features were necessary "planks" to bridge the work of the schools and teacher education programs. First, they sustained the work of the school communities, which were focused on making it possible for teachers to establish effective relationships with their students and colleagues. Second, they sustained the work of the teacher education program, providing an academic focus for learning about communities and the intellectual side of what it means to be engaged in the civic life of a community.

At the heart of the UTTC partnership is an internship model that pairs the interns who are master of arts in teaching (MAT) degree candidates with experienced mentor teachers with whom they coteach in classrooms for the academic year. The yearlong internship allows the interns to establish the kinds of relationships with colleagues, mentors, students, and families that are necessary for student achievement in urban schools. Interns in the UTTC schools are fully immersed in the life of the school and take on the role and functions of their teacher mentors. They coteach, participate on teacher teams and in faculty meetings; they meet with families and support services in the school and community; they coadvise advisory groups that meet three times a week; they conduct whole-school activities and field trips; they organize science fair and math exhibitions, plan college visitation days, and evaluate senior essays; they coach athletic teams, and develop after-school activities.

To support the work of the interns on the school sites, the UTTC developed the roles of *site coordinator* (a member of the faculty of the school site) and a *professor of the practice* from Tufts' teacher education program to work on each site at least one day per week. The site coordinator and the professor of the practice cofacilitate a site seminar one afternoon per week. A key component of this site seminar is teaching the interns how to uncover the resources and richness of the neighborhoods from which their students come to school. From January 2002 through June 2003, with grant support from the MetLife Foundation and Jobs for the Future in Boston, the UTTC developed a curriculum called Preparing Urban Teachers: Uncovering Community. This curriculum "refined and expanded the [UTTC's] efforts to deeply acquaint its interns, [and eventually all its preservice teachers], with the diverse communities and cultures from which their students come" (Shakespear, Beardsley, and Newton 2003, 3). This seminar curriculum becomes one of the ways the UTTC is responding to the recommendation from the Carnegie Corporation that schools of education should strengthen civic dimensions of preservice and in-service education for teachers (Carnegie Corporation and CIRCLE 2003). A study funded by the Carnegie Foundation and supported by the American Educational Research Association, synthesized the aspects of teacher preparation that are known to produce successful teachers. According to the panel of authors, it "appears that PDS have a positive impact on teacher and pupil learning" (AERA 2005, 1). Other promising practices in teacher education include "school and community fieldwork that positively affects candidates' attitudes, knowledge, and beliefs and confidence about teaching culturally diverse learners" (AERA 2005, 2). The UTTC community curriculum, continues to be vital to modeling civic engagement in the community and teaching teachers the importance of seeking support and knowledge about the resources in a community to strengthen their teaching.

The Uncovering Community Curriculum

How does "uncovering community" and acknowledging teaching as civic engagement strengthen one's teaching? In the *MetLife Survey of the American*

Teacher (MetLife 2000), students expressed "feelings of alienation" from their schools and a lack of real connection with their teachers. The founding headmaster of the Fenway High School described the connection between a student's willingness to learn academic subjects and positive relationships with teachers of those disciplines: "In urban teaching, my sense is we [teacher and student] have to look each other in the eye, to figure out as soon as we can what we mean to each other. Whether it is going to be a respectful relationship. Where are you going to take me? What can I learn from you? Once we figure all that out, the human-to-human stuff, then we can get to the calculus. If we don't do the relationship building first, we can never get to the calculus" (Teitel 2003, 29).

Significant, caring relationships between teachers and their students can draw students into learning material and absorbing new ideas and perspectives that encourage them to grapple with intellectually rigorous curriculum and sophisticated analysis (Steinberg and Allen 2002; Hollins 1996; Northeast and Islands Regional Educational Laboratory 2002; Nieto 2003; Shakespear, Beardsley, and Newton 2003). Developing significant relationships, particularly with the increasingly diverse student population in our nation's schools becomes increasingly challenging for teachers, especially at the high school level. It requires that teachers learn to know the neighborhoods and community issues that frame a students' experience. As Nieto (2003) writes: "Even though most teachers enter the profession for noble reasons and with great enthusiasm, many of those in urban schools know little about their students and find it hard to reach them. Thus, despite their good intentions, many teachers who work with students of racial and cultural backgrounds different from their own have limited experience in teaching them and become frustrated" (7). The UTTC Uncovering Community curriculum addresses this critical need for teachers to become knowledgeable about their communities so they can teach in ways that demonstrate their civic engagement and enhance student achievement.

The curriculum includes seven half-day seminars conducted in the fall semester as the interns begin working at their school sites. The seminars are designed to teach the interns about their students' urban neighborhoods and to allow them to experience personally the sounds, sights, and people of those neighborhoods. Urban neighborhoods are very complex, and they have long histories and civic concerns that often frame the values and concerns that the families have for their children's education. In Boston, certainly, as well as in Malden, the histories of the neighborhoods can be framed as the history of how various racial and ethnic groups have influenced the life of the community and the struggles that certain groups have faced in order to be accepted as part of the larger urban scene. The sessions are designed to help interns reflect on assumptions they may have about urban areas and the role of the schools within the urban landscape. In many instances, the seminars help the interns see beyond the "deficiency" of an urban area and look to the support systems that may be in those areas to guide young people. The series encourages the interns to question the stereotypes that exist of urban neighborhoods and, in turn, value the lifestyles of urban students and their families.

The seminars also serve to model a path that interns can follow throughout their teaching careers to become acquainted with the communities in which they teach and to understand the issues with which a neighborhood is grappling on a day-to-day basis. This knowledge helps teachers better understand their students' daily lives by better understanding the context of student life outside of the classroom. Through a range of experiences, the seminar expects the interns to do a great deal of thinking about the social and civic issues that influence learning in the community, particularly the impact that race, ethnicity, and culture have on the lives of their students and their classrooms. And finally, the seminars provide an opportunity for the interns to acquaint themselves with "wise people" of the neighborhoods and community agencies that support families and youth throughout the community (Shakespear, Beardsley, and Newton 2003; the complete seminar series can be downloaded from: www.ase .tufts.edu/education/projectcs/main/asp).

These seminars would just be another interesting preservice experience, a grand "field trip" of sorts if the PDS learning community did not value this introduction to civic engagement as critical intellectual work. Both the faculty of the Tufts teacher education program and the faculty of the school sites value the work of uncovering community and weave its experiences and themes into the work of other courses and discussions. Dr. Joan Connolly, the superintendent of the Malden Public Schools speaks eloquently of how this curriculum has guided the Tufts teacher education programs into a new era of professional growth and awareness of civic responsibility and community:

Each year there are approximately 6400 students in the Malden Public Schools. They speak 52 languages; they are one of the most diverse school populations in the state of Massachusetts. I don't think I am being dramatic when I say that the future of our democracy will rise or fall based on the quality of education for students like those in Malden. And the quality of education they receive may rise or fall on how well the teachers in the classrooms understand the history of Malden and the neighborhoods from which their students come to school and the cultures that can enrich their learning.

How Do We Know the UTTC is Fulfilling Its Mission?

Back to Emily Dickinson's planks. Since its slow and cautious beginnings in 1998, the UTTC has had a number of successes as part of its experience. The number of people of color who matriculate in the MAT program has grown from 2% in 1998 to 36% in 2005. The education department has added three faculty of color as well as an urban education tenure-track position to support research in Critical Race Theory and urban education reform. The Provost and the Tisch College of Citizenship and Public Service have supported stipends for the interns as well as scholarships for students. The Diversity Committee has funded precollege experiences for the students of the UTTC schools. But that "precarious gait" that the participants in the partnership are developing represents a coming together of scholarship and practice, a shared commitment to seeing schools, at all levels, as places for civic engagement and problem solving. How do the partners evaluate whether or not the efforts and commitment are having positive results? There are myriad methods and measures to use to evaluate the successes and disappointments of a partnership, especially a PDS (Teitel 2001; 2003; with Abdal-Haqq 2000). But as much as the evaluation of a partnership that sees teacher education as civic engagement is about evaluating a university program's work and impact on public schools, it is also a story about the people who have shaped and lived and been influenced by one another within this collegial learning community. As evaluators measure the success and challenges of such partnerships, it is critical to include interviews of the teachers who have been prepared in the partnership. The success or disappointments of the partnership can be best described by those who commit to teaching as civic engagement and whose careers unfold as examples of activism in their schools and communities.

Interviews indicate that for many of the UTTC participants who are white (interns, university faculty, mentor teachers, supervisors) the work of the UTTC has brought them closer in relationship to people of color than they had ever been before. For some, it has been the first time they have had to accomplish something very important with people whose ideas, roots, values, and culture are very different from their own. In some cases, those ideas, roots, values, and culture were more reflective of the UTTC sites than the experiences of the white participants. In the relationships that have been forged through the partnership, people have experienced firsthand the truly transformative effects of that educational change best experienced through the relationships we build as we face our challenges. This PDS model, this close collaboration between a university and public urban high schools, has inspired one hundred new teachers to see their profession as inextricably linked to the life of the community in which they are teaching.

Chad, a graduate of Morehouse College, surprised his family when he matriculated into Tufts UTTC program. He had decided to follow his mother's example and become an urban high school math teacher. After his first year of teaching, he spoke eloquently about the social activism that had awakened for him in his internship year. "I felt the idea taking shape and becoming real for me. It was a spiritual experience, but it was also part of the hard work of being present for my students every day." This same activism is with him into his fourth year of teaching math in Boston. He articulates clearly his vision of the relationship between teaching math and social activism; teaching students to be thorough problem solvers instructs young people to think critically about a host of issues, including social issues and civic life. Katherine's story is somewhat different. A white, middle-aged resident of Boston whose children attend a local public school, Katherine decided to become an urban teacher after a career in community development. Her experience in the UTTC helped her to understand her own racial history as it compared and contrasted with the racial history of the students enrolled in her high school history class in Boston. She "dared" to take her urban students—reluctant writers all—on a field trip to a local beach and challenged them to "write" their ideas about how they fit into the current history of their city. She was gratified by the evaluations her students wrote that term; they reported that history had become very important to them, especially as it related to their lives in the city.

Kari also decided to turn from pursuing an engineering career to becoming a math teacher in middle school. He taught statistics to his eighth-grade students by having them compare data of various Boston high schools. The students published that data in an information booklet to help their peers and their families choose a high school in Boston that would best meet their needs and prepare them for success. Now teaching in a Boston charter school, Kari has taught Saturday classes to involve students and their families in learning algebra and other high school mathematics. As algebra is still considered one of the "gatekeepers" to higher-level math and the career choices required by that math, Kari sees connecting mathematics to the community as a significant contribution to the well-being of that community. Camille, a native of Jamaica who received her undergraduate degree in mathematics from an elite liberal arts college in New England, also wanted to share her love of higher mathematics with urban students. She developed and piloted the first calculus course for Fenway/Boston Arts Acacemy students during her internship year. She is now studying for a Ph.D. and teaching math in a Boston high school, she remains committed to teaching math as activism. "The achievement gap in mathematics exists and we need to do something about that," she declares.

In another interview, JD, a graduate of Fenway High School and a local liberal arts college, explained how he enrolled in Tufts UTTC program to "give back" to the young people of his community the same knowledge and belief in intellectual power that his teachers and professors had given to him. "I believe in the kids of this community." After teaching in Boston for four years, he describes how it still takes him a long time to walk down the corridor of his school because he is always stopping to check in with students. "I can't understand how teachers can walk by students and not say anything. We have got to show them, in every way, that they are the future of our neighborhoods. They can make [our communities] better." Kevin, who grew up in Philadelphia and who taught humanities and drama during his internship at Boston Arts Academy, started a troupe of young street actors who give performances on the challenges and joys of urban community life. Continuing to combine his love of drama with a sense of community involvement, Kevin now teaches in California and continues to include acting and community theater as part of his curriculum.

Interviews with these teachers, as well as with the other 90% who have remained in teaching after five years provide evidence that the UTTC alumni are connecting what they learned in their UTTC intern experience to the realities of the urban communities in which they teach. Because they learned that teaching *is* civic engagement, they teach *through* civic engagement and raising the awareness of their students about the powerful impact they can have on their communities. The impact of their work and the contributions they make to the young members of the urban communities in which they teach cannot be overshadowed by the debates and dilemmas that separate teacher education from more traditional studies in the academy. Their contributions can best be understood by seeing their work as evidence of the civic engagement of the UTTC—as the bridge that has been so cautiously yet purposefully built.

Teaching for Civic Engagement

Awareness of community and a commitment to reaching their students through developing lessons and curriculum that reflect the lives of their students typifies the success that the UTTC has had in preparing teachers to view teaching as civic engagement. Larry grew up in Virginia and graduated from Morehouse College. He came to Tufts UTTC program after volunteering in the Atlanta public schools. He was fascinated to learn about the history of Boston, the rich history of black people in Boston, as well as the controversial history of school busing and the impact it had on neighborhoods. He came to understand how that history engendered distrust and concern about the quality of education in Boston in so many families, of all races and backgrounds. As he learned to be a teacher, he wanted to find ways to bring families into the educational experience of their children, to develop trusting relationships with families. Here he describes how he developed a humanities curriculum that used powerful texts and local neighborhoods to accomplish what he believed is critical for urban student achievement:

We spent a lot of time studying the neighborhoods and our families. The different ways we had been successful or not in becoming a strong community. We read *All Souls* and *Raisin in the Sun*. They looked carefully at their own families and the strengths in those families. The students talked to their parents, brought in artifacts that represented their family. It really got some families very involved in the project. I also used a parent contact–type strategy. All parents want their children to be successful in school. But they need time to understand what students are doing in school so they can understand how best to support their children. I asked students to interview a family member about something we were studying in class so that we could have different ideas about material represented in our discussions. It gave some parents a whole different level of information about what was happening in school and how they could discuss some of these topics with their kids.

Another example of using current issues in a community to engage students in learning is this example from Danny, who grew up in Oakland, California, and was familiar with the impact of gentrification on neighborhoods in the San Francisco area.

As a history teacher, I am always looking for current issues to help students understand the issues that make up history. Studying colonization can have little meaning for students unless they understand underlying issues of power and economic gain for outsiders. My mentor teacher and I talked about this a lot. We decided to begin the unit by having students research gentrification in their neighborhoods from many different vantage points. I asked them to think about someone from the outside coming in and changing the neighborhood. They involved their families in the discussions. Some of the grandparents even got into it! There were many different perspectives presented, and these debates and perspectives always played out in the classroom. Some students wanted to encourage bringing in new money, new economic opportunity to the neighborhood. Some wanted to prevent new development that would price those who lived there now out of the community. We encouraged them to discuss openly, to be activists for their perspective; to ultimately think about issues that could help them find common ground. When we began the unit on colonization, the students had a great deal of information and experience in which to ground their understanding of the impact and implications of colonization. The whole theme of our curriculum was about teaching students to become active in their communities.

The UTTC has tried to forge a substantive collaboration between a university and urban schools. It has attempted to prepare future teachers by engaging them deeply in the cultures and lives of the schools and their communities. The UTTC prepares teachers to see themselves as public intellectuals for the public good. As the twenty-first century begins, young people are distracted by many things; they may ignore the politically and socially charged issues that face their communities. Teachers should be teaching their students to see themselves as developing intellectual lives. They should be helping young people learn the benefits of using their knowledge and talents to strengthen their communities. Teachers can accomplish this by being public intellectuals themselves, by modeling how their own ideas and their own interests and energy can help the communities in which they teach (Shor 1992). They can begin on the first day of school by opening the school year with a discussion of why the government mandates that we go to school at all (Meier 1990). Connecting intellectual endeavors and study to the idea that our own communities, our present as well as our future, depend on well-educated, thoughtful contributors, we create a sense of the importance of education, of the noble purpose of our schools, and the work that goes on in all levels of our institutions devoted to learning. Collaborations like Tufts UTTC present the work of training teachers as critical civic alliance, and engenders trust among stakeholders who have not always trusted one another. "When there is a high level of trust among teachers, parents, principals, these key players are more committed to the central tenets of school improvement. Teachers in high-trust settings feel loyal to the school, seek innovative approaches to learning, reach out to parents, and have a deep sense of responsibility for students' development" (Putnam 2000, 305). Only when teacher education programs see teacher education as civic engagement and build experiences that bridge the knowledge-pedagogy and K–12/academy divides, can our public school systems, our children, our families, and our community truly fulfill their potential.

References

American Educational Research Association. 2005. "Studying Teacher Education: What Do We Know?" Accessed July 20, 2005, from http://www.aera.net/uploaded Files/News_Media/News_Releases/2005/STE-WhatWeKnow1.pdf.

Apter, D. E. 1977. "Political Life and Cultural Pluralism." In *Pluralism in a Democratic Society,* edited by M. M. Tumin and W. Plotch, 58–91. New York: Praeger.

Baratz, S. S. and J. G. Baratz. 1970. "Early Childhood Intervention: The Social Science Base of Institutional Racism." *Harvard Educational Review* 40:29–50.

Banks, J. A. 2001. "Citizenship Education and Diversity: Implications for Teacher Education." *Journal of Teacher Education* 52, no. 1:5–16.

Beardsley, L. V. and L. Teitel. 2004. "Learning to See Color in Teacher Education: An Example Framed by the Professional Development School Standard for Diversity and Equity." *The Teacher Educator* 40, no. 2:91–115.

Carnegie Corporation of New York, and CIRCLE. 2003. "The Civic Mission of Schools." Accessed July 19, 2005, from http://www.civicmissionofschools.org/cmos /site/campaign/cms_report.html.

Cochran-Smith, M. 2000. "Blind Vision: Unlearning Racism in Teacher Education." *Harvard Educational Review* 70, no. 2:157–90.

———. 2003. "Assessing Assessment in Teacher Education." *Journal of Teacher Education* 54, no. 3:187–91.

Comer, J. 1980. *School Power: Implications of an Intervention Project.* New York: Free Press.

Connolly, Joan. 2005. Personal interview at Tufts University.

Delpit, L. 1995. *Other People's Children: Cultural Conflict in the Classroom.* New York: New Press.

Dewey, J. 1916. *Democracy and Education: An Introduction to the Philosophy of Education.* New York: Macmillan.

Dickinson, Emily. 1924. *The Complete Poems of Emily Dickinson.* Boston, Mass.: Little, Brown. Bartleby.com, 2000. www.bartleby.com/113/.

Enos, Sandra, and Keith Morton. 2003. "Developing a Theory and Practice of Campus-Partnerships." In *Building Partnerships for Service Learning,* edited by Barbara Jacoby, 20–41. San Francisco, Calif.: Jossey Bass.

Goldring, E., and P. Sims. 2005. "Modeling Creative and Courageous School Leadership through District-Community-University Partnerships." *Educational Policy* 19, no. 1:223–49.

Goodlad, J. 1988. "School-University Partnerships for Educational Renewal: Rationale and Concepts." In *School-University Partnerships in Action: Concepts, Cases, and Concerns,* edited by K. Sirotnik and J. Goodlad, 3–31. New York: Teachers College Press.

———. 1993. "School-University Partnerships and Partner Schools." *Educational Policy* 7, no. 1:24–39.

———. 1997. *In Praise of Education.* New York: Teachers College Press.

———. 2000. "Education and Democracy: Advancing the Agenda." *Phi Delta Kappan* 82, no. 1:86–89.

Greene, M. 1988. *Dialectic of Freedom.* New York: Teachers College Press.

Gross, R. and T. Dynneson. 1991. *Social Science Perspectives on Citizenship Education.* New York: Teachers College Press.

Haycock, K. 1994. "Higher Education and the Schools: A Call to Action and Strategy for Change." *Metropolitan Universities* 5, no. 2:17–24.

Heath, S. B. 1983. *Ways with Words: Language, Life, and Work in Communities and Classrooms.* New York: Cambridge University Press.

Hollins, E. R. 1996. *Culture in School Learning: Revealing the Deep Meaning.* Mahwah, N.J.: Lawrence Erlbaum.

Jensen, A. R. 1969. "How Much Can We Boost IQ and Scholastic Achievement?" *Harvard Educational Review* 39:1–123.

Katz, M. B. 1975. *Class, Bureaucracy, and the Schools: The Illusion of Educational Change in America.* New York: Praeger.

Levine, M., ed. 1992. *Professional Practice Schools: Linking Teacher Education and School Reform.* New York: Teachers College Press.

Maher, F., and M. K. Tetreault. 2000. "Knowledge versus Pedagogy: The Marginalization of Teacher Education." *Women's Studies Quarterly* 28, nos. 3 and 4:194–201.

Meier, D. 1990. "Taking Children's Opinions Seriously: A Talk with Bruno Bettleheim." *Teacher* 1:6–7.

Meier, Deborah. 2004. "Community." In *Keeping School: Letters to Families from Principals of Two Small Schools,* edited by Deborah Meier, Theodore R. Sizer, and Nancy Faust Sizer, 97–103. New York: Beacon Press.

MetLife. 2000. *The Metropolitan Life survey of the American Teacher, 2000.* New York: MetLife.

National Association of Secondary School Principals (NASSP). 2006. *Breaking Ranks II.* Accessed May 3, 2006, from http://www.nassp.org/s_nassp/sec.asp?CID=563 &DID=48223.

Nieto, S. 2003. *What Keeps Teachers Going?* Teachers College Press.

———. 2005. "Public Education in the Twentieth Century and Beyond: High Hopes, Broken Promises, and an Uncertain Future." *Harvard Education Review* 75, no. 1:43–64.

Northeast and Islands Regional Educational Laboratory. 2002. *The Diversity Kit: An Introductory Resource for Social Change in Education. Part II: Culture.* Providence: LAB at Brown University.

Ogbu, J. U. 1987. "Variability in Minority School Performance: A Problem in Search of an Explanation." *Anthropology and Education Quarterly* 18:312–34.

Ogren, C. A. 2000, "A Large Measure of Self-Control and Personal Power: Women Students at State Normal Schools during the Late-nineteenth and Early-twentieth Centuries." *Women's Studies Quarterly* 28, nos. 3 and 4:211–32.

Pickeral, Terry. 2003. "Partnerships with Elementary and Secondary Education." In *Building Partnerships for Service Learning,* edited by Barbara Jacoby, 174–91. San Francisco, Calif.: Jossey-Bass.

Putnam, R. D. 2000. *Bowling Alone: The Collapse and Revival of American Community.* New York: Simon and Schuster.

Shakespear, E., L. Beardsley, and A. Newton. 2003. *Preparing Urban Teachers: Uncovering Communities.* Metlife Foundation.

Shor, I. 1992. *Empowering Education: Critical Teaching for Social Change.* Chicago: University of Chicago Press.

Spring, J. 1972. *The Rise and Fall of the Corporate State.* Boston: Beacon Press.

Steinberg, A., and L. Allen. 2002. *From Large to Small: Strategies for Personalizing the High School.* Boston: Jobs For the Future, Inc.

Tatum, B. 1992. "Talking about Race, Learning about Racism: The Applications of Racial Identity Development Theory." *Harvard Educational Review* 62, no. 1:1–24.

Teitel, L. 2001. "An Assessment Framework for Professional Development Schools: Going beyond the Leap of Faith." *Journal of Teacher Education* 52:57–69.

———. 2003. *The Professional Development Schools Handbook: Starting, Sustaining, and Assessing Partnerships that Improve Student Learning.* Thousand Oaks, Calif.: Corwin Press.

———, with I. Abdal-Haqq. 2000. *Assessing the Impacts of Professional Development Schools.* Washington, D.C.: American Association of Colleges for Teacher Education.

Westheimer, J., and J. Kahne. 2004. "What Kind of Citizen?: The Politics of Educating for Democracy." *American Educational Research Journal* 41, no. 2:237–69.

8

Race Matters in Civic Engagement Work

In her keynote address "Civic Engagement: The University as Public Good," delivered at a 2004 AACU symposium on practicing liberal education, Nancy Cantor, chancellor of the University of Illinois, Urbana-Champaign, noted that the university has a critical role to play in civic engagement because the university has the means to foster culture-changing work in society. Cantor suggested that this work is best done when scholars and learners feel both empowered to examine their world and responsible for making change in it. At the same time, she pointed out that the most common operational aspect of civic engagement in the university—that is, service or volunteer work—while "valuable in the connections it makes and the people it helps, does not undertake to inform students about systemic sources of inequities." She went on to urge that we "immerse ourselves in environments of genuine exchange and interdependence."

I agree with Cantor's observation that civic engagement education about systemic inequality is too limited, and I would pick up where she leaves off to observe that scholars and learners cannot feel empowered to examine their society and take responsibility for action to change it if they are not solidly grounded and skilled in how to identify and analyze social systems of inequality. They will otherwise feel insecure, at the very least, about genuine exchange and interdependence. I shall focus my reflections on one of the major systems of inequality in contemporary society—race—and on its relationship to civic engagement work.

W. E. B. Du Bois's (1903) declaration that the problem of the twentieth century is the problem of the color line, though made at the beginning of that century, has not lost its relevance at the dawn of the twenty-first. While the centrality of race as a constituent element of Western modernity is widely accepted (Gilroy 2003; Holt 2002; James 1996), and while the persistence of racism in U.S. society is well documented (Guinier and Torres 2003; hooks 1994; Matsuda

1996; Omi and Winant 1994; Winant 1994 and 2004), too many scholars and teachers remain averse to critical race thinking (Matsuda 1996; Tatum 2003). Both intentionally and inadvertently, many avoid the explicit teaching of race and racism as these relate to their subject matter as well as to everyday lived experiences, their own and their students'. Ruth Frankenberg (1993) has named this kind of practice both race-evasive and, as a necessary consequence, power-evasive. Unfortunately, civic engagement scholars and practitioners have not escaped this aversion. Marschall and Stolle (2004) discuss such evasion and its implications for understanding and practice in their critique of Robert Putnam's (2000, 2002) works on social capital, a concept that has been central to contemporary discourse on civic engagement. They argue that Putnam's conclusions are flawed because he does not take the role of racial difference into account in his explanation for the decrease of social capital in the last three decades or more. Their view is that taking race into account would lead to different foci for research, interpretations, and outcomes.

The lack of meaningful attention to race in civic engagement teaching and the resultant impact on the quality of that education have led to calls from many scholars and community activists for corrective efforts (hooks 2004; Kivel 2002; Matsuda 1996; Omatsu 2000). To a number of scholar practitioners in the academy whose work focuses on how to analyze and combat systems of inequality, it is becoming increasingly clear how important it is to teach and talk about race—and especially one of its most potent social manifestations, racism—in the work of civic engagement. While the examination of race as a system of inequality itself is rarely a major focus, in recent years it has begun to be implied and included in discussions of service learning that explore the importance of diversity, consciousness of social justice, and the impact of different positionalities in service learning education and delivery (Boyle-Baise 2000; Deans 1999; Galura et al. 2004; Pompa 2005; Robinson 2000; Rosenberger 2000). I would argue that because race is central to our individual and group identities and to our social relations, effective civic "teaching and learning" must at the very least engage us in the in-depth study of how our own assigned and chosen racial identities, privileges, and disadvantages shape the ways we engage across identity lines. Knowledge or ignorance in this area will definitely affect our ability to be effective in crossing racial and other social boundaries in our work. Yet equally important is providing a solid grounding in the history of race, its construction, and how it operates as a system of inequality along with other similar systems, such as that of socioeconomic class. Only with such theoretical understanding of the social institution of race can our students be expected to make meaningful progress working on issues of racism, as a major system of inequality, in their civic engagement education.

We are living in a complexly diverse world in which racial politics increasingly are deeply contradictory. How is it, for example, that the "culture" of

Asian groups, as represented in their food, music, and clothing, can be considered the height of "chic," emulated and consumed in larger society, and Asian athletes Michelle Kwan and Zhao Yang be celebrated nationally, while the brutal anti-Asian violence acted out on the bodies of Asians and Asian Americans across the nation continues to rise and to be tolerated? (Dang 2000). How is it that even as universities and political leaders tout the positive values of diversity, multiculturalism, and globalization, social groupings and communities continue to be separated along stark racial and ethnic lines, and both overt and covert racist activities pervade the lives of college students, shaping their experience both as individuals and in groups? Why do some racialized ethnic enclaves exist? Why do racial privilege and disadvantage persist despite the common postmodern insistence that race is a thing of the past and that we are in fact "post-race"? Civic engagement research and scholarship can make valuable contributions to our understanding and eventually working for change regarding these kinds of issues, but in order for this potential to be realized, race and the differential impact of race on different lives and communities must be explicitly and frankly addressed. Simply put, it is imperative that we link pedagogies of race to pedagogies of civic engagement.

In this essay I attempt two tasks. In both cases, I draw upon my experience of six years teaching and learning in an undergraduate civic engagement course within a liberal arts curriculum. First, I use my own course as a case study to illustrate how the teaching of race and its impact on lived experience is critical to effective and ethical civic learning. Second, I step back to ruminate on my experience and speculate about the kinds of research that will be needed to improve both the effectiveness and the ethics of current work in civic engagement theory and practice.

Because there is no established definition of civic engagement in contemporary scholarship or practice, for the purposes of this writing, I shall use a simplified definition of my own. It is one that has been shaped by continuing efforts to find ways to help college students understand a complex concept. I define civic engagement as the actions of informed individuals and collectives to respond to the needs created by systems of social injustice in the communities in which they live and work. These actions can take many forms, but in every case they must be requested or approved by the communities themselves, and executed in collaboration with community participants. Finally, these actions must involve some form of ethical practice within the community aiming to create a more just and humane world. Since on most campuses much of the work of civic engagement at the undergraduate level is referred to as "service learning," it is important to point out here that although the definition of civic engagement I am using may encompass activities found under the rubric of service learning (for example, tutoring ESL [English as a Second Language] to new immigrant populations), it is nonetheless *distinct* from them. Not all service learning activities have as their goal addressing the underlying structural problems of social injustice nor are they always requested and approved by, or made in collaboration with, the communities in which they take place. Civic engagement as I understand it must strive to fulfill both requirements.

. . .

Six years ago, I had the opportunity to design and teach a college-level course in which enrolled students would work regularly in Boston Chinatown on community-designated projects at nonprofit organizations, as well as participate in a weekly university seminar in which they learned theory and reflected on practice. I entitled the course "Active Citizenship in an Urban Community: Race, Culture, Power, and Politics." Its stated goal was to help students acquire the practical skills, competencies, and habits of mind to be effective and ethical lifelong community participants, working for a more just society. Objectives included (1) familiarizing students with the racial, economic, and political history of the community; (2) teaching them how to identify the contemporary problems confronted by the community; (3) analyzing the systems of inequality operating in the creation and maintenance of those problems; and (4) helping them develop strategies for working in and with community partners to confront the issues through direct service and advocacy. Students were expected to be willing to address community concerns through studying and applying theories, engaging in the kinds of activities assigned by community organizations, and ultimately reflecting on their practice.

. . .

Boston Chinatown is located in downtown Boston. It comprises a small neighborhood in which some 5,000 residents, predominantly Asian American immigrants, currently struggle to coexist with numerous ethnic businesses serving both the community and the tourist trade, a large hospital complex, and a major medical school. Over the past four decades, much of the community's original residential housing has been torn down to make way for the institutional expansion of the hospital and medical school complex, as well as for federal and local highway projects and, in recent years, the construction of luxury high-rise condominium residences. All three forces have combined to drive property values sky-high, making it increasingly difficult for low-income residents to find housing or continue to live in the neighborhood.

A special aspect of Boston's Chinatown is that it has long been both regarded and used as an urban-based center serving the social, cultural, and political needs of Asian Americans of different ethnicities within an approximately 100-mile radius of the city. As a consequence, Chinatown offers one of the very few locations in the Greater Boston and northeastern New England region in which new Asian, and occasionally even other, immigrants with limited language skills and little social and financial capital can gain a foothold from which to acquire access to life resources. Thus the problems confronting this community—and they are of crisis proportions—include but are not limited to a lack of affordable housing, of health care, of employment, and of many other services especially in demand among new immigrants. Environmental pollution and marginalization from city politics are harsh daily realities as well. In the view of a significant number of community workers, the community even faces the possibility of extinction, as the number of affordable residential spaces diminishes. Nonprofit community organizations that provide both direct service and advocacy work are severely understaffed and underresourced. They welcome the assistance of informed individuals from the academy in a host of projects: for example, teaching adult ESL, translation services, and staffing campaigns for fundraising, for voter registration, and for environmental heath and sustainable development. Assistance in research related to community planning, sustainable development, social policy, public health, political participation, and education is valuable as well.

. . .

Students in the course range from those in their first year to seniors. They come from a variety of academic majors, and are of different racial identity locations. The majority of them identify their socioeconomic status as middle- or upper-middle-class, and a little more than two-thirds in each class have grown up in suburban, predominantly white communities. Most come to the course without any preceding experience in civic engagement work in an urban, racialized ethnic community. Some may have volunteered in their own communities. Almost none have had prior formal coursework on race, racial construction, and other systems of inequality. None ever have prior knowledge of the history and contemporary issues of the particular community that they are about to enter.

The Course as a Case Study in the Process of Teaching and Learning

In this section, I employ excerpts from students' written communications to me during their involvement with the course in order to illustrate patterns of thinking, feeling, analyzing, and synthesizing that can emerge from a civic learning experience of this sort. Each student communication I have selected is also representative of a significant number of others across the six years I have taught this course. Communications range from the occasional electronic message to weekly entries in course journals and field notes. For each excerpt, I include the student's racial identity location.

Phase 1: Before the Course Begins

As courses with required community involvement are relatively uncommon in the undergraduate curriculum at my institution, I receive many inquiries about the course before the first class. The following electronic mail from one student requesting information about the course is representative of an attitude I often see in students deciding whether or not to enroll:

Hello Professor, I am told this course is about volunteering in Chinatown so I am not sure why the course subtitle is: RACE, CULTURE, POWER, AND POLITICS. Doesn't Chinatown have Chinese people in it? So why would we be talking about race and power? I can see how culture would be relevant. Actually, I want to find out what we will be reading ahead of time because I hope we do not talk about things like race and power. I had a lot of these discussions in high school and they just go nowhere and set people against people. I think we should be talking about what's positive. I am sure the students who want to take this class are not interested in race issues but are full of good will and energy. I want to be learning about the culture of the Chinese people. That's one of the reasons I want to take the course. (Latino male junior)

I hazard a guess that most readers would agree with me that were this student considering a course involving students working in a predominantly black or African American community, it is unlikely he would have made exactly the same statement. He might still have stated that he did not wish to discuss race and power in a "volunteer service" course, but he would not have questioned that race, if not power, existed and was relevant to working within a black community in the United States. In the context of a course based in an Asian American community, however, this student's confusion is not extraordinary. Contemporary racial discourse in the United States continues to be dominated by a black/white paradigm (Ancheta 1993), even though race in the United States has never been limited to black and white, either historically or in the present. From the perspective of the black/white paradigm, Asian Americans—neither black nor white—are frequently considered to be not "raced." In addition, it is a deeply embedded habit of mind in the United States to see Asians, regardless of their naturalization status, as "foreign" and "not American." The "difference" that being Asian represents is thereby relegated to a matter of "culture." In this case, it is, of course, a culture considered "foreign" to that of the United States; that is, a culture that is non-American. "American culture" is nearly always, if not always, referred back to a white European-based tradition.

During the first day of class in which students are "shopping" around for courses, an Asian American female student wrote on a student information form I collected:

Why do you say that there is racism in Chinatown? I don't understand. Who are the bad guys? Do you mean Chinese against other Chinese? I had actually chosen this course because it wasn't going to be in a ghetto community. I am an Asian Studies major so I wanted to learn more about Chinese people and Chinese language. I am not looking for a course about race or racism. I actually don't want to study American society or Americans this semester. I want to prepare for going abroad to China next year.

A white European American student commented:

I have always admired the Chinese race and am looking forward to my working in Chinatown. I had several friends in school who were Asian and I remember them as particularly smart and respectful so I think that I would be interested in seeing the kind of culture in their community, which must be so different from my white middle class, middle American suburb. Given the chance, I would choose to live in a culturally rich community like Chinatown.

The preceding two reflections reveal that the students clearly (1) do not include Asian Americans in their definition of "American"; (2) assume that only Chinese are to be found in Chinatown; and (3) do not consider Chinatown an American or U.S. community. Again, their confusion is quite common in the larger society. An emblematic experience of Asian America, against which it struggles constantly, is one of having Asian America conflated with Asia in the American mind. This deeply embedded habit of thinking is one of the principal reasons that Asian Americans are viewed and regarded as "perpetual foreigners" or "aliens" in the United States. It results in their lived experiences of violent nativistic anti-Asian targeting as well as marginalization—if not entire omission—from the American body politic. In the case of the Asian American student, who uses the racially coded term "ghetto community" to mean a predominantly black community, "American" must be thought to apply to both black and white individuals but not to Asian Americans—even though, ironically, she herself is a second-generation U.S. citizen.

Needless to say, I have by now learned to incorporate as standard practice for the first day of class a brief definition of Asian America, its origins, its racial location in U.S. society, and its communities. The discussion ensuing from this definition inevitably includes a clarification of what the course "is" and "is not" about. It *is* about an urban U.S. community and the experience of its members as racialized "others" in U.S. society; it *is not* about China, the Chinese, a Chinese community, or Chinese culture.

Phase 2: First Contact with the Community

One of the first assignments that enrolled students must carry out is a "mapping" exercise in Chinatown. Students are dropped off in pairs at a central point in the community with a set of questions to be answered through observation and interaction with individuals that they encounter. And one of the first content lessons students receive is a formal orientation to the community, in which community-based cultural and political workers are their teachers. As students share their reactions to both learning activities, it becomes clear that ignorance about the realities of the community does not prevent students from holding and voicing some strongly preformed stereotypes and beliefs about the community and its residents.

A white European American student wrote:

My image of the Chinese as very self-sufficient and clan-like is supported by the experience of walking around the community during our mapping exercise. They do not want to talk to outsiders, and though my mapping partner is Asian, she also got the brush-off. The people who did not speak English looked at us with curiosity but also with what I felt to be distrust or suspicion. I can see it's going to be difficult to break into the community since there is not much friendliness (I am comparing it to what I think I would get if I were a stranger asking for information in my own community [an upper-middle-class, predominantly white suburb southwest of Boston], and I think people would be eager to share information about the community). But I have heard that Chinese are culturally reserved, so I should not judge too much right now.

Another white European American student shared these thoughts:

I was kind of disgusted by how dirty the streets were. I noticed that people in the community (I'm assuming they live there since they were Asian looking) didn't seem to care too much about throwing litter on the street and there was a lot of not very well packaged garbage out in front of the businesses. Some streets looked like they had not been cleaned for years. I don't understand how the hospital wouldn't want the area cleaner. I've noticed that a lot of minority neighborhoods are dirty in this kind of way and I guess I wonder if there are different cultural standards for cleanliness. Can we discuss this?

A third student, biracial African American and European American, noted:

One of the speakers giving information during the orientation seemed to be saying that there is overcrowding in the residences. I read in other places that it is not unusual for 12 or more Asian people to live in one or two rooms, so is this a standard because of larger Asian families? The speaker seemed to be saying that the overcrowding leads to unsanitary conditions and to higher rates of infectious diseases such as tuberculosis. If that is the case, then why do people continue to live in this way? Should there be regulations about how many people can live in a certain amount of space?

An Asian American student, not unfamiliar with the actual site of Chinatown, was more specific about where some of her assumptions about aspects of the community originated:

The first week of getting to know Chinatown is not without tensions for me. I've grown up going to Chinatown with my parents every other weekend to eat and get groceries, etc. But I have never considered why there is Chinatown other than some enterprising Chinese do their businesses there. My parents always referred to the people who are in Chinatown most of the time as poor Chinese, of lower class, rural "country bumpkin" type background. They also told us to be more careful down there because of higher crime and drugs and other such unsavory items. For the most part, this is what I know and what I believe about Chinatown. So I am nervous about going there regularly. My immediate questions are: How dangerous are the streets down there? And will they take advantage of me like charging me more because I am middle class and a college student?

The four statements quoted above suggest that students, regardless of their own racial locations, can come to civic engagement endeavors full of alarmingly misleading information, biases, stereotypes, and myths about the community and people they will engage with. It may be obvious to many readers that what the students put forth mirrors the misinformation, cultural essentialisms, and racial biases circulating in the larger society with reference to Asian Americans and "the Chinese." But it is equally important to note how their statements point to the glaring lack of any formal history and theory that might inform their attempts to make sense of lived realities very different from their own. Critical thinking and analytical skills are extremely limited. What gets drawn on are their own embedded assumptions and values, shaped by personal family experiences, popular myths, racial location, and socioeconomic class status, just to list the most important items of influence.

The confusion and ignorance revealed by students point to a dire lack of explicit education about the history of race and racial America throughout their educational experiences, both formal and informal. In discussing the way university students relate to race and racial differences, Beverly Tatum (2003) comments that one of the most common problems on contemporary college campuses is how little information students of all racial identity locations have about race and different racial histories in general. She explains that most whites, occupying racially dominant positions, have very little knowledge either about the lives and experiences of targeted or subordinate populations or about their own unmarked, unnamed white racial privilege. Some students of color in racially targeted populations may know that their white peers enjoy race privilege. They may even know of direct or indirect racist actions against people of color, including themselves. Still, these "knowings" do not translate into deep content knowledge about different racial groups' histories and experiences or about the profound impact of a racial system on our society. For many students of color, another form of racism— namely, internalized racism—leads them to hold the same essentialized racist stereotypes and myths about themselves that larger society does. Tatum argues that the only remedy for these vast ignorances is systematic pedagogy in which educators are committed to talking and teaching about race, especially as a system of inequality, in their formal curricula, without evasions and euphemisms.

Phase 3: Studying Systems of Inequality, Community History and Contemporary Realities

Early in the semester, while students are having their formal community orientations, they study the histories of Asian America in general and Boston Chinatown in particular, and they learn how to analyze current community conditions and politics by applying theories of race and economics. Toward the third week of the semester, the most common student response to the curriculum is one of shock or astonishment. The following responses illustrate the different areas in which students find themselves taken by surprise, as if unaware of their own preconceptions.

An African American student wrote about the almost universal surprise of discovering that Asian America is American, that Asians are raced in the United States, and that they experience racism:

I had no idea that I was going to be learning about racism, and then institutionalized racism and environmental racism. I guess I had thought of this course as my "relax" course this semester—a way to get away from campus and do something fun in a cultural community. I have other courses in American history and environmental issues, and this course actually fits tightly with those, except I had never thought of Chinatown as "American" in its history and never realized it even suffered any racism!! What a surprise! I don't think I'm going to be able to relax in this course though!!!

Most students are also startled to find that Chinatowns across the nation have a long history in America and are residential enclaves born out of anti-Asian racial exclusion. A biracial Latina and white European American student wrote:

I had no idea what to expect—all I knew about Chinatown is going there for dim sum on the weekends and sometimes at night because food is cheap and places are open late. Until the orientation and this week's readings, I didn't know that people lived there. I thought it was just restaurants and stores. I was really surprised to look up and see that people lived in apartments above the businesses and I discovered several housing projects that were quite big. I was most surprised to learn that Chinatown came about because of racial exclusion and forced segregation. I always thought that places like Chinatowns, Koreatowns, Little Saigons exist because the Asian people wanted to segregate themselves and live together. I am familiar with the barrios and I am getting the idea that there are similarities between our communities.

An Asian American student reported both puzzlement and dismay over her lack of knowledge about the concerns that plague Chinatown communities:

Even though I am Asian and parts of my family lived for a long time in San Francisco Chinatown, it is shockingly eye-opening for me to see how much large institutions and highways destroyed the kind of community that was in Boston Chinatown in the 40s and 50s, and how little the needs and wishes of the community are listened to, then and now. I had no idea of any of this and want to talk with my parents about what they know about the history of San Francisco Chinatown. Our readings talk about how every Chinatown in the U.S. has been targeted by gentrification and environmental racism. How could I have not known about any of this?

A fourth student, white European American, described with refreshing honesty her astonishment at her own racial and cultural biases, fueled by the omission of any examination of Asian America in her education:

I have to admit I always thought it was in the culture of the Chinese to not care about cleanliness. I guess I always just considered Chinese restaurants to be kind of dirty and messy. I am *embarrassed* that I was so biased—where did that kind of view come from? And why didn't I consider the Asian immigrants as Americans? I have learned that black culture is not separable from the kind of racism that has dogged blacks throughout American history, so why didn't I make that link? I feel like I am just a BIG BLANK inside when it comes to thinking about Asians. I don't believe I ever had ANY information or course about Asians in any of my classes in high school or college up till now. I guess I have a lot to learn, and I better learn some of it fast before I go to work in the community and make a fool of myself and offend just about everybody around me. I really need to think about the fact that I am a white person and that I will never have to deal with what Asians have to, and I need to look hard at my own values and start changing some of them.

Clearly, the students' novel, and for the first time explicit, access to curriculum content that (1) focused on the history of the racialized ethnic community, (2) articulated the impact of race and institutionalized racism within it, and (3) provided racial and economic analyses of contemporary problems was critical to the very obvious shift in their understanding. Nearly all turned from a view of the community partner as some "exotic, fun-filled cultural enclave" to one of it as a marginalized urban U.S. community of color, born of racial exclusion, and with current problems stemming from institutionalized racial discrimination. The last student's reflection underscores how crucial it is that, before students venture into their civic learning activities, the formal curricula of civic engagement not only explicitly address systems of inequality but also require students to examine their own social locations, to think about how they are shaped by these locations, and to speculate on what their own locations might imply for their interaction in the community.

Phase 4: Working in the Community

Students start working in the community a month into the semester. The readings, reflections, and analyses required up to this point have given them a basic knowledge of the history and contemporary issues in the community and of theories of race, racism, and systems of inequality, as well as a few opportunities to apply what they have learned to analyses of their own social locations and core values with regard to systems of inequality. As students begin their work in the field, they commonly find themselves trying to navigate unfamiliar terrain. Some face language and cultural barriers; some face a lack of resources to engage in the assigned tasks; and all experience insecurity in the face of ambiguity about the criteria by which they will be judged on their sensitivity to the community and their competence in practice. Thus, while students have by this point developed a fledgling awareness of their own race and class privileges and of several basic stereotypes and myths targeting Asians, immigrants, and low-income communities, their first true encounters with the activities of civic engagement usually lead to a further surfacing of their own deeply held biases as they are pushed out of their "comfort zones" of social expectation.

A bilingual Asian American student assigned to assist in services to new immigrants wrote:

I started doing taxes for immigrants today. I have never been so frustrated in my life. I find out that after attending hours of tax-prep training for this, the software I learned at the tax center cannot be used with the computer at the agency. The agency computers are way too old. So my supervisor asked me to do my work by hand. I was panicked. The doors opened, and immediately the lines formed, and most were older women.

I was very disturbed and irritated when the older immigrant women wanted me to "just do" their taxes for them. I thought you're supposed to teach someone to fish instead of giving them the fish. That's what I learned in my high school volunteer program. I think people *should* learn to help themselves. I thought they would be curious as to how to do it and want to learn so that they are not dependent on others doing it. But when I asked them to look at the forms with me, they became agitated—and pushed it at me—saying "just do it," and "I don't want to learn this, what if I do it wrong?" When the time came for the end of my 3 hour session, I tried to tell those still in line that I had to go and if they would come back another day, someone else would help them. They got panicked and said "Just do mine—I can't take time from work again." I never expected them to be so aggressive and demanding. They seem to be demonstrating a kind of "small" mentality that is very Chinese—just take care of me. I've heard that immigrants should be forced to learn English and use it, and this is a case where it is very true.

For a Latino student, language usage triggered this response:

I think I had a terrible day at the agency because I was eager at first and then I got upset since all the staff around me spoke mostly Chinese to one another. I found this very rude—they know that I don't speak any Chinese. I know they can speak some English. I thought they would at least try to use some English when I'm around. When we were stuffing envelopes at the same table, I think they were talking about me. Of course I do look like I don't belong there—this college student who has weird hair and clothes and who absolutely isn't an Asian. My Asian roommate told me that Chinese people are very arrogant and rude, and maybe this is what I'm encountering. It makes it difficult to think that I am supposed to be there to help out but they don't want me there?

A number of students served as classroom aides, tutors, and mentors in the only public school in Boston Chinatown. The youth they worked with, ranging from sixth to eleventh grade, were immigrants of color, or children of parents who were immigrants of color. Students' stereotypes about racial others and their own unquestioned values about the appropriateness of the behavior they witnessed, ranging from classroom deportment through educational aspirations and cultural assimilation to parental involvement, came through starkly as they reacted to their experiences working in this public school.

A white European American student wrote after meeting her after-school mentoring group:

One of the kids we're supposed to work with after school said that he couldn't attend any after-school club. We found out that his grandfather, who is from Haiti, would not let him stay after school at all. The grandfather wants the kid back at home as soon as school is over to help him with a family business in another town. I talked about this with my partner and we feel the grandfather is standing in the way of his own grandson's acculturation and involvement in American society. Since he chose to be in this country, he needs to let his family be involved here.

A white European American student was assigned to assist the teacher in classrooms. She observed:

I had a really strange introduction to the school. While I expected that the students who were going to be the least respectful were black, and they were, I was surprised to see that the Asian students were almost just as crazy. I think it's going to be a challenge for me as a white female trying to get their attention. I'm surprised at how difficult the Asian students were because I had expected that they would be easy to deal with. I have volunteered during high school in a school with a lot of African American students and I'm not surprised at their rambunctiousness but I had always assumed that Asians were the best students—quiet, well behaved and certainly not troublemakers. The Asians in my high school pretty much fit this bill.

A biracial African American and white European American student lamented:

I was upset that every student I asked told me that they didn't like school and they didn't see any real point in getting good grades and going to a good college. One kid said that he just isn't going to make it to college and become like "white people." When I asked him why, he said, "My uncle told me that I'm Chinese and people won't trust me and won't expect me to be the best in English and I just don't understand how things really work here." I think his uncle is really destructive to tell him that, maybe the guy is bitter or something, but he's killing his nephew's dreams and chances of succeeding. I expected that he would want the second generation to succeed even if he couldn't.

A biracial Asian American and white European American student reported in frustration:

I don't know how to deal with this one student who is always acting out, always threatening about beating others up or being beaten up or running away. I found out that she is the oldest of six kids and goes home to do all the housework and cook. She is angry because of all this, and I think I would be angry too if I were in her place. Is this considered a case of abuse; it may not be physical but it could be mental?

Another biracial Asian American and African American student wrote:

I just can't believe that so many of the parents are so uninvolved in their children's education. They don't seem to ask to see their homework and anything that the school sends home. I recall my parents were always involved and going over stuff with me. Both my parents worked full time, but they still seemed to spend a lot of time with us. The students I'm working with tell me that none of their parents have ever come to the school. All the kids I'm working with are Asian, and I guess I thought Asian parents were really intense about their kids education, almost too intense, if you know what I mean, so I'm really surprised.

Stuart Hall's (1996) observation that race often provides the language through which class conflicts find expression reflected in many of the students' statements. While race and class intersect and compound many of the community youths' experiences, my students did not have the habit of mind to recognize these intersections and sort out the different components. Instead, they tended not only to conflate experiences and values related to class and race but also to read them both as simply aspects of culture. Most commonly, students took "culture" to be the explanation for what they found unfamiliar. I have discovered that unless such conflations are thoroughly and painstakingly pointed out, and then analyzed and critiqued, students remain unaware of their problematic interpretations. In that case, their strongly embedded racist and elitist personal theories can actually be reinforced rather than dismantled by their work within the school.

Phase 5: Revelations and Reevaluations

By the middle of the second semester of the course, five to six months after their initial contact with the community, most students have had ample opportunity to gain theoretical knowledge as well as more particular insight into their own social locations and values through structured reflection on and analysis of their experiences in the field. Students have thus begun to feel much more involved in their community contexts and to infuse their work with their own talents and creativity. Their reflections on civic learning at this point frequently refer to "what they did not know" when they started the course. They speak about which parts of the curriculum they found most useful in correcting previously held biases. Frequently, they mention titles and authors of readings that were critical in transforming their thinking, as well as activities that led them to seek alternative explanations for their encounters. Their reflections give us valuable insight into what could be not just useful but even necessary components of effective civic engagement curriculum and pedagogy.

The student who had complained about the cleanliness of the community in a quotation given above offered this reflection:

I complained a lot about how dirty Chinatown was and how little people there seemed to care about their environment, but what I am learning about environmental racism in urban areas like the Chinatown community has totally blown me away. I never even included the city in my consideration of environment before now—it was the forests and rivers—and I had never thought of the word "racism" attached to environmental issues. I am seeing how race and especially race and class combined are so absolutely at the center of this issue. Who are the people who get to make environmental policy? Who are the people who get to choose where they want to live? Why should it surprise us that a community that is almost 100% new immigrant, with language and cultural barriers, with one of the lowest income brackets in the city, is always targeted for all the mess that people who have clout and money know how to avoid in their communities? I think these issues are right in front of our nose, except that unless we are *forced* to see them, we don't.

A white European American student who had been especially uncomfortable with and resistant to reading and discussing the role of white privilege in the system of racism reported her analysis of her own socialization and how it shaped her views:

I was taught at home and in school to stay away from talking about controversial topics like "social injustice," so talking about racism is just one of those big no-no's. I didn't like the readings about race, especially about white privilege. If the course had not forced us to look at how race plays a major role in communities, I would have learned a totally different set of things with this community work. I think some of the biases I had—e.g., that immigrants should be forced to learn English—would have been stronger. I would have seen it as a choice whether immigrants learn English and want to participate in American society. Even the canvassing from door to door in the community would not have changed my views—it would just have made me feel that the Chinese residents were very exclusive and suspicious. The community speakers were crucial to changing my mind. After listening to them, I would go back and read about race privilege and the article from *The Possessive Investment in Whiteness* [Lipsitz 1998] and then I began to change my mind.

An Asian American student who had been especially challenged by the Asian American youth he tutored wrote about the turning point in his work:

I think the Asian boys thought they could get away with a lot because I'm an Asian male, but once I started to call them out on their behavior, they actually calmed down and I think I am developing a relationship with them. The article by Lisa Delpit [1995] on "Silenced Dialogues" helped me in a way that is truly *life-changing*. I grew up in the only Asian American family in an upper middle class white neighborhood and I was judging the students by what I had learned to do all my life to survive as the "other" in my own community. It took her article to wake me up. I am glad to be working with these boys because we do have a relationship and they don't get to see older Asian Americans who are teachers and professionals too often.

The student who had authored the electronic mail questioning me about the appropriateness of including the study of race and power in the course wrote specifically to address his earlier missive:

I don't know if you remember but I'm the one who sent you an email in the summer about the course and I asked you why we had to talk about race and all that. In the beginning, I had not understood why the course had "race, culture, power, and politics" in its title and almost didn't take the course because these topics were a turn-off. Just working at the agency alone would not have convinced me that race, culture, power, and politics are required for understanding community—any community. If we had not read about how racism works against Asians and how people's race affects their access to political participation, or even just clean air and green space, I don't think I could see how the lives of the people and the existence of this whole community are all based on the inequalities of race, culture, power, and politics in our society. My own parents are immigrants in a very Latino neighborhood and I think I actually began to let myself see what they faced because of taking this course. I think maybe I was trying to deny that racism is real or that it really can affect you. I am reading another book in another class called *Savage Inequalities* by Jonathan Kozol—it is about inequality of access to education, and if I wrote a book about Chinatown, I would also call what I have seen there "savage inequalities" in access to housing, safety, space, political voice, the list goes on.

Phase 6: Reflections on a Year of Civic Learning

Finally, I turn to students' reflections at the end of their yearlong experience of civic engagement and learning. A few themes repeatedly emerge from students' written communications. Students comment frequently on the absence of information about systems of inequality in their formal education. They are able to identify these systems and analyze how they operate, and they recognize how they themselves are implicated within the systems. They identify the process of civic learning that has led them to transformed perceptions of themselves and of the community and its residents. Many students, especially seniors, share informed reconsiderations of their career and life choices.

A white European American student reflected on how his overall education had failed to provide him with critical knowledge about systems of inequality and teach the dangers of uninformed, well-intentioned "good works":

I am one of those people who went to a diverse school and did a lot with diversity education in the school. One thing I never learned till working specifically in this community and taking the course is that racism can be expressed in very different forms. I never learned about the institutional kind of racism, the kind that you can't see because it is just in the way that things are set up and done—in policies and laws and practices. I guess I did grow up on a diet that said that racism is mostly concentrated in those that are ignorant, uneducated, and that it's about being afraid of and hating or looking down on those that are different from you, but I realize that I never really figured out what drove it other than warped human nature. And so it is with both relief and terror that I am beginning to understand that racism is "a system of advantage based on race," that it is not just ignorant people being mean. I never saw how embedded things are in the structures of our society. So even good intentioned people like me, like other students in this class, could actually be performing out of racism and not even realize it. This is something entirely new to me. I think I've never understood this aspect of service—it's not about cleaning the streets, teaching English, getting people out to vote—I mean it is about all of these things, but that they are really individual pieces that only make real sense if you group them under the kind of action that seeks to fight to stop racism acted on one community by larger society around it.

A biracial African American and white European American senior confessed:

I have always wanted to go into law. I come from a family where there are a lot of people in law. So I still do want to go into law—I think. The only thing that is very different is the image I have in my own mind of what is possible with a law degree and what I want to do with it. My uncles all work in prestigious law firms and I guess I always thought I'd like that kind of setting. But the kind of work they do is not even remotely connected to what I've been learning about this year in community involvement. Over break I went to visit my uncles in the law firms, and I found the things they were working on to be about protecting wealth and power for those who already have it and want more—like the luxury condo developers who want to tear down Chinatown. At the same time, it is so clear to me that without the help of people who really know the law, some of the battles for community justice would have been futile. So I want to be able to use the law to do battle for community justice. That's really clear to me. I don't know how to get there yet. I can't be more blunt than that. But I do know that I want to put any education I get towards doing something that makes those who don't have access to what they need come closer to getting it. I made an appointment with the community lawyer who came to speak to us. He was incredibly down to earth but inspiring. He had mentioned that he would be willing to talk to us outside of class about the choices that he made both in and after law school.

A white European American student who had been fearful of teaching students of color appeared to have shifted her stance after her experience tutoring and mentoring:

I no longer think that I can't work with kids who are very different from me. Whenever I thought of teaching in the past, I had pictured myself teaching in a school just like my own, which I now realize is one of the richest and best suburban publics. Now I want to work in schools where there are students of color, immigrants, poor white kids, and other kids who are really "disadvantaged" by the way the school systems are set up. I don't think I'm so naïve as to think I'll have a great time because I've seen how hard and punishing it is and how many people burn out. But I need to try to do this. I'll be teaching for a year with a program in New York where I'll be working with ESL students. I am ecstatic. I am also scared out of my mind. But I've learned in this course that it's a good thing to be scared. It will take away some of the cockiness and arrogance that I realized I have. I learned that being scared doesn't mean I can't go ahead and still do something and make it work.

An Asian American student poignantly traced the trajectory of his movement from recognizing his own internalized racism and elitism to taking on a newfound sense of responsibility for using his awareness in future work to combat racism and oppression:

I don't know what would have happened if I had gone to work in Chinatown without taking the course at the same time—the research on race and health and environmental racism made the greatest impact on me. I have been to Chinatown all my life and was very critical of those who lived there, learning these views from my parents—I always thought that the Chinese who lived in Chinatown came from poor social status and were not civic minded—that they had no concern about the larger welfare of their streets and community. I really thought that the streets were dirty because they were particularly "bad citizens," as in "I only look out for myself and my front steps." I think I've been somewhat embarrassed and apologetic about "my people" whenever I go to Chinatown to eat with my non-Asian friends and I will make comments about the people there being ignorant and uneducated. I wanted to separate myself from them.

Now that I have learned about how unequal the services are in different communities it is like seeing the world through *totally new lenses*. I was stunned to hear about how Chinatown was targeted as the place for all the highway ramps, for huge hospital complexes, for the sex industry—it is as if the residents of this community are just not considered "human" as other Americans are—this feeling that they will absorb everything because they are Asian/Chinese, poor, new immigrants without language and cultural capital, and no one will stand up and fight for this community. I realize how I didn't know anything about the history of what I now consider my own racial community here in this society. And that most people I come into contact with have no idea!! This is eye-opening because I feel very differently about this idea of working within a community. I am leaving this course feeling that given what I now know, I absolutely have a responsibility to continue to do this while I'm in this area and then wherever I go I should seek out other Chinatowns and communities like it to give my time and energy to. You had talked about life-long education and goals before, and I feel that I am really clear about these now.

Ruminations on What I Have Learned and Where We Need to Go

Civic engagement is the most recent expression of the historic liberal arts mission of preparing students for public life as civic participants (Latham 2003). I want to think that we have become involved in our work as scholars and teachers because one of our main goals is to swell the numbers of individuals in the generations to come who are not only willing but also intellectually and practically skilled enough to make a lifelong ethical commitment to working with communities and populations most marginalized so that in the end all involved are empowered to create more just societies. While the last few student statements in the prior section might give us some hope that our efforts toward this goal are not entirely futile, much remains to be done.

I have learned from the students I have worked with in the last six years that the transformations they underwent over the duration of the course could not have occurred without a curriculum and pedagogy "forcing" them to study community history and systems of inequality. Their comments and reflections all suggest that had they engaged in community work alone, without the more academically oriented work that helped them see the conditions they encountered in the broader context of institutionalized injustice in our society, the risk would have been very high that their experiences would have reinforced the embedded biases, assumptions, misinformation, and ignorance pervading U.S. society and, thus, their own knowledge base. Civic engagement educators and their community partners are all too familiar with a common scenario in civic engagement teaching and learning in which the unexamined biases and values that students (and teachers) bring with them into a community context result in negative interactions that engender conflict, avoidance, patronization, or moralization.

The result is that "well-meaning" teachers and learners avoid—perhaps even strongly oppose—further forays beyond the traditional classroom into unfamiliar communities. Community partners, already stretched thin for human and material resources, find themselves suffering from the loss of time and energy they have spent educating and nurturing both outside learners and a community-academic partnership. The expectations they had that their academic partners would "do no harm" are thus shattered. Plans and projects are stalled or aborted, contributing to the development of a great deal of cynicism about any positive role for the academy and academics in the community.

I have also learned from students who caution that absent an understanding of the systems that reproduce inequality, even "positive" civic engagement work may leave underlying problematic values and gaps of knowledge unchallenged. For example, students could have a very successful experience of cleaning up neighborhoods and creating more green space in a community without ever being challenged in their belief that the residents in the neighborhood do not care about the physical environment and ultimately are the ones to blame for any poor conditions they live in. Students might therefore never come to understand institutionalized environmental racism that targets certain communities for "beautification" and others with unwanted toxic waste. Explicit theoretical instruction integrated into civic engagement education is necessary to avoid these destructive endings.

The Work Done since I Began

Six years ago, my involvement with the field of civic engagement as an educator began when a couple of administrators at my university consulted me about why a two-year-old civic engagement project they had implemented was failing. The attrition rate for the university students who had made yearlong commitments to mentor/tutor weekly in a public school program in Boston Chinatown (the same school mentioned earlier in this essay) was 60% by the end of the first semester and 90% by the middle of the spring. In a focus group I set up with the student volunteers, I learned that they had all broken their commitments out of a sense that they had nothing to contribute to the public school youth. They felt they could get the youth neither to focus on their schoolwork nor to involve themselves in after-school interest activities. They felt that the youth were "not bound for college" or were too poor at English to benefit from the help that was offered.

While the university students had been given a handbook and four hours of a tutoring workshop prior to their engagement at the school, they had no background knowledge of the students and their home communities, or of the history and culture of the school and the community in which it was located. Furthermore, the university students (all except one identified themselves as white

European Americans of upper-middle-class backgrounds) had not been asked to consider their own social identities or those of the students they worked with (all Asian American and black/African American of working-class or low-income first-generation immigrant parents) and how these different social locations influenced lived experiences. Further exploration in the focus group revealed that a plethora of misinformed and misguided assumptions and values about the race and class status of the youth—which the university students had brought with them into the project—were strongly reinforced by the actual service work in the school. In one university student's words, he had "expected the inner city poor kids would not care as much about doing well in school as middle-class kids in the suburbs because parents of the two groups have different values about education"; and in fact, his time at the school "proved these expectations to be grounded in reality."

As an outcome of this consultation and the focus group, I agreed, somewhat reluctantly, to develop a yearlong course for credit in the formal university curriculum to prepare and continue to educate the next group of university students as they enlisted in this project the following year. As an instructor of comparative race studies and Asian American studies in the American Studies Program, I had two motivations for engaging in this endeavor: my sense of affiliation to and concern for the immigrant communities that the youth of the public school came from (including the Asian American community in which the school was located) and my sense that "learning through interactive and reflective practice" might be a meaningful way to educate university students about race and related social identity differences that matter in larger society. My reluctance came from my lack of experience in how to create an academic course in which civic engagement in an off-campus community played a central role.

My prior teaching experiences had shown me the truth of Tatum's observation (mentioned earlier in this essay) that the majority of today's students come to university without formal education in the meaning of race and racism as institutions in society and with a great deal of misinformation about racial realities, both their own and that of their different peers. At the very least, I wanted students in my class to enter the school and its racialized ethnic community of new immigrant populations with a basic knowledge of the history of both, as well as with education not only in the meaning and impact of race and class differences on people's everyday lives but also in the cultures of social institutions.

As I embarked on research to design the course, I was both surprised and disappointed to discover the absence of race and race-related issues in the literature of civic engagement education. Moreover, the occasional reference to race invariably employed a black and white racial paradigm. In that first year of teaching, I ended up drawing on content developed in other courses I taught on comparative race in America and Asian America, adapting it (in some cases without much success) for use in the area of civic engagement. For pedagogy, I employed, with a great deal of trepidation and at high risk of disservice to the public school youth and their communities, a trial-and-error approach to how best to teach in order to ensure that university students would have an opportunity for meaningful learning while providing constructive and ethical contributions in this very fragile and tenuous partnership between the academy and the public school community. For the purpose of evaluating the effectiveness of both curriculum content and pedagogy, I used the following questions as measures of acceptability:

1. Were the choices for theoretical and historical content and pedagogical strategies informed by the needs of the students being tutored, the school community, and the larger community in which the school was located?
2. Did the individuals, the school, and the community consider their needs served by the efforts of university students?

In the intervening years, I have come to understand that one of the many factors dissuading university faculty from taking on civic engagement projects, especially in contexts they deem unfamiliar, is the lack of readily accessible researched and tested deep-content knowledge and pedagogy to guide them in their design and implementation of this kind of educational experience.

The Work that Lies Ahead

Six years down the road, my experiences with the field of civic engagement lead me to make the following observation: As racial differences increase and their complexity of meaning deepens in our society, I am more convinced now than ever that scholars defining the field must (1) recognize the pervasiveness of racism as a system of inequality in contemporary society and (2) systematically include and pay attention to race and its impact on lived experiences as central to their research, theory construction, and knowledge production.

Several avenues of research and scholarship offer potential benefits to the field. First, exploration of the meaning(s) and practices of civic engagement in different racial/ethnic/cultural communities in the contemporary United States would generate further interest in the field and promote its usefulness among a broader and more diverse audience than is now the case. In the last two decades alone, the establishment of communities with new racial/ethnic/cultural/linguistic/religious populations has become the norm rather than the exception across the United States. Many of these communities have significant transnational populations. Do members of these new and evolving communities consider the discourse in the field of civic engagement relevant and applicable to them? How do they, for example, relate to the criteria by which traditional studies have evaluated social capital? How would they define and identify social capital in their communities? How do they react when their realities are omitted from discussions of theory, policy, and practice in civic engagement literature, and what are the implications of these omissions in their lives? How does culture-making in these new communities reshape social, economic, and political culture in society at large? In this area, cooperation and collaboration between those in the field of civic engagement and those in the field of race and ethnic studies could prove exceptionally productive. Within my own field of Asian American studies, for example, the last decade has seen an abundance of new knowledge production on numerous aspects of social, political, economic, cultural, and racial experiences in emergent Asian American communities across the United States. This scholarship, however, can be profitably exploited only if civic engagement scholars and teachers make decisions to build it into their own knowledge base and include it in shaping their own research and formal coursework.

Second, sorely needed is critical examination of the practices of civic engagement education and dissemination of the results. We have to have empirical confirmation of precisely what procedures effectively integrate content knowledge and various pedagogies relating to race and systems of inequality. Unless scholars, educators, practitioners, and community partners are committed to continuing, systematic, and active reflection on "how" civic engagement work is implemented and improved, we run a great risk of unethical practice that further harms and silences populations marginalized by institutional structures to begin with. We also stand likely to fail in the education of university learners.

Third, and finally, assessment criteria for civic engagement research, education, and practice must be developed for *all* of us in the field in order to hold us accountable for meeting our espoused goals. In this research, longitudinal studies that follow the impact of civic engagement education on learners and the communities they were or are involved in would be an important first step in allowing us to gauge whether involvement with civic engagement indeed leads to lifelong commitment to effective and ethical work. When it comes to civic engagement education, we must always keep the end in mind. What we are ultimately aiming for is productive efforts at transformative education, both theoretical and practical, through which everyone engaged, inside and outside the academy, is empowered to envision and build a more just society.

References

Ancheta, Angelo. 1993. *Race, Rights, and the Asian American Experience.* New Brunswick, N.J.: Rutgers University Press.

Boyle-Baise, Marilynne. 2002. *Multicultural Service Learning: Educating Teachers in Diverse Communities*. New York: Teachers College Press.

Cantor, Nancy, 2004. "Civic Engagement: The University as Public Good." Keynote speech at Association of American Colleges and Universities symposium, Practicing Liberal Education: Deepening Knowledge, Pursuing Justice, Taking Action. January 21.

Dang, Janet. 2000. "Anti-Asian Hate Crimes on the Rise." *AsianWeek*. January 12–18.

Deans, T. 1999. "Service Learning in Two Keys: Paulo Friere's Critical Pedagogy in Relation to John Dewey's Pragmatism." *Michigan Journal of Community Service Learning* 6:15–29.

Delpit, Lisa. 1995. *Other People's Children: Cultural Conflict in the Classroom*. New York: New Press.

Du Bois, W. E. B. 1903. *The Souls of Black Folk*. Chicago: McClurg.

———. [1935] 1997. *Black Reconstruction: An Essay toward a History of the Part Which Black Folk Played in the Attempt to Reconstruct Democracy in America, 1860–1880*. New York: Atheneum.

Foos, Cathy. 1998. "The 'different' voice of service." *Michigan Journal of Community Service Learning* 5:14–21.

Frankenberg, Ruth. 1993. *White Women, Race Matters: The Social Construction of Whiteness*. Minneapolis, Minn.: University of Minnesota Press.

Galura, J.A., P. Pasque, D. Schoem, and J. Howard, eds. 2004. *Engaging the Whole of Service-Learning, Diversity, and Learning Communities*. Ann Arbor, Mich.: OCSL Press.

Gilroy, Paul. 2003. *Against Race: Imagining Political Culture beyond the Color Line*. Cambridge, Mass.: Harvard University Press.

Guinier, Lani, and Gerald Torres. 2003. *The Miner's Canary: Enlisting Race, Resisting Power, Transforming Democracy*. Cambridge, Mass.: Harvard University Press.

Hall, Stuart. 1996. "New ethnicities." In *Stuart Hall: Critical Dialogues in Cultural Studies,* edited by D. Morley and K.-H. Chen, 441–49. London: Routledge.

Holt, Thomas, 2002. *The Problem of Race in the Twenty-first Century (The Nathan I. Huggins Lectures)*. Cambridge, Mass.: Harvard University Press.

hooks, bell. 1994. *Teaching to Transgress: Education as the Practice of Freedom*. New York: Routledge.

———. 2004. *Teaching Community: A Pedagogy of Hope*. New York: Routledge.

James, C. L. R. 1996. *C. L. R. James on the "Negro Question."* Edited by Scott McLemee. Jackson, Miss.: University Press of Mississippi.

Kivel, Paul. 2002. *Uprooting Racism: How White People Can Work for Racial Justice*. British Columbia: New Society Publishers.

Latham, Andrew. 2003. *Liberal Education for Global Citizenship: Renewing Macalester's Traditions of Public Scholarship and Civic Learning*. Macalester University report.

Lipsitz, George. 1998. *The Possessive Investment in Whiteness: How White People Profit from Identity Politics*. Philadelphia: Temple University Press.

Matsuda, Mari. 1996. *Where is Your Body? And Other Essays on Race, Gender, and the Law*. Boston, Mass.: Beacon.

Marschall, Melissa, and Dietlind Stolle. 2004. "Race and the city: Neighborhood context and the development of generalized trust." *Political Behavior* 26, no. 2:125–53.

Omatsu, Glenn. 2000. "The 'Four Prisons' and the Movement of Liberation: Asian American Activism from the 1960s to the 1990s." In *Asian American Studies: A Reader,* edited by Jean Yu-wen Shen Wu and Min Song, 164–96. New Brunswick, N.J.: Rutgers University Press.

Omi, Michael, and Howard Winant. 1994. *Racial Formation in the United States: From the 1960s to the 1990s.* New York: Routledge.

Pompa, Lori. 2005. "Service Learning as Crucible: Reflections on Immersion, Context, Power, and Transformation." In *Service Learning in Higher Education,* edited by D. Butin, 173–92. New York: Palgrave MacMillan.

Putnam, Robert. 2000. *Bowling Alone: The Collapse and Revival of American Community.* New York: Simon and Schuster.

———, ed. 2002. *Democracies in Flux: The Evolution of Social Capital in Contemporary Society.* Oxford: Oxford University Press.

Robinson, Tony. 2000. "Dare the School Build a New Social Order?" *Michigan Journal of Community Service Learning* 7:142–57.

Rosenberger, Cynthia. 2000. "Beyond Empathy: Developing Critical Consciousness through Service Learning." In *Integrating service learning and multicultural education in colleges and universities,* edited by C. R. O'Grady, 23–43. Mahwah, N.J.: Lawrence Erlbaum.

Tatum, Beverly. 2003. *Why Are All the Black Kids Sitting Together in the Cafeteria?* New York: Basic Books.

Winant, Howard. 1994. *Racial Condition: Politics, Theory, Comparisons.* Minneapolis, Minn.: University of Minnesota Press.

———. 2004. *New Racial Politics: Globalism, Difference, Justice.* Minneapolis, Minn.: University of Minnesota Press.

Three Major Foundations and the Decline in Funding for Higher Education Civic Engagement, 1995 to 2005

In the mid-1980s and into the 1990s, debates raged about a critical decline in civic participation in America especially among young people. Higher education and philanthropic foundations rose to the challenge, "inspiring hundreds of institutions to explore and act upon their vision of a civic mission" (Holland 2001, 1). By the end of 1999, Campus Compact's ambitious "Mapping Civic Engagement" project (funded by the Surdna Foundation) compiled fifty-six national and regional initiatives in higher education devoted to "developing civic skills, inspiring engaged citizenship, promoting a civil society, and building the commonwealth" (www.compact.org/mapping/).

The mapping project reported "growing evidence of a national social movement for civic renewal in higher education [with] potential to not only strengthen American democracy, but also to make higher education more effective in meeting its main goals." The report also identified two main "gaps in the field." These two issues turned out to be prescient in anticipating the subject of this essay: the recent decline in major foundation support for higher education civic engagement. First is the question of whether civic education actually results in an increase in civic skills and active civic participation among college students, including a rise in voting rates. Second is the unequal power relationship between universities and the communities, with higher education showing little willingness to engage communities as full partners in setting the direction for campus-community initiatives (www.compact.org/mapping).

Data for this study come from monitoring the Web sites of selected foundations, over approximately a year and a half beginning in August 2004. Changes were evident by the spring, summer, and fall of 2005 when older programs and grant guidelines disappeared or were substantially changed. Published reports from these foundations were also reviewed, plus reports and Web sites related to civic engagement activities at some colleges and universities and national organizations (such as Campus Compact) that support higher education civic engagement. Published literature on foundations and higher education civic engagement, both scholarly and practitioner-based, was reviewed. Perhaps most important, confidential interviews with ten key informants who are national leaders in this field were conducted between September 2004 and April 2005: six from higher education and four from foundations. Within the limits of confidentiality, it is possible to say that all four of the foundation informants had been or currently were in senior positions providing support for higher education civic engagement. Of the six national civic engagement leaders interviewed, all are well known and highly respected academics or other practitioners holding senior posts across the United States, either at colleges and universities or related support organizations. Gender pronouns used here for interview subjects are sometimes varied to further safeguard confidentiality.

Overall, these data show a decline in foundation support for higher education civic engagement among three major foundations that have been most likely to provide support. These changes in funding appear to have occurred largely for reasons that are *internal* to the expectations these institutions set for themselves and how they see what the public demands of them: measurable outcomes of the results of the programs they support, innovative solutions to pressing social ills, and accountability to local community needs and constituencies. These demands may reflect a larger crisis of purpose that charitable foundations today are experiencing about their role in modern democratic societies as earlier roles have shifted and changed (Anheier and Leat 2002).

Following a brief discussion about why foundations in the 1990s began funding higher education civic engagement, the remainder of this essay documents the shifts in funding for higher education civic engagement among three foundations commonly identified as major sources of support: Carnegie Corporation of New York, Pew Charitable Trusts (now a public charity that continues to make grants), and the W. K. Kellogg Foundation. In contrast to the "big 3" I also discuss a fourth, Surdna Foundation, whose grants to higher education civic engagement differ both in approach and in its apparent continued level of commitment. The essay ends with conclusions and implications for obtaining outside support for higher education civic engagement.

Why Did Foundations Support Higher Education Civic Engagement Initiatives in the First Place?

It follows from foundation history that these funding institutions would be interested in supporting civic engagement initiatives by colleges and universities. Foundations have long been important to the historical development of higher education in the United States (Bulmer 1999; Hammock 1999, 5; Rothschild 1999), including support for social science research aimed at developing ameliorative measures for urgent social problems.

From the time of the New Deal into the 1960s and 1970s, U.S. foundations such as the Ford Foundation sought to contribute to widespread social reform by devoting portions of their resources to building and testing model social programs intended to be taken up by the then-expanding federal welfare state. (O'Connor 1999) But in the 1980s and 1990s as the welfare state declined and then devolved social support to state and local governments and to community nonprofit organizations, foundations too sought more locally based community *non*governmental ways toward social reform. They began to emphasize funding to build civil society and the capacity of local communities (G. Smith 1998; J. A. Smith 1999). In this context, campus-community "partnerships" between higher education institutions and their host communities were appealing (Silver and Boyle 2005).

Given the rise in public concern about civic and political engagement by college-age youth, and a growing interest in supporting local community-based nonstate solutions to problems previously addressed by government, it is not surprising that foundations in the 1990s sought to support changes in curriculum and teaching intended to both build a more engaged generation of young people and address problems in local communities. Foundation initiatives such as the National Commission on Civic Renewal (funded by Pew) called for expanded efforts to increase civic participation, strengthen democracy, and provide more "close to home" opportunities for citizens—including college students—to be more civically engaged (Babcock 1998). On the campus side, given the decline in government funding for higher education overall, schools had little choice but to turn to private sources like foundations to support new initiatives. In a mutually reinforcing pattern, increased resources from foundations likely contributed to the growth of university civic engagement (Bowley and Meeropool 2003).

I now piece together a story of changing directions at three major funders of campus civic engagement.

Carnegie Corporation of New York: A Change in Focus from Civic Education of College-Age to K–12 Students

Carnegie's civic education funding initiatives have been typical of what was perhaps until recently the most common approach to civic engagement efforts on campus today: educating students in civic values, skills, and social and moral responsibility. While this emphasis is consistent with Carnegie's founding mission "to promote the advancement of knowledge and understanding," (www.carnegie.org), the foundation apparently considered a range of approaches before selecting its emphasis on civic education. In 1999 Carnegie convened a Stanford University conference of youth development specialists to guide its thinking (Gibson 2001, 13). Two years later, Carnegie issued the report *From Inspiration to Participation: A Review of Perspectives on Youth Civic Engagement,* authored by the then-program officer of Carnegie's "Strengthening U.S. Democracy" Program.

The 2001 report outlined three perspectives on civic education (Gibson 2001, 1). The first came from service learning advocates who had shifted their own thinking from designing youth volunteer experiences to identifying and addressing the larger sociopolitical conditions that underlie the problems volunteering had sought to address. Some urged a move away from service to political action, advocacy, and social and community change (Gibson 2001, 10). A second perspective came from political scientists who focused on the need for strategies to increase voting rates. The last perspective, and the one Carnegie chose, came from youth development specialists who favored a developmental and educational experience they believed would best promote youth active citizenship. Its focus was on the development of a strong sense of personal identity, responsibility, caring, compassion, and tolerance as part of youth moral development (Gibson 2001, 12).

In 2001, Carnegie's "Youth Civic Engagement" project defined the problem of civic engagement as a substantial decline in young people's participation in democracy at the same time as young people were becoming more involved in community service. The main solution was education for citizenship through "school-based civic education"; the favored approach included "instruction in the fundamentals of democracy," and "experiential opportunities—including community service, service learning, and/or political engagement . . . integrated into the school curricula" with "time for reflection and analysis regarding these experiences." Carnegie affirmed this particular approach to creating "free and responsible citizens [through] educat[ing] for active citizenship" in the 2002 report *The Civic Mission of Schools*—though by the time this report was issued, Carnegie was beginning a shift away from funding higher education civic engagement to focus on K–12 education.

By 2004, Carnegie had turned its school-based civic engagement grant-making almost entirely toward K–12 initiatives in civic education. An informant from the campus side that I spoke with in the summer of 2004 told me, "The whole [higher ed] program at Carnegie has been eliminated. They've moved to voting and K–12." In fall 2004 a key foundation informant told me that Carnegie would "not go back to higher education civic engagement." Why the shift? One reason I was given was increasing concern about the preponderance of foundation monies going to higher education institutions, including extremely affluent ones like Harvard University, while K–12 schools were "starving for money."

By spring 2005 the program officer who had authored the 2001 report and who was pivotal in defining the direction of its higher education civic engagement initiatives left the Carnegie; around that same time someone from the foundation world knowledgeable about higher education civic engagement funding told me, "Carnegie is in transition and I have no idea where the work is going there."

Pew Charitable Trusts: From Youth Engagement Education to Increasing Youth Voting

In 1996, Pew funded the high-profile National Commission for Civic Renewal and apparently took to heart one of the commission's recommendations for "renewed attention to civic education for young people as a key means of boosting their knowledge, understanding, and engagement." In 2001, Pew established a "Youth Engagement Initiative" aimed at increasing the amount and quality of young people's involvement in American life. This initiative exemplified a student learning and youth development approach to higher education civic engagement. This approach was evident in a news release announcing the creation of the Pew-supported Center for Information and Research on Civic Learning and Engagement (CIRCLE) housed at the University of Maryland. CIRCLE's mandate was described as putting the "question of how young people acquire civic attitudes and habits back on the research agenda" (www.puaf.umd.edu, July 2001 press release).

While the civic education aspect of Pew's funding has been in some ways similar to Carnegie's earlier emphasis, the approach at Pew seems never to have been so focused on student learning and youth development. For example, even at the beginning of Pew's 2001 Youth Engagement Initiative, Pew made a grant to the University of Richmond for its "Election Reform Information Project" (oncampus.richmond.edu). Pew's civic engagement initiatives, unlike Carnegie's, have also emphasized community and social change through campus-community partnerships along with its youth focus. The Pew Partnership for

Civic Change housed at the University of Richmond states its purpose as being to "catalyze community solutions" to community problems. A recent book sponsored by the Pew Partnership "outlines the key strategies used by thousands of leaders to create a better future for all the community citizens" (Morse 2002; www.pew-partnership.org). Further evidence of this more community-centered approach is the 2003 Pew report *University and Community Research Partnerships: A New Approach,* which aims "to identify document, and disseminate information about successful efforts to address tough challenges in communities across the country" (Dugery and Knowles 2003, 2).

In 2004, Pew began to focus its efforts on "encouraging young people to vote" (www.pewtrusts.com). A key grant went to George Washington University's "New Voters Project," "the largest youth voter mobilization effort in U.S. history" (www.newvotersproject.org).

What was it that brought about this shift at Pew from civic education to youth voting? One informant on the campus side told me, "Pew gave up on building a movement. It had no larger strategy. There was heavy pressure from Pew on measurables. They came in like the 800 pound gorilla, and then they just pulled out. Now in addition to youth vote, it's all moved to community-based stuff." When I asked someone knowledgeable about Pew why the shift from community change and youth development to voting, that person said, "There was less money so there had to be more focus. It's easier to tell if you make a difference in voting. It's more practical, more tangible. It's too hard to establish impact in communities. There had to be a focus on where we could actually make some change."

The New Voters Project was reported as a success in raising youth voting in the 2004 presidential election (CIRCLE online newsletter, April 2005), and Pew's 2005 grant guidelines "encourage inquires from potential partners committed to strengthening American democracy specifically through programs that will increase young people's interest in voting" (www.pewtrusts.com). In addition to voter turnout, the project also seeks to influence political parties and other political organizations to include youth as an important constituency in their appeals. Changes in the staffing at Pew in summer 2005, like at Carnegie, suggest that future funding directions in this area are again shifting and unclear.

The W. K. Kellogg Foundation: From Transforming the Academy to Making Change in Low-Income Communities

Kellogg's higher education civic engagement funding seemed for a while in the mid-1990s and into the early 2000s to focus on the societal problem of colleges and universities as viable institutions and their ability to adapt to major changes in their external environments. Kellogg exhorted campuses to "take charge of their futures [and] develop the capacities to change" as a condition of their [own] survival" (Eckel, Green, and Hill 2001, 3).

Indicative of their earlier emphasis on changing the academy as a way to affect the larger social good—a quite different approach from that of either Carnegie or Pew—Kellogg launched a major initiative in 1995 along with the American Council on Education (ACE) called the "Kellogg Network on Institutional Transformation." The aim was "to learn and work with institutions, helping them to transform themselves to be more flexible, accountable, collaborative, and responsive to students, faculty, the communities, and the regions they serve" (Eckel, Green, and Hill 2001, 31). Desired indicators of transformation included changes to curriculum, pedagogy, student learning outcomes, faculty rewards, and new organizational structures such as teaching centers and new forms of faculty governance (Eckel, Green, and Hill 2001, 8–9). As one key informant on the campus side told me, "A decade or so ago, funders were very interested in this kind of work. Higher ed was at the table then and the argument was that higher ed should be in the forefront of change in society, the purveyor of knowledge for society. [Three years later] funding for higher ed was already waning at Kellogg." Someone knowledgeable about Kellogg characterized this as a "university in service to society focus" with the idea that "universities would need to change themselves to better serve communities."

The upshot of the institutional change project was that Kellogg concluded that while a few faculty and students and some schools would rise to the challenge, large-scale changes in the institutional culture and structure of the American academy were probably not realizable. As one key informant put it, Kellogg "realized that large-scale institutional change was probably not going to happen." As one campus key informant told me, "About a decade ago, there was an idea that higher eds could affect society. There were some projects that had social goals but no results so it does not surprise me that foundations have pulled out. So that's led to an anti-university rhetoric in foundations. Foundations said that higher education did not get results. That's what I heard."

Frustrated, then, with the slow work of changing universities as a way to change communities and society, Kellogg turned its funding toward affecting societal change and "social good" more directly. Decrying the erosion of "higher education as an agent of social change and civic renewal," and mourning "retreat from public life" especially by research universities (www.thenationalforum.org), Kellogg shifted its funding to initiatives that focused directly on *community* issues and concerns. The foundation decided to support colleges and universities only when they served as resources to address community issues and concerns. As one campus key informant put it in the fall of 2004, "Kellogg saw that they did not need to go through higher eds. They could go directly to the community." Suggesting that Kellogg is not alone in this conclusion, another key informant in touch with the national funding scene told me: "There's a feeling [among foundations] that making change in higher education is very slow, and funders have shifted to problems in the community and to giving monies directly to communities not higher ed. There's a place for higher ed if the higher ed's focus is on community needs. So the focus is now on outcomes in the community, not on student learning outcomes." A person knowledgeable about Kellogg confirmed this direction, saying, "It was decided not to start with higher education institutions, but to start with the community, to not go through higher ed but go directly to the community."

Indicative of this shift, a 2003 report of the Kellogg-supported National Forum on Higher Education and the Public Good, announced a *community-centered* social change–oriented direction for Kellogg initiatives around Youth and Education. While not entirely abandoning the value of civic education and transformation of the culture and structure of the academy, Kellogg's newer interest is in campus initiatives explicitly as means to larger societal ends; that is, the "public good." The National Forum, for example, newly funded by Kellogg until 2006, planned an October 2004 Wingspread conference on the topic "Higher Education Collaboratives for Community Improvement and Engagement"—a title that clearly reflects a shift toward *community* benefits of campus initiatives (www.thenationalforum.org).

Kellogg's 2004 written grant guidelines for its Youth and Education program explicitly discouraged new proposals. They criticized the common "unilateral outreach" of higher education civic engagement initiatives in relation to local communities, and identified eight characteristics of campus-community partnerships they would support. The guidelines were unambiguous: they would *only* fund requests "jointly sponsored by and providing resources to [higher education] institutions and community partners" that provide "evidence that the institution and the community are committed to long-term engagement. To receive a grant, such a partnership must be developed *before* approaching the Foundation for funding support and strong evidence of mutual benefits, accountability, and respect" must be clearly shown. (*Engagement in Youth and Education Programming*, www.wkkf.org: 3 and 8).

In 2005, Youth and Education programming at Kellogg has taken another turn to a focus "on improving learning for young people, especially those most vulnerable to poor achievement." While Kellogg at this writing continues to provide some support to postsecondary education institutions, such support is offered only in relation to local communities. Especially telling in regard to foundation operating trends overall, the guidelines clearly state, "The Youth and Education team is not accepting proposals for these initiatives, which are focused on identified grantees" (www.wkkf.org/Programming/Overview). Indicative of ongoing changes in direction at Kellogg, one person knowledgeable about funding for higher education civic engagement told me in the summer of 2005, "I have no idea where Kellogg is going."

The Surdna Foundation Staying the Course? Youth Direct Action for Community and Policy Change

Surdna has for some time supported higher education to act as a social change agent to affect positive change in host communities and society. Since 1995, the stated goal of Surdna's Effective Citizenry program has been "to support young people to take direct action to solve serious problems in their schools, neighborhoods, and the larger society" (www.surdna.org/programs/citizenry.html). In 1999 Director Edward Skloot speaking at a conference at the University of Wisconsin said, "We don't have an educational focus. . . . We now believe that infusing democratic principles in individuals is only a start." Skloot explained that the origins of the Effective Citizenry program lie with one of Surdna's original funding initiatives: the Community Revitalization Program established in 1990 and now closely linked with youth engagement efforts. In contrast to changes at Carnegie, Pew, and Kellogg, Surdna's grant priorities and guidelines in these areas remained the same as of summer 2005.

Surdna's Community Revitalization Program's primary goal is "to transform low income, urban communities into vibrant, economically diverse communities of choice" (www.surdna.org/speeches/service.html). Early support of Trinity College's Center for Neighborhoods in Hartford played a role in leveraging a sizable grant from the Kellogg Foundation. The mission of the Trinity center was to revitalize the neighborhood around the university, and a main focus of their work was to support community organizing (www.trincoll.edu). The Trinity College project also supported a variety of community-based institutions such as a job training center and a day-care center for residents of the surrounding neighborhood. One of the reasons Skloot gave in 1999 for why Surdna supported Trinity's early efforts is that the school showed its commitment by investing more than six million dollars of its own endowment in the surrounding neighborhood.

Higher education Surdna grants in 2002 and 2003 that exemplify an institutional reform/university as social change agent–approach to higher education civic engagement went to the Center for Greater Philadelphia at the University of Pennsylvania "to support college students engaged in a course-based study of public school financing aimed at achieving greater equity"; and to the Center for Democracy and Citizenship at the University of Minnesota to expand programs in city schools where young people act to address local problems (www.surdna.org/grants/citizenry.html). In 2004, Dartmouth College received a grant from Surdna to conduct a campuswide public impact initiative that urged students to pursue public service careers. New York University obtained a Surdna grant to train community groups engaged in youth organizing, and the University of Wisconsin received one for research on youth governance of community nonprofits.

Information posted on Surdna's Web site as of summer 2005 and a conversation at about that time with someone knowledgeable about Surdna suggests that they plan to stay on this course of emphasizing "young people taking direct action," paying special attention to youth of color and to issues of juvenile justice reform, and emphasizing policy and behavioral change that will both benefit and empower youth leaders today.

Summary of Findings

Evidence from foundation Web sites and publications, conversations with key informants knowledgeable about foundation funding for higher education civic engagement, and with past and current campus grantees shows that monetary support for higher education civic engagement has declined or even been eliminated at foundations that had been major supporters up until 2004. Where funding from the "big 3" does still exist, the emphasis is on "direct action" by young people, including voting, and on dealing with underlying causes of social ills. As one foundation informant said, "[Instead of supporting service learning], we would rather focus on why these problems are so intractable, why is there so much poverty, what does it mean and what can young people do to step up and address that." This person's orientation is consistent with the interest that some foundations still have in funding campus-community partnerships when they center on community benefits and address community-defined issues.

While the effects of this decline in funding cannot be yet determined, as one academic leader stated pointedly, "When Pew moves in and then moves out, it has an impact. The same is true with Carnegie, Kellogg, and Ford." Another campus informant told me,

I think [the foundations] made a mistake. They've left the whole field in limbo. There were some impacts . . . and now they can't keep doing the work. It's the kind of work there doesn't seem to be any other support for. There's no government money and corporate funding is not likely. It's long-term work. Civic skills, citizen knowledge development—it doesn't happen overnight. It's hard to measure, not tangible. To have young people become actors in their world there has to be a planned intervention to make that happen. They can't do it on their own. Most of what can happen has to have staff. Institutions can't pick this up.

When I suggested that foundations were telling me that it was time for colleges and universities to support this work from their own resources, he said:

"That's partly true, but the issue is how long do you try to seed something? High schools say there're not rewarded for this work, for citizenship education—higher eds too. It's not what families and students pay tuition for so it's harder for colleges and universities to justify paying for it." When I asked this well-placed academic who in the foundation world he thought had made the decisions to eliminate support for higher education and why the decisions were made, his answer was telling in relation to the apparent lack of discussion or even preparation by funders for what was about to happen to their grantees. He said simply, "I don't know. . . . It's only been in the last decade that they were interested in civic engagement, and only then because of all those studies that showed a decline." Another successful grant-getter in higher education put it this way: "The winds change." His choice of imagery suggested he had no more influence or control over what foundations decide to fund or not than over the continually shifting forces of nature. On the other hand, a key figure in the foundation world, in explaining why they did not support funding for higher ed civic engagement, told me, "I don't see a clear road map at the college level."

A Crisis of Purpose in Foundations Today and Internal Foundation Practices Affecting Changes in Funding Campus Civic Engagement

Recent scholarly writing about philanthropic foundations has argued that these charitable institutions are experiencing a crisis of legitimacy and purpose. No longer clear about their role in modern democratic societies, foundations today are struggling to respond to challenges about their value in relation to their privileged tax status, demands for accountability and transparency, and questions about their relationship to a declining and devolving welfare state (Anheier and Leat 2002; Anheier and Toepler 1999).

Some of the factors identified in this study as playing a role in the decline of foundation funding for higher education civic engagement seem indicative of this larger struggle. They suggest considerable ambiguity about the place of private foundations in supporting—and acting themselves as agents—in civic engagement and building civil society. There may well have been valid external reasons for the major foundations that had previously supported campus civic engagement to shift or eliminate their support. The difficulties in demonstrating actual behavioral changes as a result of civic education, the slowness of change in the academy, the unwillingness of universities to share power with local communities, growing skepticism about the will and capacity of colleges and universities to affect community change—all are cause for legitimate concern. Still both the current research and research by others cited in this essay suggest that frequent shifts in funding directions are to be expected regardless of how successful the outcomes of funded initiatives. Why?

Because they appear to occur more in relation to factors that are more *internal* to these foundations and how they operate than they are external in relation to impact on outside targets for change such as universities and local communities. What are some of these factors that constitute common practices and ways of thinking internal to private foundations today, factors that were very evident in the current study?

Getting Something Started and Moving On

Following trends and shifting when they shift seems almost a matter of pride in the foundation world. As one foundation staffer told me, "Foundations change all the time. It's 'Let's do something different today?'" Sometimes foundations follow trends because they see it as their role to get something started and then move on, expecting that some other source of support should step forward once foundations have provided the "seed." One foundation staffer I spoke with clearly implied that schools that were serious should by now be funding campus civic engagement themselves, and those who were not were perhaps "doing this work to chase the money, not because it was a real commitment."

Conducting Independent Studies and Convening Leading Thinkers

A not uncommon practice among foundations today is conducting their own internal research into areas in which they have identified an interest. While such research has long been a defining practice of operating foundations, it seems to be becoming more common in private/independent foundations as well. This practice is in contrast to earlier ones where private foundations circulated requests for proposals to the wider research community. Today a foundation program officer is more likely to survey the research literature herself, perhaps consult with a few researchers that she knows through her own networks, and develop a focus for funding. Sometimes the foundation convenes meetings of people foundation staffers consider leading thinkers. These invitational gatherings may be cosponsored with grantee organizations; in the case of campus civic engagement funding, cosponsoring has occurred with various colleges and universities who were recipients of large grants, and with national organizations who work with campuses such as Campus Compact and CIRCLE. Reports of the proceedings, perhaps authored by a consultant hired by the foundation, may be published and circulated to a list of other key people and organizations identified by the foundation and posted on Web sites.

Pulling Out When Results Are Not Evident or Too Slow in Coming

The perceived failure to alter the culture and structure of the academy, which the Kellogg Foundation set out to do, was apparently an important factor in shifting to what seemed more readily apparent and manageable changes in community outcomes. As foundations face declining revenues and increased public scrutiny in the early part of the twenty-first century, they are more and more prioritizing short-term, well-marked impacts that provide clear evidence of having made some readily observable practical difference. Foundations are under more and more pressure to explain the impact of their grants; for a while the shorter-term impacts in local communities may seem to offer an advantage over longer-term impacts of student learning for active citizenship (which could not be effectively measured until young people matured). While there may be some debate within foundations about how short a time frame makes sense, the general feeling is that effects must be shown quickly—within five to seven years—to make the investment worthwhile.

As one informant told me, as she explained the need to show short-term results, "The downside is that some issues don't respond well in a time frame of five to seven years." Another informant told me that a foundation that used to support the larger goal of "expanding democracy" later decided that this kind of project would take too long and so not be able to provide the "proof of success" needed to sustain the effort. "It's hard to find measures of an expanding democracy when it may take years and years to do that." Along the same line, a somewhat frustrated program officer said that he was concerned that larger systemic issues like improving voter access, getting the media to foster open political debates, consideration of proportional voting initiatives and other electoral reform projects were not being addressed by foundation priorities.

Foundation support for initiatives to increase voter turnout in the 2004 election, especially among young people, seemed to be caused at least in part by this need to show results quickly, which it appears they succeeded in doing (the CIRCLE, April 2005). Youth voter turnout is more easily and rapidly measured than either student learning or community outcomes, and voter turnout can be more easily affected than less tangible approaches to strengthening democracy such as increased opportunities for public dialogue and deliberation. At the same time, a focus on this one aspect of civic engagement may be detrimental to the overall goal of increasing civic participation not only in electoral politics but in other aspects of civil society. As one academic leader told me, "I would not apply to [Pew-funded] CIRCLE for a youth engagement grant because their only focus is voting."

Making Decisions Based on Staff Changes or for Personal Reasons

Staff changes and other more "personal" factors appear to have a good deal of impact on shifting grant priorities. One key informant traced the change in emphasis from student learning to more community-based issues specifically to changes in foundation staffing; another said that the "real engine that drives" grant priorities is "who is in place" at the foundation. When I asked key informants why various decisions got made, they would often name a strategically located individual who successfully argued effectively for his or her "personal" interest area. Or they might explain a change of direction by referring by name to someone who had recently left the foundation or someone who had just arrived. When I asked if it might not instead be that changes in staffing were an effect rather than a cause of changes in overall organizational direction at a foundation, key informants said that was not typically the case. One informant even offered that a major grant initiative came about because people high up at the foundation knew the director of the program that was funded and "they liked what he does." These ideas support a common view of foundations as somewhat idiosyncratic and subject to individualized more than organizational priorities.

"Contract" Grantmaking

While not a major feature of the evidence gathered for this study, philanthropy that might be called funder-determined and grantee-preselected appears to be a growing trend. It shows up on the Kellogg Foundation's Youth and Education program guidelines (previously quoted), which state explicitly that they do not accept proposals but rather identify grantees in advance. A leading academic doing civic engagement work told me, "Where there is still some funding, the foundation decides its own niche [and comes to the grantee]. They identify who and what [gets done]."

In this same vein, another key informant I spoke to on the academic side said:

Foundations today do their own research. They decide what they want to fund and they maybe have chosen ahead of time who they want to fund. It used to be you could have broader discussions with them, but now they're looking for something specific that fits *their* agenda. They have it all set out. They've commissioned a white paper and they have their program all laid out. It makes sense from their point of view, but it means that who gets the money is already in place with the programs foundations are looking for so your university either has that fit in place or they don't They're less interested in having conversations with potential grantees. Some grantees get money every year once they're in the door.

Another key informant's description of the "debate" and "dialogue" that occurred as her foundation set its grant priorities—a debate limited to staff within the foundation with occasional invited consultation with invited outside experts—suggests that higher education grantees will have a hard row to hoe in efforts to influence foundation decision-making.

. . .

What does my research suggest for the future funding of campus civic engagement initiatives? A framework of three approaches to campus civic engagement based on my 2001 study of five schools (Ostrander 2004) identified three major emphases: (1) civic education rooted in theories of social and moral development where students learn skills, values, and attitudes for active citizenship (Colby and Ehrlich 2000); (2) direct efforts to strengthen democracy by developing new or revitalized processes, structures, and/or actions and projects (Boyte and Kari 1996); and (3) higher education as an agent of larger community and social change operating through campus-community partnerships with an emphasis on improving the quality of life in local communities (Harkavy 1998). While these approaches are, of course, not mutually exclusive and fully developed campus engagement initiatives encompass them all, findings from my earlier five-school study suggest that schools typically emphasize one more than others at any given time (Ostrander 2004).

The present study of foundation funding for higher education civic engagement suggests a clear decline in support for the first approach on civic education; considerable skepticism about the second approach on building democracy through campus efforts (with the exception of youth voting projects); and some continuing interest in the third approach on funneling support for societal and community change through universities (when the focus is on funding communities directly to work with campuses in addressing community-defined issues). Some of what seem like valid reasons for shifts in foundation support may provide some tentative lessons about what kinds of civic engagement overall are seen by foundations as most valuable.

First, in terms of opportunities for ongoing support, unless colleges and universities can connect student learning outcomes explicitly to clear and observable benefits to local communities (especially low-income communities), and to direct and measurable impacts on strengthening democratic *behavior* (especially youth voting), these institutions will have a difficult time obtaining private foundation support for their engagement efforts. Schools whose initiatives emphasize student-centered civic education are at a significant disadvantage compared with those who have already established strong relationships with local community organizations and who have framed their teaching and research in relation to pressing community issues along with academic concerns.

Second, given the apparent decline in foundation support, schools will need to seek support from sources other than large private foundations—including from wealthy alumni and their school's own regular budget. Convincing university trustees and administrators to invest hard money will require senior university faculty as well as student leaders to make persuasive arguments about the importance of civically engaged teaching and scholarship to the mission of the academy. The beginnings of this intellectual rationale lie in the writings of leading thinkers past and present including John Dewey (1916, 1927), Jane Addams (1938), Ernest Boyer (1990), Ira Harkavy (1998), and Harry Boyte (Boyte and Kari 1996). The essence of the rationale is in the role of the academy in producing relevant new knowledge, both basic and applied—knowledge that must, for both good theory and practice, be rooted in the pressing issues of the day as they are experienced and addressed by people in local and global communities.

References

Addams, Jane. 1938. *Twenty Years at Hull House.* New York: Macmillan.

Anheier, H. K. and D. Leat. 2002. *From Charity to Creativity: Philanthropic Foundations in the 21st Century.* Near Stroud, U.K.: Comedia.

———, and S. Toepler, eds. 1999. *Private Funds, Public Purpose: Foundations in International Perspective.* London: Kluwer Academic / Plenum Publishers.

Babcock, P. 1998. "The Role of Foundations in Influencing Public Policy." *National Civic Review* 87, no. 2:117-27.

Bolduc, K., P. Buchanan, and J. Huang. 2004. *Listening to Grantees: What Nonprofits Value in Their Foundation Funders.* Boston: Center for Effective Philanthropy.

Bombardieri, M. and W. V. Robinson. 2004. "Nation's Charitable Foundations Favor Wealthiest Nonprofits." *Boston Globe,* January 11.

Bowley, R., with J. Meeropool. 2003. *Service-Learning in Higher Education.* Medford, Mass: Massachusetts Campus Compact.

Boyer, E. 1990. *Scholarship Reconsidered.* Princeton: Carnegie Foundation.

Boyte, H. C., and N. N. Kari. 1996. *Building America: The Democratic Promise of Public Work.* Philadelphia: Temple University Press.

Bulmer, M. 1999. "The History of Foundations in the U.K. and the U.S." In *Private Funds, Public Purpose: Philanthropic Foundations in International Perspective,* edited by A. Anheier and S. Toepler. London: Kluwer Academic/Plenum Publishers.

Colby, A., and T. Ehrlich. 2000. "Higher Education and the Development of Civic Responsibility." In *Civic Responsibility and Higher Education,* edited by T. Ehrlich. Phoenix, Ariz.: Oryx.

Cruz, N., and D. E. Giles. 2000. "Where's the Community in Service-Learning Research?" *Michigan Journal of Community Service Learning* (fall):28-34.

Dewey, J. 1916. *Democracy and Education.* New York: Macmillan.

———. 1927. *The Public and Its Problems.* Denver: Allan Swallow.

Dugery, Jacquline, and James Knowles. 2003. *University and Community Research Partnerships: A New Approach.* Richmond, Va.: University of Richmond, Pew Partnership for Civic Change.

Eckel, P., M. Green, and B. Hill. 2001. *Riding the Waves of Change: Insights from Transforming Institutions.* Washington, D.C.: American Council on Education.

Edwards, B., and S. Marullo. 1999. "Universities in Troubled Times—Institutional Responses." *American Behavioral Scientist* 42, no. 5:754–65.

Eisenberg, P. 1998. "Philanthropy and Community Building." *National Civic Review* 87, no. 2:169–77.

Ferman, B., and T. L. Hill. 2004. "The Challenges of Agenda Conflict in Higher Education—Community Research Partnerships: Views from the Community Side." *Journal of Urban Affairs* 26, no. 2:241–57.

Frumkin, P. 1999. "Private Foundations as Public Institutions." In *Philanthropic Foundations,* edited by E. C. Lagemann. Indianapolis, Ind: Indiana University Press.

Gibson, C. 2001. *From Inspiration to Participation: A Review of Perspectives on Youth Civic Engagement.* Berkeley: Grantmaker Forum on Community and National Service.

Goldman, A. 2005. "Encouraging Innovation: A Task for Congress." *Chronicle of Philanthropy,* March 17. http://www.philanthropy.com.

Hammock, D. 1999. "Foundations in American Polity, 1900–1950." In *Philanthropic Foundations,* edited by E. C. Lagemann. Indianapolis, Ind.: Indiana University Press.

Harkavy, I. 1998. "Organizational Innovation and the Creation of the New American University." In *University-Community Collaborations for the Twenty-First Century,* edited by R. Lerner and L. A. K. Simon. New York: Garland.

Holland, B. 2001. "Measuring the Role of Civic Engagement in Campus Missions: Key Concepts and Challenges." Prepared for the ASHE symposium, Broadening the Carnegie Classification's Attention to Mission: Incorporating Public Service." November 18.

London, S. 2003. *Higher Education for the Public Good.* Ann Arbor, Mich.: National Forum on Higher Education for the Higher Good.

Maurrasse, D. 2001. *Beyond the Campus: How Colleges and Universities Form Partnerships with Their Communities.* New York: Routledge.

Morse, S. W. 2002. *Smart Communities: How Citizens and Local Leaders Can Use Strategic Thinking to Build a Brighter Future.* Richmond: Pew Partnership for Civic Change.

Neilson, W. 1972. *The Big Foundations.* New York: Columbia Press.

O'Connor, A. 1999. "The Ford Foundation and Philanthropic Activism in the 1960s." In *Philanthropic Foundations: New Scholarship, New Possibilities,* edited by E. C. Lagemann. Bloomington, Ind.: Indiana University Press.

Ostrander, S. A. 2004. "Democracy, Civic Participation, and the University: A Comparative Study of Civic Engagement on Five Campuses." *Nonprofit and Voluntary Sector Quarterly* 33, no. 1:74–92.

———, and P. G. Schervish. 1990. "Giving and Getting: Philanthropy as Social Relation." In *Critical Issues in American Philanthropy,* edited by J. Van Til. San Francisco, Calif.: Jossey-Bass.

Ostrower, F. 2004. *Attitudes and Practices Concerning Effective Philanthropy.* Washington, D.C.: Urban Institute.

Rothschild, M. 1999. "Philanthropy and American Higher Education." In *Philanthropy and the Nonprofit Sector,* edited by C. T. Clotfelter and T. Ehrlich. Indianapolis, Ind.: Indiana University Press.

Silver, I., and H. E. Boyle. 2005. "Poverty, Partnerships, and Privilege: Elite Institutions and Community Empowerment," *City and Community* 4, no. 3:233–53.

Smith, G. 1998. "Strategic Grantmaking and Community Building," *National Civic Review* 86, no. 2:111–16.

Smith, J. A. 1999. "The Evolving American Foundation." In *Philanthropy and the Nonprofit Sector,* edited by C. T. Clotfelter and T. Ehrlich. Indianapolis, Ind.: Indiana University Press.

W. W. Kellogg Foundation. 2004. *Engagement in Youth and Education Programming.* http://www.wkkf.org.

Index